*A Field Guide to*

# HOME
*Schooling*

*Christine M. Field*

Fleming H. Revell
A Division of Baker Book House
Grand Rapids, Michigan 49516

Published by Fleming H. Revell
a division of Baker Book House Company
P.O. Box 6287, Grand Rapids, MI 49516-6287

Second printing, June 1999

Printed in the United States of America

Library of Congress Cataloging-in-Publication Data

Field, Christine M., 1956–
A field guide to home schooling / Christine M. Field.
       p.        cm.
    Includes bibliographical references (p. ).
    ISBN 0-8007-5653-3 (paper)
    1. Home schooling—United States—Handbooks, manuals, etc.
2. Home schooling—Law and legislation—United States—Handbooks, manuals, etc. I. Title.
LC40.F54        1998
371.04'2—dc21                                      97-44913

Unless otherwise indicated, Scripture quotations are from the HOLY BIBLE,
NEW INTERNATIONAL VERSION®. NIV®. Copyright © 1973, 1978,
1984 by International Bible Society. Used by permission of Zondervan Publishing House. All rights reserved.

Scripture quotations identified KJV are from the King James Version of the
Bible.

The list of statewide home school organizations in appendix B is used with permission of *The Teaching Home* magazine.

For current information about all releases from Baker Book House, visit our
web site:

http://www.bakerbooks.com

This book is lovingly dedicated to Mark Field—my husband, my best friend, my partner in life, love, parenting, and home education.

# Contents

# *Acknowledgments*

To Dr. Louis Diaz and his wife, Shirley Diaz, who inspire and teach me, and keep me on the right path; to Rose Marie and Irving Alton Field, who guide me and pray daily for my family; to my dear friend Ruth Gibson, who helps keep me focused on enduring biblical principles; to my friend Jackie Wellwood, who encourages and challenges me; to all the ladies in my home school support groups who help keep me going; to Bill Petersen and Linda Holland, who gave me a chance and the proverbial "kick in the pants" when I needed it; to Mary Suggs, Becky Warren-Van Arragon, and Melinda Van Engen, who make me sound like a much better writer than I am; to Marci DeVries and Karen Steele, who help keep me busy and out of trouble; to my children, who educate me every day while I try to teach them; and to my husband, Mark, for his invaluable contribution to the material herein on home schooling fathers.

# 1

# *How We Fell into Home Schooling*

*I* could never do *that!*"
 That is the response I am likely to hear the first time I
 tell someone that we are a home schooling family. Next
comes at least two of the following reasons for not home
schooling:

"I don't have enough education."
"I'm not organized enough."
"I'm not patient enough."
"I'm not sure it's legal."
"I couldn't stand to be with my kids all day."
"I have to work."
"I can't afford all that expensive curriculum."
"What about socialization?"

Before our children were born, I had never heard of home
schooling. As I read more about it and met home schooling
families, I argued through each of these points, claiming them
as my own reasons for not home schooling.

Some families seem to sense right from the birth of their
children that they will be educated at home. Their children

are born with certainty of that educational future. For us, the decision was not so clear.

We came to parenthood late. Our first daughter was adopted when I was thirty-four. Our biological daughter was born seventeen months later. Our third daughter came to us from Korea less than four years after that, and we recently adopted the fourth and final Field—a baby boy from Korea.

I attacked motherhood like I had my former profession as a lawyer—with a vengeance. I had to do the "mother-thing" right. That has varying definitions, I soon learned, depending on your priorities. Where I live, the good moms send their kids to the best schools and most expensive ballet lessons. I was in training to join their ranks, so I dashed with my children from one activity to another in our minivan.

My children learned ballet steps with ease and grace. They were preparing to look and act just like the other young school girls in their pink-hued, age-segregated setting. I wanted my daughters to learn to be their own thinkers with creative minds; they wanted to be just like all the other suburban kids—cut out of a mold with identical dreams and desires.

One day, I turned to yell at them in the van and suddenly realized that I did not know them. They were interested in things that I sensed might be less than wholesome, such as the latest TV fad. I didn't approve of the values they were learning, such as placing friends before family. They were growing apart from our close-knit little family and becoming "cultured" in a society whose values I questioned.

We reduced our schedule and returned to basics. Why go to library story hour when you can read anytime, anyplace? Why go to messy painters class when you can make a perfectly good mess at home? Does a three-year-old really need a ballet class, or might it not be fun to put on tutus, turn on the music, and have a goofy dance time in the living room? Slowly and without stress, we took advantage of teachable moments at home. Cooking, cleaning, and family living proved to be fertile fields of learning. The children became more relaxed and imaginations began to flourish once again.

Still, the formal decision to home school was fraught with agony. We saw our daughters thriving under individual attention. We knew home schooling might be the spiritual, social, and academic answer. Yet we were drawn to the quaint neighborhood public school down the block, which was also one of the country's last "walking" schools (hardly any children ride a bus to school). Like a magnet, the school attracted us with fun group projects, cheerful classroom decorations, and a sense of being part of a community. We simply desired normal, happy kids—or so we thought. Why was this such a difficult decision?

Part of the problem was defining "normal and happy." As we looked around, we observed that some normal, happy kids were disrespectful, were doing a marginal job academically, possessed bad attitudes, had little, if any, faith training, were more interested in peers and television than anything else, and had a host of other questionable values.

We wanted something different for our children. We don't want them to be dependent on how the world and other children perceive them. We want them to be concerned primarily with how God views them, and he is not invited into their classes at the public school. We want them to view God and family as the most important things in their lives. These values are not being fostered in the course of trying to raise normal, happy kids—especially in our culture.

The fall when Clare, our oldest, was ready to enter school, we reluctantly enrolled her in kindergarten. Our school district possesses a reputation of having the finest schools in the country, and our local school has many fine Christian teachers. What harm could come of this? We reassured ourselves that it was a good decision. It didn't matter much academically because Clare had already completed all the work from a kindergarten curriculum at home and we were delightfully engaged in a first grade program when she enrolled in public school kindergarten. Our middle child, Caitlin, was working through a kindergarten program, and our baby, Grace, was progressing nicely. Why not try this small foray into public education to see what would happen?

Clare, perhaps due to her personality, became totally dependent on the approval and friendship of other school children. The opinions of the little pack of girls she "ran with" became her gospel. She was only six years old. I shuddered to think what the teen years would bring if we did not help her to achieve grounding in more enduring values.

The children in Clare's class came from a variety of economic, social, and religious backgrounds. Some were from Christian homes and some were not. Some were from two-parent homes and some were not. Some had behavioral disorders and some did not. One teacher was expected to help twenty-four diverse boys and girls develop and learn. Under these circumstances, much was made of collaborative learning and group activities. One teacher could not tutor twenty-four students one-on-one, so the children learned together and did everything as a group. The impact this had on my daughter was to make her all the more willing to merely "follow the herd." She was thinking less and less for herself and becoming totally immersed in the school culture. That conditioning included frequent use of the phrases "stupid" and "shut up," phrases strictly forbidden in our home, as well as the emergence of some words not fit to print.

The bad language and the hardening of Clare's heart caused us sufficient concern. Then one day she came home to announce that some little girl had "had sex with her boyfriend." We asked our then five-year-old what that meant, and she was clueless. But she was delighted to broadcast this tasty bit of kindergarten gossip to the household and to our neighborhood.

Other stories came home that were equally troubling. Our daughter began to complain that certain children would kick her every day at gym time. She also continued to make up stories about other things that proved to be totally baseless. The mere idea that she was thinking about such things was disconcerting enough.

Slowly and prayerfully, doubts were resolved. It was an extremely difficult personal family decision to home school. I wish I could say it was simple, but it wasn't. When God puts something on your heart, he does not guarantee the task will be easy. Nothing good in life is ever easy. But the difficult times are a dim memory when considered in light of the joy that the lifestyle of home schooling can bring.

As we lived through our one and only semester of public school, any doubts that we had about our path were removed. We told our daughter and the school authorities that she would no longer be attending as of that Christmas. The new year found us engaged in the exciting, enriching, perfectly legal practice of home schooling.

## The Law and Home Schooling

Home schooling is legal in all states, although it is subject to some regulation. States possess the inherent right to control home schools, within reason. Although the United States Constitution does not delineate the right to home school, it is a right derived from the Fourteenth Amendment, which guarantees all citizens the right to "liberty." That liberty cannot be withheld without "due process."

When parents home school for religious reasons, their right to do so is also protected by the First Amendment of the United States Constitution, which guarantees citizens the right to freely exercise their religious beliefs. Home education, under certain circumstances, is a form of the exercise of religious beliefs.

Predicated on the basis of a right to liberty, courts have held that parents have a fundamental right to home school. In *Pierce v. Society of Sisters* (268 U.S. at 534–535, 1925) the court held that parents have "the fundamental right . . . to direct the upbringing and education of their children."

We are not alone in taking our children home from school. The Home School Legal Defense Association estimates that in 1994 there were between 750,000 and 1.2 million home educated children in this country.[1] It is impossible to give a totally accurate number because of the varying reporting requirements for each state. It is possible that this figure is quite conservative and that the actual numbers are higher because home schoolers, for a variety of reasons, are not likely to share much information voluntarily.

Researcher Dr. Brian Ray has demonstrated that the number of home school families is growing at the rate of 15 percent to 40 percent per year.[2] *U.S. News and World Report* claims that the number of children being home schooled is 1.2 million in a year and is growing by 25 percent annually.[3] Author Mark Weston says, "Estimates of students now being educated at home range from 500,000 to two million, or between 1 and 4 percent of the entire American student population. The Home School Legal Defense Association, a membership organization of home-school families, claims at least 25 percent growth in each of the past 10 years."[4] Clearly, the numbers are growing.

Authors Clay and Sally Clarkson say, "Christian Home Education is the original 'Designer' education. More than any other approach to education, each new Christian home school bears the imprimatur of *The Designer*."[5] That is an appropriate analogy in our consumer-oriented society. Many parents willingly buy into purchasing designer jeans and tennis shoes for their children. They are focusing on what adorns their children's bodies instead of training them to adorn their hearts and souls with the love of God—the imprint of the *true* designer.

The results of home education are impressive—well-adjusted children who score much higher than their public school counterparts on standardized achievement tests. These children come from average families and yet *clearly* outperform children educated in public schools. Scott Sommerville, an attorney with the Home School Legal Defense Association, recounts, "When a housewife with $150 worth of textbooks can outperform the public schools, then maybe it's time for a change."[6]

Perhaps most impressive is the fact that home schooled children maintain close family relationships characterized by mutual love and respect. Try finding that in a group of teenagers gathered to watch MTV!

The concept of home education is growing in acceptance. While once an underground activity of 1970s fanatics, today many (although not all) home schooling families are conservative politically and socially. Home schoolers span the political spectrum from the far right to the far left. Their shared fanaticism is in their concern for their children.

### State Regulation

Simply because parents possess a right does not mean that the state cannot regulate the activity. In a related decision, the court ruled that the state retains an interest in home schooling and can exercise some control. In *Wisconsin v. Yoder* (406 U.S. at 221, 1972) the court found the state's interest is in seeing that children grow up to be "literate" and "self-sufficient."

For states to preserve interest in home education, they can impose requirements on home schooling families who seek to exercise individual rights. Some requirements that have been tried and are the subject of much lively discussion and litigation include standardized testing, teacher certification, curriculum approval, and home visits, all of which will be discussed in this book.

At this early point of discussion, suffice it to say that it *is* legal to home school in the United States. The restrictions and regulations of the individual states may vary, but each recognizes the validity of home education.

### Teacher Certification

One of the first matters to be investigated with regard to your state law is whether teacher certification is required. Even when certification is required, most state laws provide a way for parents to circumvent the requirement, such as through affiliation with a satellite school. Chris Klicka, an attorney and author of *The Right Choice,* notes, "One of the most significant studies in this area was performed by Dr. Eric Hanushek of the University of Rochester, who surveyed the results of 113 studies on teacher education and qualifications. Eighty-five percent of the studies found no positive correlation between the educational performance of the students and the teacher's educational background. Although 7 percent of the studies did find a positive correlation, 5 percent found a negative impact."[7]

From a home educator's perspective, the solution may be to study how well students are doing rather than how "qualified" the teachers are. Test results and the many areas of success of home schooled children speak for themselves.

Dr. Brian Ray of the National Home Education Research Institute studied two thousand families in all fifty states: "The research revealed that there was no positive correlation between the state regulation of home schools and the home schooled students' performance."[8]

The current trend in laws is to lessen such requirements. Most states do not require parents to have specific qualifications; a few require a GED, a high school diploma, or a bachelor's degree. Only recently, Michigan struck down the teacher certification requirement as unconstitutional (*People v. DeJonge,* 501 N.W. 2d at 127, 1993). In this case, the parents were teaching their children successfully but were not certified teachers as required by Michigan law. They were criminally prosecuted and convicted. Ultimately, the Michigan Supreme Court reversed their criminal conviction with this holding: "We hold that the teacher certification requirement is an unconstitutional violation of the Free Exercise Clause of the First Amendment as applied to families whose religious convictions prohibit the use of certified instructors. Such families, therefore, are exempt from the dictates of the teacher certification requirements" (501 N.W. 2d at 144). This victory for home schoolers in the state of Michigan is a landmark case that bodes well for the future of home education and the freedoms of home educating families everywhere.

## Home School Demographics

Most home educators are not extremely wealthy or highly educated. Dr. Brian Ray studied these variables in a wide sample of home schooling families and learned that the average family had 3.2 children, fathers with three years of college, mothers with two years of college, and a median family income of $35,000 to $49,999. Only a handful of these parents were certified teachers. Dr. Ray concluded that these factors had little if any bearing on the academic success of the home educated student.[9]

In the decision-making process about home schooling, a part of me reasoned that I had already made a commitment to full-time mothering. What could be so difficult about adding home schooling to that equation? Many full-time homemakers see teaching our children at home as more important than what we did in the workplace. Home teaching adds a new and different dimension to motherhood. I was prepared for the nurturing and the tears, the crafts and the chores, but home schooling has stretched me to take on new roles and skills as I am actively involved in my children's minds and hearts.

Isabel Lyman, a Massachusetts home school mom, describes herself as follows: "I'm a modern-day Hispanic-American version of Laura Ingalls Wilder with a personal computer, minivan and advanced college degree. Part schoolmarm, part activist, part pioneer, part entrepreneur, part entertainer and dedicated wife."[10]

Home schooling has been a learning experience for me as a teaching mom. It was for Linda Dobson too: "As the children acquired basic skills . . . their interests expanded. Their sense of wonder blossomed. So did mine. Their abilities multiplied. So did mine. Their confidence increased. So did mine."[11] Teaching my own children has been as much a blessing for me as for the children.

As my children have tried their hand at art, ballet, sports, singing, or reading the classics, I have rediscovered my own childhood interests and developed new ones. I am remembering much of what I had forgotten of my own education and adolescence. Parents who send their children to school outside the home may only have this reflective experience at their child's Christmas play or concert. It is a daily experience for us in our home schooling.

Home schooling demands monetary and time commitments. In home schooling or any other endeavor, the cost must be measured against the benefit. In financial terms, the cost of child care and private school must be weighed against the benefit of a second income. As you research home schooling and search your heart, you may come to the conclusion that paying someone to educate your child makes little sense. Why work to pay others to raise your children? The job might be better done by you at home.

Home schooling author and speaker J. Richard Fugate notes, "Many husband and wife teams find, upon careful examination, that the wife's net income (after all work-associated expenses have been deducted) is only 10% to 25% of her total salary. . . . Thus, the average working mother who earns between $800 to $1500 probably only earns $200 to $300 per month. This is an amount that a family business might be able to produce while teaching the children about work at the same time. Many home school families have even discovered that decreasing their standard of living to an amount within the husband's income was possible."[12]

This was our experience as well. I left a full-time practice of law to stay home full time. We transitioned from being a double-income family with no children, to being an old-fashioned one-income family with the mother at the domestic helm. There were financial sacrifices and many adjustments to my self-definition and identity, but each member of our family is flourishing under this new arrangement.

Not to say that all women work for sheer enjoyment; many have no choice. Yet even those who work outside the home may be able to home educate. Julie Stahler, a single mom acquaintance, teaches her eleven-year-old son at home with a creative arrangement. Her parents offered to keep her son with them during the day if there was any chance of her considering home schooling. So she teaches before and after work and on weekends and leaves assignments for her son during the day.

Those of us who *do* have a choice about working and do not exercise it are cheating our families and ourselves. In the history of women, many have fought long and hard so that we might all have choices. If we are too embarrassed to make a choice that seems old-fashioned, then we have no real choice at all.

The editor for the prestigious *Forbes* magazine analyzed it this way: "You have three kids, private day school at, say,

$10,000 each. Let's say one of the parents earns $50,000 a year and the other considerably more. If the lower paid one stays home with a computer, a blackboard, and the kids, eliminating the tuition bills would more than compensate the loss of after tax income. Not considering the psychic benefits."[13]

The psychic benefits are the most important for our family. We call them the spiritual benefits. They manifest themselves in a greater commitment to family and faith. No price tag can be placed on this phenomenon. It is ultimately more valuable than fancy vacations, new cars, or bigger homes. There is a cohesiveness to our family that would not exist if we did not all share in this adventure of home education. Author Mary Hood notes, "Many parents in the home schooling movement were originally full-time workers, too, but they have rearranged their priorities and their schedules in order to be at home with their children. . . . These parents have learned that their increased freedom and control far outweigh the things that they have had to give up."[14]

The prestigious publication *The Economist* had these recent comments about home schooling: "In a society where two-income families are becoming the norm, and where parents pay for public schools whether they use them or not, home schooling involves considerable sacrifices of both time and money. The fact that more and more parents are turning to it implies something worrying about the state of public education."[15]

Something worrying indeed—such as increasing violence and decreasing test scores, increasing delinquency and decreasing value placed on morals. Public education is in a sorry state that money can't repair. Money cannot implant values, nor can it improve reading and math scores. In dollar terms, researcher Dr. Brian Ray estimated that the average family spends $489 per year per child to home educate.[16] You can spend far more, and some families spend far less. Regardless, the cost is minimal when compared with the benefit.

Some people are still afraid to take the plunge into home schooling. They are afraid they will fail and that their children won't measure up. But a family that has as its primary commitment the training of its children cannot help but do as well or better than the schools. Parents need to allay their fears and take the plunge into home education. As you read further and ask God to guide you in your decision-making process, you will gain more confidence for your convictions.

Author Susan Schaeffer Macaulay says, "There has never been a generation when children have so desperately needed their parents' time, thoughtful creativity, and friendship. The surrounding culture is deeply out of step with the Word of God. Other pressures threaten to take away sanity, stability, and simple humanity."[17] Now may be the time when it is imperative for your family to consider home schooling for the very survival of the family unit.

French writer Ferenc Mate said it best: "The only concentrated attention our children get now is when someone is trying to sell them something."[18] In the home education arena, where your children receive focused one-on-one tutoring, your children have the opportunity to absorb your morals, values, and knowledge. Moreover, the age of your child does not matter. You may have a middle school child who is drifting away from you and your values. Or you might be the parents of beautiful preschoolers and you want to preserve their spark and love of learning. Home schooling can be for each age—and for any age. Although it is true that the earlier you begin, the easier it will be, any child can be gracefully, freely, and lovingly brought back into the home learning environment.

The decision may be a difficult one for you, as it was for us. Is it the best thing for your family? Will the children be able to compete academically should they return to a traditional school? What will neighbors and relatives think of our decision? These issues and many others will be explored within these pages.

This is the story of our joy and struggle, as well as those of many other families. Our culture is in a state of moral decay. Our families are in disrepair. Many of us know that home schooling is one way for us to snatch our families back from culture and raise them the way God intended—at home, under our own tender, loving care. There is no more effective way to strengthen the family nucleus than to home educate. God did not give your children to educational bureaucrats; he gave them to you. It is my hope that you will see the clear blessings and advantages of the home school lifestyle. It could be the most significant adventure your family ever takes.

How is "home school" spelled? Some people spell it "home school," some "homeschool." It is becoming increasingly popular to spell it "home's cool."

Our home may seem a bit out of step with our culture, but our family is flourishing in so many ways. Our home's cool.

# 2

# *Why Home School Now?*

ome schoolers are indeed a diverse group. While current estimates suggest that 85 percent of home schooling families are evangelical Christians, there are also many others, including New Age home schoolers. Collectively, they have been described as "strange bedfellows of religious conservatives and political libertarians," by author Joel Riemer; he also stresses the beauty of what these groups have in common: "the family-centered aspect of home schooling. Both find that home schooling offers an experience that strengthens families and . . . broadens children's horizons."[1]

There are innumerable reasons to home school. Your primary reason may be to teach your children strong Christian values, whereas your neighbor may home school because she is radically anti-government and does not wish to entrust her children to the state. Despite your disparate reasons, you will find many more things in common with other home schooling families than you might imagine. First and foremost, you probably share a strong belief that the family should be the primary setting for education. You might also believe that closeness and building family relationships are major goals. You undoubtedly share an indescribable passion for your children that will compel you to make sacrifices that others might find too dear.

Your life tapestry, however different from that of your neighbor, will be woven through with the strengthening thread of home education. Though the overall pictures on the tapestries may differ, they will share many of the same threads of strength. The choice of home education adds color, pattern, beauty, strength, and character to the tapestry of family life. In a society characterized by mass production, home schooling is the work of the individual craftsman—the work of God within the family. It is personal handicraft as opposed to the mass production of the schools. If God is calling your family to home educate, he will give you the tools, strength, ideas, imagination, and inspiration to create a unique brand of education best suited to your family.

God, the Master Craftsman, created your family. Home schooling is a work of master craftsmanship that we mere mortals can give to our children's lives. In no small way, we are shaping human character and helping determine destiny. Will you give your children the benefit of your time to do so?

## Why Home Schooling Might Be the Answer

### Keeping the Faith

Many Christians interpret Scripture as providing a biblical mandate to home school; they view home schooling as a matter of obedience not preference. Home schooling mom and author Helen Nelson shared with me in a survey for this book, "This is an adventure, and if God is calling you to do it, do it with an obedient heart, looking for his help in all you do."

When Moses led his people out of Egypt after hundreds of years of slavery, he reminded them of all that God had done for them. He praised God's faithfulness and also reviewed the many commandments that God had given to the people. Then he said:

> Love the LORD your God with all your heart and with all your
> soul and with all your strength. These commandments that
> I give you today are to be upon your hearts. Impress them on
> your children. Talk about them when you sit at home and
> when you walk along the road, when you lie down and when
> you get up. Tie them as symbols on your hands and bind them
> on your foreheads. Write them on the doorframes of your
> houses and on your gates.
>
> Deuteronomy 6:5–9

Note that we are first commanded to love our God—then, *to
teach our children.* As Christian home schoolers, we must not
neglect that primary and fundamental commandment to love
God. It provides meaning and substance to all of home schooling. Having your personal relationship with God intact will
allow you to weather the many challenges of home schooling.

If we are to teach God's commandments as we sit at home
and while we walk along life's road, then parents are to teach
their children at all times and in all places. Scripture does not
say we are to entrust the training of our children to a government school system. Teaching is really another form of dis-
cipling. Our children are our first mission field. We need to
do that job to the best of our ability before we send them into
the world or before we try to disciple others. It is always a
tragedy to see people who are so active in a ministry that they
neglect the nurturing of their own children. The Bible reminds
us of the priority of the parent-child relationship. As we teach
our children to be faithful servants of God, we are promised,
"All your sons will be taught by the LORD, and great will be
your children's peace" (Isa. 54:13). In our family, this peace
is more important than top grades, stellar athletic performances, or awards. This is indeed what will endure.

If we are a "success" in home schooling, then we will have
godly children. If we have any boast, it is in knowing God and
passing that on to our children. As it says in Jeremiah 9:23,
"This is what the LORD says: Let not the wise man boast of his

wisdom or the strong man boast of his strength or the rich man boast of his riches, but let him who boasts boast about this: that he understands and knows me, that I am the LORD, who exercises kindness, justice and righteousness on earth, for in these I delight." As we delight in teaching our children in faith, we can rest assured that God delights in it as well.

According to Scripture, children are blessings: "Sons are a heritage from the LORD, children a reward from him" (Ps. 127:3). These blessings come with weighty responsibilities, including the duty to "train a child in the way he should go" (Prov. 22:6). These verses are considered by many to be the Bible's explicit marching orders for parents to home educate their children.

According to author Llewellyn Davis, "The only biblical injunctions concerning teaching children are addressed to parents, particularly the fathers, and to grandparents."[2] There is no biblical granting of authority to the government to train our children. Indeed, teaching and training of children is specifically a family matter. For a large part of history, education, faith training, and home life were inextricably woven together in the fabric of everyday life. As society became more fragmented in the areas of industry and education, that fabric became worn and tattered. Home schoolers recognize home education as a means to weave that strength back into the family.

Many Christians believe that there is an actual battle for the hearts, souls, and minds of our children going on in society. Those who control public education appear at times to have the ultimate goal of banishing faith and family training in favor of government-sanctioned values and politically correct thinking. We have given schools the authority to teach values to our children by supporting drug education, violence prevention classes, and sex education. If we can't—or won't—do the training at home, it will be done by strangers in the schools. The problem is that the values imparted by our institutions are radically different from those of most Christian families.

Before I had children—and before I had much of a reason to think about such matters—I used to be somewhat amused by the alarmists who warned us to beware of creeping secular humanism. I attended a Catholic school for some of my education and my public school career was quite a long time ago, so these concerns seemed overstated to me. After all, the idea of humanism sounded innocuous—valuing human beings for who they were. I was ignorant of the other side of this argument—the absence of God and supreme deification of man as a god unto himself.

Author Christopher Klicka clarifies: "Humanism simply means that man, rather than God, is the measure of all things. Humanism does not recognize God or his Absolute moral values, but instead asserts that each person can set his own values and control his own destiny."[3] To put it another way: "Humanists deny the existence of God, the inspiration of the Bible, the divinity of Jesus Christ, life after death, and the biblical account of creation. . . . In humanism, man finds self-fulfillment, happiness, love and justice through his own experience, reason and will."[4]

Christians believe that all knowledge and wisdom come from God. He has something to say about every aspect of life in his Word, so no teaching can ever be adequate without reference to the Scriptures. Humanists, on the other hand, see knowledge as valuable and meaningful in its own right, without any reference to God. The goal of humanists "is to use education to manipulate and control masses of students."[5]

We have seen this in the philosophy of men like Horace Mann and John Dewey, who viewed education as a means of social control and societal change. In 1837, Horace Mann, the president of the Massachusetts State Senate, enacted a centralized, statewide system of public schools that were controlled by the state and financed by tax dollars. He believed that these so-called "common schools" would be a vehicle for controlling the burgeoning immigrant population by imposing the language, beliefs, and values of the dominant group on all.

John Dewey is called the father of progressive education. He was the first president of the American Humanist Association, the group that drafted the Humanist Manifesto, declaring the deification of man. His writings and teachings encouraged a belief that the government could best prepare children to function in society, officially usurping the role of family, parents, and church.

Put in the most blatant terms, here is the battle plan of the humanists, many of whom are currently teaching in our schools:

> I am convinced that the battle for humankind's future must be waged and won in the public school classroom by teachers who correctly perceive their role as the proselytizers of a new faith: a religion of humanity that recognizes and respects the spark of what theologians call divinity in every human being. Their teachers must embody the same selfless dedication as the most rabid fundamentalist preachers, for they will be ministers of another sort, utilizing a classroom instead of a pulpit to convey humanist values in whatever subject they teach, regardless of the educational level—preschool, day care, or large university. The classroom must, and will, become an arena of conflict between the old and the new—the rotting corpse of Christianity, together with all its adjacent evils and misery, and the new faith of humanism.[6]

Humanism has been taking a foothold in our schools for quite some time. A man named Charles Francis Potter, an avid supporter of the humanist movement, wrote over fifty years ago: "Education is thus a most powerful ally of humanism, and every public school is a school of humanism. What can the theistic Sunday schools, meeting for an hour once a week, and teaching only a fraction of the children, do to stem the tide of a five-day program of humanistic teaching?"[7]

God has no place in the public school that is one block down my street. In fact, he has been kicked out the door by legal and administrative edicts. Author Mary Hood says, "As long as Jesus is banished from His proper place at the center of your children's education, as long as the public schools remain secular institutions, committed to religious neutrality, Christian children don't belong there."[8] Oddly enough, we allow God on our money and in our Pledge of Allegiance, but not in the hearts and minds of schoolchildren.

To the contrary, God occupies the primary place in our home. He guides our lives and is woven through every aspect of our family life. Home schooling gives us the opportunity to imbue every aspect of our children's education with the Word of God. When we discuss current events, we can ask the children what God would think about the situation. When we discuss world conflicts, the discussion can focus on the religious as well as the political aspects of the event. As science is taught, we can focus on creation and discuss evolution as an alternate theory, rather than the limited way most schools teach about the beginning of the universe. For Christian home schoolers, faith is not just another aspect of our culture. It is the very definition of who we are as Christians.

Home schooling researcher Maralee Mayberry notes: "The home school movement, perhaps to an extent greater than other movements of the era, exemplifies the principles of individualism and self-reliance, and the attempt to live in a way that is consistent with one's worldview."[9] For Christians, it is the only way to live the Christian life—in a consistent, unified fashion where we live out our beliefs on an everyday basis.

Home schooling *works*. The spiritual benefits are just the tip of the iceberg. Home schooling is so successful that many people today are doing it less and less for religious reasons and more and more because their kids are so successful at it. As an article in *The School Administrator* states, "Nationally, it's become a legitimate option—it's the cutting edge for the big movement toward parental choice."[10]

Although viewed by many as an old-fashioned harkening to an earlier time, home schooling remains on the cutting edge in many ways—spiritually, academically, and socially. It is also the most effective way to strengthen and preserve your family values.

### Family Values

In discussing the moral failure of Israel, the author of the Book of Judges says, "In those days Israel had no king; everyone did as he saw fit" (Judg. 17:6). Although this was written many years ago, it still describes our social situation today. We are so sensitive about offending someone's rights or preferences that absolute values are nonexistent. If we hold to a standard of truth—the Word of God—we are accused of being inflexible and not keeping up with the times.

A major parental concern today is the question of "values clarification" that occurs in public schools. Exactly what does "values clarification" mean? Home schooling mom and author Mary Hood explains:

> There are no absolutes according to the authorities in question. Instead, what is right depends on the specific situation. Young children are given lessons in "values clarification," where they are systematically taught to ignore the teachings of their parents and make their own decisions. Yet they are not really encouraged to make their own individual choices, but to form a "consensus," by discussing the issues with their peers. Thus, seven year olds are being taught by other seven year olds, who are all fashioning a "new" ideal of right versus wrong that does not mesh with the belief systems of their parents. . . . There is no such thing as education without values. If you aren't teaching one set then you are teaching the other.[11]

In essence, everyone does as he sees fit, just as in the time of the decline of the nation of Israel.

In the home school setting, values are not determined by the situation, by peers, or by the latest fad. Instead, parents have a unique window of opportunity to instill their deepest beliefs and values in their children. By avoiding the value-neutral school system, parents can give their children a firm foundation on which to base the rest of their lives.

Children are not the only ones to strengthen their values and character through home education. Author J. Richard Fugate notes that two generations receive an education in home schooling—both child and parents: "Parents become more mature by just surviving a few years of home schooling. Their pride is humbled by seeing how much they don't know. Their willfulness is controlled by self sacrifice. Their laziness is replaced with self discipline and industry when required to hold down the equivalent of a second job. . . . I believe all homeschooling parents who apply themselves to the task 'as unto the Lord' will become increasingly more mature in the process."[12] It is helpful for me to remember during difficult times that I am maturing spiritually along with my children.

Home schooling families place a high value on the fact that they are close-knit families. Attorney and author Christopher Klicka observes,

> Parents are able to spend hours interacting, teaching, sharing, and nurturing their children. Fathers, no matter what their work hours, can spend much more time with their children because the children's instruction can be adjusted. This time is far above the national average of parents spending approximately seven minutes a day with face-to-face contact with their children, according to a study from Stanford University. The children also do not become segregated from their brothers and sisters by age differences but are able to relate to all age groups.[13]

The family value of togetherness is well served by home schooling. As author Cheryl Gorder states, "The best hours of the day rightly belong to those you love, home schoolers explain. When a child goes to public school, the teachers get those hours, and parents get what's left over—usually a tired child."[14] I know my child's good times and her bad times. I can tell when she is not cognitively ready for a new task, and we have the blessed freedom to wait for readiness. I can truthfully say I know and love *all* aspects of my children because of the closeness fostered by home schooling.

In my oldest daughter's brief time in public school, she would return home with her creative energy spent and her heart closed. She would be distracted, tired, and exhausted. We got to share the dregs of the day while her best times were spent as a "part of the crowd" at school. Now we share the best *and* the worst times of the day together, and we learn from all of life's experiences.

Parents need not fear that they will do an inadequate job of home schooling. With much love, attention, and time, your child can flourish at home rather than become lost in the shuffle at school. In fact, your child will get far *more* individual attention at home than at school: "A UCLA study of 1,016 public schools found that teachers averaged a total of about seven minutes daily, all day, in personal exchanges with their students. This would allow for no more than one or two personal responses for each student. In contrast, our counts of daily responses in typical homeschools ranged from more than fifty to nearly three hundred."[15]

In your home school, failure need not even be an issue. Your child *will* learn and progress—but at his own rate and on his own timetable. Author Ray Ballman explains how public school schedules can doom some children to failure: "To cover the material, teachers need responses from students able and willing to give it, and so they pay attention to about a third of the class, largely ignoring those who need instruction most, who may be written off as failures in the early weeks of the semester. A high percentage of failure is expected and accepted."[16]

You can expect more than this from your family educational experience. You can give your child much more—your time, your attention, your values. One of the first steps in doing so is to take back the full responsibility for your child.

### Parental Responsibility

To whom does God give children? Not the government. Not even the church. He gives them as gifts to mothers and fathers; then he speaks at length about the duties of parents to their children, and children to their parents. Much debate in the home school community centers on this important issue of responsibility. Llewellyn Davis's book *Going Home to School* states it clearly:

> The central issue in education is who should have ultimate control over the child—the parents or the government. We have allowed the State to assume responsibility for our education, our elderly, our handicapped, our settlement of legal disputes; and usurp many other aspects of authority that God originally gave to the family and to the Church. It is right for Christians to "render unto Caesar what is Caesar's," that is, allow the State to assume those functions that legitimately are within its realm of authority. However, we must be careful not to give the government God's portion.[17]

God's portion is our hearts and minds—and the hearts and minds of our children. Home schooling mom Norma Kunda shared her beliefs with me this way: "We believe God has given the primary responsibility for the upbringing—religious and academic education and socialization—of a child to his parents. It is a responsibility for which we will be held accountable and which we must not take lightly. It is only with the greatest caution and forethought that we should delegate any aspect of this upbringing to any other person or entity."

Along with that responsibility comes the ominous task of education. Many home schoolers rely on Deuteronomy 6:6–9 as their touchstone in this respect. How can children be taught diligently when they are away from the home for seven to eight hours per day being indoctrinated in a primarily humanistic, non-Christian environment? Attorney Christopher Klicka notes: "Nowhere in Scripture can a reference be found in which God delegates to the state the authority to raise and educate children. . . . Parents can delegate their *authority* to raise and teach their children to someone else (i.e., tutor or church school or private or public school), but they can never delegate their *responsibility* to teach their children to anyone else."[18]

Schools encourage parental involvement. In fact, one of the tenets of Goals 2000, a federal attempt to control public education, is to increase parental involvement in their children's schools. Unfortunately, that parental involvement often takes the form of baking cookies. We are not allowed to be involved in our children's education in any significant sense. That is to be left to the experts. We are competent to run the copier and decorate bulletin boards, but not much else.

Who is really raising our kids? When we send them off to school, we give someone else authority over their day. We have no control over their primary caretakers or their use of time at school. At the 1996 Illinois Christian Home Educators convention, Christopher Klicka reminded us that there are forty million children in public school who spend twelve hundred hours a year in a classroom. From kindergarten through grade twelve, seventeen thousand hours will have been spent. During that time, somebody's values are going to be taught. Home schoolers want *their* values taught. The schools have the power to "mass-manipulate," and we put our children at risk when we put them in that situation.

Paul Blanshard, writing for *The Humanist* in 1976, said, "Our schools may not teach Johnny to read properly, but the fact that Johnny is in school until he is sixteen tends to lead toward the elimination of religious superstition."[19] When we willingly give over our authority by allowing our children to go to public school, we relinquish our control to an educational establishment that views our cherished religious faith as mere superstition.

Gregg Harris, one of the leading writers and speakers in the field of home education, puts it this way: "We've been convinced over the years that others outside the family can do a better job of providing things that the family had always provided for itself in the past. Institutions that specialize in everything from fast-food to fast times, from public schools to public health, have wooed us with a promise that they can meet our needs at lower prices and with better quality. What we've found, though, is that the farther we get away from the family unit, the higher the prices go up and the poorer the quality gets."[20]

With an individually designed home environment, children can receive a dramatically different education of fine craftsmanship rather than mass production. We need to embrace the reality that, when it comes to our own children, parents are the real experts—not bureaucrats, not social engineers, and not researchers of the educational establishment.

An American educator, William P. Faunce, summarized the flaws of the public schools in this way: "We have in America the largest public school system on earth, the most expensive college buildings, the most extensive curriculum, but nowhere else is education so blind as to its objectives, so indifferent to any specific outcome as in America. One trouble has been its negative character. It has aimed at suppression of faults rather than the creation of virtues."[21]

In home schools, we can "major" in values and virtues, "minor" in educational twaddle, and give our children a superior academic experience as well.

*Academic Excellence*

Research on the academic success of home schoolers is impressive and prolific: "Dr. Brian Ray, president of the National Home Education Research Institute, conducted an analysis in 1994 of the standardized test results for 16,320 home-school children nationwide. He found these children to average at or above the 73rd percentile in all subject areas. (The national average of all conventionally schooled children is the 50th percentile.)"[22]

In addition, Ray Ballman notes, "Statistical analysis of more than eighty studies demonstrates that a student taught individually achieves on the average thirty percentile points higher in norm-referenced standardized achievement tests."[23]

Superior academic preparation is a compelling motivation of many home schoolers. According to a 1996 Florida Education Department survey, "61 percent of parents ranked dissatisfaction with public school environment and instruction as the primary motivation for homeschooling—topping religion, listed by 21 percent."[24]

It is interesting to note that this academic excellence is achieved with less stress and less time wasted than in a traditional school setting. Richard Rossmiller, a researcher from the University of Wisconsin, studied students with an eye toward estimating how much time is wasted each year within the institutional setting. "According to his research," writes Christopher Klicka, "the typical student annually spends 367 hours (more than two hours a day) in activities such as lunch, recess, attendance-taking and class changing, and 66 hours in 'process activities' during which teachers answer questions, distribute material and discipline students."[25] Conversely, home schooling is so efficient that the average student needs to spend only two to three hours in formal instruction, leaving unlimited time for learning in the rest of life and the rest of the day.

The home can provide the ideal learning environment. Researcher Maralee Mayberry analyzed "effective learning environments" and concluded that such places have three variables in common: commitment to academic excellence, pleasant and orderly atmosphere, and the teacher's confident attitude in his or her ability to help students achieve. These three factors—academics, atmosphere, and attitude—are precisely the factors that set most home schools apart. "Mayberry asserts, the qualities associated with effective learning climates are embodied in the home school setting."[26]

Another academic advantage of home education is that you can choose the amount of structure for your child. Many families start out with an approach that is close to that of a formal classroom. As they gain confidence, they may choose to loosen the structure and follow their children's interests more. A home school is not tied to a clock or a calendar and thus affords delicious freedom to pursue passions.

In a home school setting, you are able to deal with your child's individual personality. If the child is stubborn or needs to work on patience, this can be dealt with much more effectively at home than in the assembly-line atmosphere of school, where the child simply might be labeled as having a behavior disorder.

In your home school, your child won't be branded with a lifelong label, such as "slow learner" or "hyperactive." Because you can tailor education to your child's unique needs and requirements, you won't be subject to the interference and control of "specialists" in the school system. Even if your children have already received a label, you can spare them the long-term harm of that experience by withdrawing them from school and learning to deal with their challenges at home.

Many home schooling families are successfully meeting the needs of their special needs children in the home setting. Parents with such a child should not automatically assume that the public school with its resources is best equipped to handle their child.

Resources are available to help you evaluate your situation. Joyce Herzog, a learning disabilities specialist, has written a book specifically for home educators called *Learning in Spite of Labels*. A Christian organization of parents called NATTHAN (National Challenged Homeschoolers) provides a quarterly newsletter, a resource guide, and referrals to local support groups. They may be contacted at NATTHAN, 5383 Alpine Road SE, Olalla, WA 98359, or by phone at 206-847-4257.

In your home school, perpetual learning can take place anywhere, anytime, all year long. You are not subject to the school calendar or the bus schedule. Vacations, travel opportunities, or family business can be accommodated by your school schedule. Your life can be your classroom. You are not stuck sitting at a desk. You can study nature while basking *in* nature, rather than reading a book about it. You can read the classics while resting under a shade tree. The possibilities are infinite and exciting.

Academic excellence should not be the main reason to home school. Christopher Klicka says, "Our goal is not to have geniuses here on earth, but rather to have righteous children for the kingdom of God."[27] Parents who choose home schooling for religious or spiritual reasons find that superior academic performance is a wonderful side benefit. While focusing on training their children's character, they also enjoy outstanding academic results, precisely because home schools are such effective learning environments.

What about college? Home schoolers fare as well as others in the college academic environment. About 50 percent of home schooled students attend college—about the same rate as public school students. Many institutions actively recruit home educated graduates "because of their maturity, independent thinking skills, creativity, and extensive academic preparation," says Inge Cannon, executive director of Education PLUS.[28] The subject of home schoolers in college will be covered later in greater detail. For now, know that colleges across the country, both public and private, have accepted home school graduates. You and your child can expect this trend to continue.

### Social Perspective

We took a hard look at our lives and decided we didn't want what was newer, faster, brighter, and improved. Our society seems to espouse such things. Quantity has replaced quality as a standard of success. We're looking for things to go faster and more efficiently, and our children are caught up in the haste.

Child psychologist David Elkind describes them as "hurried children." He believes, "The concept of childhood, so vital to the traditional American way of life, is threatened with extinction in the society we have created. Today's child has become the unwilling, unintended victim of overwhelming stress—the stress borne of rapid, bewildering social change and constantly rising expectations."[29]

Home schooling offers the twenty-first-century family a unique alternative to get off the world's materialistic, hurried merry-go-round. Authors Terry Dorian and Zan Peters Tyler call this the gift of time: "The gift of time God gave me with my son during the first year of homeschooling was precious. A deciding factor in our decision to continue homeschooling was the chunk of time school takes children from the home. School takes their prime."[30]

Susan Schaeffer Macaulay is a contemporary proponent of the Charlotte Mason philosophy of education. Charlotte Mason was a turn-of-the-century British educator who believed children should be involved in real-life experiences rather than merely reading textbooks. Ms. Macaulay, in compliance with Ms. Mason's philosophy, notes, "Six-year-old children are as pressurized as executives."[31] We rush them from here to there in a strict schedule that enables us as parents to cope with all the pressures of our lives. We want children, but then we want them to become self-sufficient adults as soon as possible. In the process, we rob them of a child-hood—their time to dream and dawdle. Ms. Macaulay says, "School hours are like a monster . . . gobbling up the treasure of time. Careful now! We only get to be a child once!"[32]

During that vast time that our children are away from us, they are subject to the random socialization of school. We hold fast to the mistaken notion that our six-year-old needs to be with other immature six-year-olds in order to be "nor-mal." This is nothing more than group immaturity. What good can come from this?

The Bible says, "Do not be misled: Bad company corrupts good character" (1 Cor. 15:33), and, "He who walks with the wise grows wise, but a companion of fools suffers harm" (Prov. 13:20). Sue Welch and Cindy Short, editors of *The Teaching Home,* note, "Young children are more likely to be influenced by the majority than to be a testimony to them. Children who receive their education outside the home are prone to accept their peers' and teachers' values over those of their parents. Some advantages of freedom from peer pressure can be self-confidence, independent thinking, the ability to relate to peo-ple of all ages, and better family relations."[33]

It is almost a joke among the home schooling community. The first question we are likely to be asked is, "What about socialization?" The question itself indicates an assumption that the school is the sole dispenser of social skills. On the contrary—school is where our children are exposed to drugs, alcohol, tobacco, sex, guns, and violence. We want our chil-dren to be positively socialized, not randomly socialized in a values-free school zone. David Guterson, author of *Family Matters,* says, "*What about your children's socialization?* is a ques-tion homeschooling parents are often asked as if surely they can have no decent answer. Perhaps it is time for the parents of school-children to begin to ask themselves the same ques-tion in tones of equal concern."[34]

The reality is that "the positive side of socialization—shar-ing, respect, communication, getting along, and relating to others can be wonderfully fulfilled in a home-school setting."[35] Nothing can be more normal or healthy than learning socialization skills in the confines of a warm, loving home atmosphere. It is absurd to assert that a six-year-old needs the company of other immature children in order to be properly socialized. School is not even intended to be a social experience. Children meet with other children, but their contact is superficial and their interaction is shallow. Just because other people are present does not mean social skills will be developed.

Home schooled kids are not locked away in isolation. Author Ray Ballman explains:

> A study by Seattle University researcher Linda Montgomery found that home schoolers between the ages of ten and twenty-one were just as involved in social events like music, dance lessons, scouting, and 4-H as those conventionally schooled. Further, she found that home schoolers show leadership skills equal to or better than their public school peers. A Washington state home school research project surveyed home schoolers and found that more than half spent twenty to thirty hours a month in community or volunteer activities. About 40 percent spent more than thirty hours a month with friends outside their families. Home schoolers are not usually isolated from society, and they learn how to effectively live and work in it.[36]

Keeping family values, keeping academic excellence, and keeping social sanity are a few good reasons to home school—but many, many more exist.

### Sparking Creativity

The negative socialization of the school setting does more than impair a child's ability to relate to others. It also has a negative impact on his creativity and initiative. Children need freedom to spark creativity. They need to experience nature and the great outdoors. A group of children confined to a classroom cannot accommodate this need. A structured nature walk to the local park to look at the trees is at least an attempt, but it does not provide the opportunity that children need to really explore and savor nature. In your home school, you can spend entire days out of doors, chasing insects, catching tadpoles, and collecting leaves. The freedom to explore and learn cannot be matched in a classroom setting. Author Cheryl Gorder notes:

> Through fear, the child loses his identity. Through his loss of identity, he loses his creativity. He is afraid to try anything new, to examine the world on his own. There is no initiative left. School has led him to believe that he must be taught in order to learn and that there is no learning without specified answers. For him, learning is something given, not taken. . . . What the child really learns in this entire process is how to avoid true learning while appearing to be busy, how to look industrious while the teacher is looking, how to sneak a note to his friend while the teacher's back is turned, and how to turn in mediocre work just to get by.[37]

Time and again, I have seen the progressively bad attitude of young students. Kindergartners start out excited and enthused about school and learning. By third grade or so, the children are sick of school and bored with education. Their attitudes are poor and it appears the light has been extinguished from their eyes.

As the mother of girls, I am particularly compelled to home school. Although teachers try to be fair with all children, the fact is that girls are often shortchanged in the classroom. Boys who are more aggressive, vocal, and disruptive are likely to receive the lion's share of the teacher's attention. In addition, the classroom teacher's time is often gobbled up by dealing with "problem kids." Most teachers will admit that 90 percent of their time is taken up by 10 percent of their students. Either these 10 percent need extra tutoring or they have behavioral issues. What happens to the rest of the children? They learn to waste time and to wait. In a home school, your children receive 100 percent—and often 110 percent—of your energy and attention.

Consider also the well-documented "Pygmalion Effect." Psychologists who were researching self-fulfilling prophecy gave teachers false information about their students. They noted that the teachers thereafter treated the students in a manner consistent with this false information. If the teacher was told that the student was gifted, the child was treated as gifted. If the teacher was told that the student was a problem child, he was treated as a problem child—even though this group of students was in reality a "normal" group.[38] What has your teacher been told about your child? Subtle negative impressions on the part of a teacher can have a profound impact on the treatment your child receives at school.

### Safety

In some schools, a child's actual physical safety is threatened on a daily basis. (This will be discussed in more detail later in this book.) Some families choose to home school in order to secure their children's safety from physical harm and danger.

One mom, who was illiterate and first had to teach herself how to write before taking on the task of teaching her own children, reminds us, "Whenever people mention the problem of gang membership, I mention that the common factor amongst all gang members is that they attended school at some time in their lives."[39]

Violence is all too prevalent in our schools. In my own area, a home schooling mom sent her children to school for the first time this year. Her boy was beaten up in shop class and required stitches on his head. This doesn't just happen in the inner city. It happens anyplace where young people without adequate, positive adult influences in their lives gather together.

## The Intangibles

Home schooled kids are healthier. They are not subjected to every virus or contagious disease that floats by. The downside, for our family, is that we were unable to catch chicken pox. We wanted our children to catch it and be done with it. Every time it swept the neighborhood or the school, it missed our door. Since home schooled children are healthier, they miss less instructional time. If a child has special health concerns, such as food allergies or asthma, these can be dealt with more effectively at home. You can rely on your own mothering expertise rather than trusting a stranger to look after your child.

Families can spend their prime time together. Shari Henry, editor of *Heart of Homeschooling,* says, "I realized there is something the public at large just won't 'get' until they know enough homeschoolers face-to-face. It's something that can't be proven or measured by statistics. It just *is.* It is, though, consistent in every homeschooling family I've met. It is the very essence of the homeschooling movement, the tie that binds us all together. It is the importance of family."[40] Authors Terry Dorian and Zan Peters Tyler elaborate on the centrality of family: "Through homeschooling, we reclaim the family and build intimate relationships with our children that will bear fruit into eternity. . . . The greatest opportunity for disciple-making parents will ever have on this earth is with their children."[41]

Home schooled children experience less stress. In a classroom setting, children are guided from one activity to the next, sometimes with great fanfare and excitement. They come to expect education to be entertaining. In contrast, home schooled students are not assaulted by the negative socialization and overstimulation of the classroom. This allows them to be calmer and less addicted to constant activity and stimulation.

Through home schooling, you can encourage your children to be independent learners and thinkers. They don't have to take what the textbooks say about history as gospel. They can investigate all viewpoints. In addition, they are not subject to the latest learning theory, method, or fad. If you believe whole-language reading instruction is inadequate and you want your child to learn phonics, you can teach phonics in your home school. You can teach evolution as an interesting theory and creation as reality—instead of the other way around. Your children can receive a broader, richer, fuller intellectual experience.

One independent learner, quoted in the *New York Times Magazine,* summarizes the benefits this way: "The biggest benefit of home schooling is that it chops away the barriers, opens up all the limits in life. Even with its trials, home schooling shows you there are alternatives. You think: Couldn't I do it a different way? You have confidence."[42]

## What about Mom?

There is an element of satisfaction in the work of home teaching that is hard to define. It is not just the pride of watching your children grow and learn; it is much deeper than that. It is a knowledge somewhere deep within your being that you are doing what is absolutely best for your child.

While the children experience less stress, however, the home schooling mom may experience more. Many are the days when I have longingly looked at the school down the street and thought, "What harm would it do to send them?" After a good night's rest, I have usually regained my perspective. Although you may have bad days, overall the experience can bring a deep satisfaction for mothers, who are most often the primary teachers in the home school.

David Guterson, author of the inspiring book *Family Matters,* says:

It seems to me that all parents must have these moments . . . to gain sustenance from what they offer. Many are so starved in this regard that they have quit looking to their children for emotional food and have begun to search for it inwardly. The result for some is a dislike of their children on an order and or a scale that befuddles their instincts and that inevitably produces the kind of guilt that yields obligatory—and stale—"quality time." . . . She has not learned how to take sustenance from them, is riven by doubts about herself as a mother, cannot understand why she prefers their absence, feels relief when they head for the school bus. The seven-hour respite school provides is in reality a hole she cannot climb from.[43]

The sustenance I gain from the daily relationship with my children is priceless. I will not barter it away for the price of some peace and quiet. Guterson concludes his discussion by saying, "To give . . . children over to an institution is to deny . . . certain elemental satisfactions that life as a parent has to offer."[44]

Parenting is indeed hard work, but it is infinitely rewarding work. Home schooling is even harder. But the rewards are infinitely (and eternally) worthwhile. Author Gregg Harris says, "Rather than ask, 'Is home schooling for everyone?' let me ask, 'Should every Christian home be a place where children are instructed?' If the answer is yes, then welcome to the home school movement."[45]

Despite doubts or fears, be encouraged that you *can* home school. If you possess the commitment and remember your main focus, you will be successful.

## When Home Schooling Is Not the Answer

There are a few situations where home schooling may not be the best choice.

*When your commitment is weak.* Each family must have firm convictions in order to withstand all of the difficult days. Discouragement and despair will impair the quality of the experience for everyone.

*When time does not permit home schooling.* Ted Wade, author of *The Home School Manual,* says, "Even if you are a trained teacher and purchase a well prepared materials package, holding a regular outside job would make responsible home schooling almost impossible."[46]

*When your husband does not support the idea.* Like any other major family undertaking, each partner must be in agreement before making the lifestyle changes warranted by home schooling. If you are not in total agreement, you will suffer disappointment.

*When you are organizationally impaired.* Ted Wade warns, "If you aren't in the habit of following through on long projects, or if you anticipate frequent periods of time during the school year when 'more urgent' tasks are apt to 'unexpectedly' take you away from your teaching, you had better send your child away to a conventional school."[47] There are some excellent resources available to help the organizationally impaired. My first book, *Coming Home to Raise Your Children,* provides lots of information on organizing your home and responsibilities. My friend and home schooling mother of seven, Jackie Wellwood, has written a book called *The Busy Mom's Guide to Simple Living,* which can help you organize and simplify your finances and your home responsibilities. Also, my friend Mary Carney has written *Looking Well to the Ways of Your Household: Practical Help for the Domestically Challenged.* This book, as well as her other helpful resources, is available from Simple Living Workshops, P.O. Box 174, Advance, IN 46102-0174, or by phone at 317-676-6049.

*When illness or other higher priority commitments cause inadequate time and energy.*

*When you are unable to manage your own children, or when your relationship with your children is tense.* Work on discipline and character first before academics are even considered.

None of these are insurmountable barriers to home schooling. If you truly desire to home school, take a month, a semester, or even a year to get heart, house, and mind in order. There are no perfect home schools or perfect home schoolers—just a number of committed people who put one foot in front of the other and step out in faith to do the job they feel called to do.

## How to Decide

From a personal perspective, this was one of the most difficult family decisions my husband and I ever made. I suggest you read as much as you can about home education, talk to others who are already home schooling, and ask yourself some hard questions.

*Do you really enjoy being with your children all the time?* When you home school, you live, eat, sleep, learn, run errands, and do *everything* together. If your relationship is strained, remember this advice from author Linda Dobson: "Remove your child from daily behavior modification, free him from external messages that contradict and drown out his internal voice and, eventually, behavior changes. Provide time, your own life and the lives of variously aged guides and friends as examples and, soon, your needy, demanding, petty child becomes a self-motivated, self-responsible, kinder individual—the kind of person with whom anyone would like to spend time. And that includes you!"[48] Contrary to what you may believe, more time spent with your child does not have to be an irritation. It can be rewarding and sustaining.

*Have you prayed and considered what the role of school is in your own child's life?* Home schooling is more than academics. In fact, most who home school say academics is not the key factor. Once you have set out goals for your family and considered whether the schools can do an adequate job in reaching them, the decision becomes easier.

*Are there home school support groups or other home schooling families in your area?* Not only is that important for parents, but it is essential that your child know and socialize with other children who are sharing similar experiences.

*Is access to out-of-school activities (such as church youth groups or park district sports activities) available?* Some families pursue many outside things, some very little. Too many might seem to defeat the purpose of home schooling, but a few out-of-school activities can provide essential social experiences.

*Have you evaluated available curriculum and made a choice that you can live with for a year or so?* To hop around from one approach to another is expensive and can be confusing for the child.

Finally, as authors Terry Dorian and Zan Peters Tyler note, "People begin homeschooling for a variety of reasons. All homeschooling parents continue for one reason: it works!"[49]

# 3

# *Why Not the Public School?*

*A*t the beginning of each school year, my husband and I watch news coverage of children returning to school. In an annual autumn ritual, teachers go on strike, bus drivers quit (leaving children stranded), and health hazards are discovered in the school buildings. Without fail, "the system" appears unprepared to greet the new year. There is a certain sense of relief that our children will not be subjected to these bureaucratic machinations.

Public education can be likened to an assembly line factory: Raw material—our child—enters one door, and a politically correct thinking semi-adult emerges at the opposite end. We have other plans for our children; ours will be homegrown. Like the gardener who carefully chooses his seeds in the winter months and plots his garden when there is no sight of spring, we are nurturing our children at home. We thoughtfully consider proper soil temperature and conditioning before planting the seeds, and then we engage in an intense season of hard work, nurturing, weeding, and continuous, consistent attention. We could easily go to the market to buy produce and flowers, but we would miss the deep satisfaction that growing our own brings.

As author Mary Hood comments, "Someone once said that if you become too open-minded, your brains may fall out. This is a good description of what has been happening in the public education sphere over the years."[1] Rather than open-minded children, we pray that ours will be God-filled children, and we have chosen to try to accomplish this within the context of our home learning environment.

David and Micki Colfax, home school pioneers who had enormous success with their own children, say this of schools: "Their primary objective is that of moving the product—school-children—on down the line with a minimum of interference from subordinates, parents, the public, or the children themselves. Control is paramount, while subservience and conformity are valued and rewarded. Ends are transformed as education is reduced to an incidental—if occasionally troublesome—element in the day-to-day operations of the organization."[2]

If our children are the product in this assembly line of educational indoctrination, what is the overall quality of that product? Not good. "Public education is 'the second largest industry in America, with 2.3 million classroom teachers; the largest union in the world; and the second-largest budget in government (second only to the welfare department),'" writes Llewellyn Davis. "Despite these impressive resources, statistics confirm declining test scores, growing illiteracy among students, incompetency of teachers, increased enrollment at private schools, and frequent defeats of bond issues."[3] When you count the cost of production, the results hardly seem worthwhile. If quality standards were to be judged against those used in the corporate sector, most school systems nationwide would experience financial bankruptcy. Yet we continue to shovel money into this inefficient behemoth, trying to reassure ourselves that everything will work out.

Part of the blame for the national educational incompetence can be rightfully laid at the feet of the National Education Association (NEA). This is the national teacher's union with some 2.1 million members. It is the country's largest union and enjoys incredible political and direct influential powers over schools and children. According to writers Peter Brimelow and Leslie Spencer, "The NEA's rise is directly linked with the 30-year decline of American education that occurred simultaneously—not just in terms of quantity, but especially in terms of quality: education's crushing, and incessantly cumulating, cost."[4] These authors track a direct correlation between children's SAT scores and the almost unanimous unionization of America's teachers. There is a direct correlation between per-pupil spending and the rise in union power as well.

The NEA stands firmly and officially against home schooling. Linda Dobson notes the following statement from one of its 1993–1994 resolutions: "The National Education Association believes that home education programs cannot provide the student with a comprehensive education experience. The Association believes that, if parental preference home schooling study occurs, students enrolled must meet all state requirements. Instruction should be by persons who are licensed by the appropriate state agency, and curriculum approved by the state department of education should be used."[5]

If the public education system has learned anything in the past thirty years, it should be that money does not inherently solve problems. Bulging budgets and bloated bureaucracies do not satisfactorily address the issue at hand—how to best educate our children. It is indeed ironic that the NEA, with all its power and ideas for reform, should be so threatened by home education. Maybe it's because home schooling works—without huge budgets and masses of highly paid professionals.

## The Academic Outlook

In 1982, the National Commission on Excellence in Education was impaneled to examine the state of public schools. Their study, entitled "A Nation at Risk: The Imperative for

Educational Reform," decries the rising tide of mediocrity in American education. It laments that the performance of children in the United States still falls short of those in other industrialized countries by nineteen measures of academic achievement. Despite some temporary gains made after the Sputnik challenge, we still perform well below other nations. The study found the most significant declines were in math and reading skills, logic, and the ability to draw inferences. The report also estimated that twenty-seven million illiterates live in our nation, most of whom are products of the public school system. As authors of the report characterized:

> The educational foundations of our society are presently being eroded by a rising tide of mediocrity that threatens our very future as a Nation and a people. . . . If an unfriendly foreign power had attempted to impose on America the mediocre educational performance that exists today, we might well have viewed it as an act of war. As it stands, we have allowed this to happen to ourselves. We have even squandered the gains in student achievement made in the wake of the Sputnik challenge. Moreover, we have dismantled essential support systems which helped make those gains possible. We have, in effect, been committing an act of unthinking, unilateral educational disarmament.[6]

During the same time period as this report, thousands of families were returning to the practice of teaching at home. The number of those families rose from 60,000 in 1983 to 244,000 by 1988.[7] In 1983, the Home School Legal Defense Association was formed for the sole purpose of protecting the rights and freedoms of families returning to home teaching.

By the 1990s, home schooling was active in all states. Home schooling families are now a formidable political force. It is a movement that is bringing families back to their place of importance and responsibility. It is an awakening that is bringing parents back to their knees as they seek to obey God's plan for the family.

After over a decade of reactionary reforms, the educational disarmament continues and not much has improved. Christopher Klicka reports a January 1992 finding: "The U.S. Department of Education released a report that showed that the reading skills of nine-year olds worsened during the 1980s when schools were supposed to be getting better due to massive reforms. . . . Meanwhile, a study was released in February 1992 which found U.S. students were below the *world* average in math and science."[8]

It is little wonder that a "U.S. Department of Education study demonstrates that public school teachers are more likely to send their children to a private school than any other group."[9] Those with inside knowledge of public education will not allow their own children to participate.

Available information on SAT scores is also discouraging. Christopher Klicka reports, "In the past five years, verbal averages dropped eight points to 422 (out of a possible 800) and math went down to 474 (out of 800) for a total of 896 out of a possible 1600."[10]

As further evidence of the intellectual dishonesty of the educational establishment, author Ray Ballman reveals: "SAT scores are being re-normed to cover government school failure. SAT scores have dropped in recent years between 25 and 78 points. So the College Board is re-norming the SAT to make the new lower scores the average. The SAT gives scores between 200 and 800. The average for students until the late 1960s had been 500 points. The average now has dropped to 475 for math and 422 for verbal, showing that modern students are performing much worse than did their predecessors. So the College Board is simply going to adjust the SAT norm. What this means is that the results are being skewed."[11]

These mediocre results have been achieved at enormous cost. Per-pupil spending has accelerated rapidly, while student performance has plummeted. "In the last decade," writes Christopher Klicka, "from 1982 to 1992, per-pupil spending has nearly doubled from approximately $3000 per student to just under $6000 per student."[12]

Compare this with a home school family's expenditure of about five hundred dollars per pupil, per year. The impressive academic performance of the home educated reveals that home education is clearly the best choice. Is it any wonder that the NEA wants to regulate home schooling out of existence? It makes them look bad.

There is also a dishonesty in the lowering of school standards. Home schooling author Ray Ballman explains: "Experts have confirmed that students today get at least 25 percent more A's and B's than they did fifteen years ago, but at the same time they know less."[13] Children are intentionally given good grades in order to encourage them and bolster self-esteem. As author Linda Dobson notes, "A forty-five minute weekly discussion of self-esteem and a list of the '10 Things I Like Most About Myself' don't lead a child to emotional stability. . . . Emptiness exists where education should fulfill our children. The inability of informatory knowledge to satisfy, to quench the thirst for knowledge every child possesses is sad enough. But the continued practice of school-style intellectual development that strips children of their natural desire to learn, and robs them of any sense of integration, or connectedness, is a sin."[14]

False grades create a false sense of self-worth in students. They are being swindled and deceived. These grades do not accurately reflect skill or achievement. Upon college admission, many of these children are woefully unprepared. Ray Ballman reports: "A survey of 826 college campuses in fifteen states by the Southern Regional Education Board found that one-third of entering freshman require remedial training in math, reading, or writing and are not ready to begin college courses."[15] This academic intellectual dishonesty can be circumvented by teaching your children at home—honestly and effectively.

I believe that sending our children off into a system that doesn't work and pretending that everything is fine is a blindness akin to sin. We are shutting our eyes to the reality that a new approach is needed. Author Mary Hood admonishes us, "It's time for most of us to stop focusing on attempts to change the old system. It is nothing more than a 'used wineskin' and can never be fixed adequately."[16]

Home schooling is not for everyone, but those of us who choose it should be left alone without harassment or interference. History and repeated attempts at reform have shown that the old way of doing things doesn't work. Maybe the ancient way is worthy of consideration. The writer Jeremiah says:

> This is what the LORD says:
> "Stand at the crossroads and look;
>   ask for the ancient paths,
> ask where the good way is, and walk in it,
>   and you will find rest for your souls."
>                                          Jeremiah 6:16

If the state of public education concerns you, the ancient path of home education could give you the peace of mind you seek.

In contrast, what are some of the solutions the educational establishment has come up with to solve the problem of public education? Goals 2000 is its best solution to date.

## Goals 2000

During his presidency, George Bush had a vision called America 2000. This was the name given to his plan to improve education by increasingly involving the federal government.

After Bill Clinton became president, he directed the Department of Education to continue to pursue many of these ideas under the new name of Goals 2000. President Clinton said, "Goals 2000 is a new way of doing business in America. It represents the direction our government must take in many problems in the 21st century."[17]

Goals 2000 may sound like a laudable effort to the less informed. Such sweeping social reforms often sound promising on the surface. Let's take a closer look at the six original goals, the two goals that have been added, and the specific plan of Outcome Based Education.

## The Goals

### 1. ALL CHILDREN WILL START SCHOOL READY TO LEARN.

Teachers are frustrated by unprepared children who have not been exposed to learning readiness activities. This goal seeks to remedy this by providing government intervention in child rearing long before the child reaches kindergarten.

Readiness is a complicated issue. In their early years, children need love, lots of attention, proper nourishment, exposure to the world, and an introduction to the greatness of God. Few—if any—of these requirements can be met by the government. Their attempt to usurp these tasks will only compromise our freedom and individuality as families. The goal of educators seems to be to fix the whole family, not just teach the child. Such an encompassing goal gives the government too much control over family life. Mark and Helen Hegener, leading thinkers in the home school movement, warn:

> This misguided goal could be used to justify all kinds of powerful early childhood educational programs, governmental intervention in homes of children who have not yet begun school, programs for testing and keeping portfolios on children who have not yet entered school, etc. . . . Trying to solve

complex social problems under the guise of preparing children for school shifts the emphasis from support for families to a justification for outside intervention, the merging of social services with educational services, a move toward state-controlled education, and a strengthening of the idea that the role of children is to serve the schools and the state.[18]

The merging of social services with educational services is troubling. At earlier and earlier ages, children are being subjected to what author Cathy Duffy calls government's "cradle to grave agenda." She notes that "the percentage of three-to-five-year-olds enrolled in preschool nearly doubled between 1973 and 1992. Even more telling is the money that the federal government has poured into the expansion of preschool programs: it has nearly doubled in the past four years (1989–1993), growing from $10.3 billion to $21 billion."[19] The granting of this money is often tied to the expansion of health and social services, along with social workers to supervise whether we are adequately parenting our children.

These programs fall under the heading of what Mrs. Duffy calls the "Need Some—Force All" principle.[20] Because some irresponsible families need government intervention to do the right thing, we will all be forced to raise our children according to government guidelines.

For responsible parents the potential intrusion and control of this plan is offensive. To be supportive of families is one matter—to seek to dictate their lives is quite another. The Christian Home Educators Coalition explains how this plan might work:

> The Goals 2000 plan offers local schools and day care centers incentives for providing programs by which parents learn how to work with their preschoolers. In these *Parents as Teachers* programs, the "home visitor" evaluates the home and parent-child relationship, and a comprehensive plan is set up. These home visitors are certified teachers, social workers or

psychologists. Usually, they are "mandated reporters" who are required by law to turn in anyone who they may consider to be abusing or neglecting children. If the children in the homes are "at risk" of not meeting their highest potentials, special attention is given to that family.[21]

It is deeply problematic that almost any child can be classified as "at risk." There are well-defined parameters, such as a child who has been handicapped from birth. Other criteria become increasingly subjective, such as overindulgence of a child or a low level of communication with a child. Finally, there is a catchall category of "other." This might include lack of routine, too few toys, too many toys, or over or under stimulation of a child. There is anecdotal evidence that even a messy house has been construed to be a detrimental environment that places the family at risk. Once a family has earned a negative label, they are stuck in the social service system, subject to unwanted interference and intimidation. Every family experiences distress at some point. This does not, however, warrant social intervention that frequently ignores parental rights and privacy.

Early education is important. A loving home environment free from government interference is more important. The Bible provides ample advice on how to teach and train our children. We don't need a government program when we have access to the greatest book ever written on how to train up a child.

## 2. THE HIGH SCHOOL GRADUATION RATE WILL INCREASE TO AT LEAST 90 PERCENT.

Society would be wonderful if there were no youngsters who had to work, if there were no broken homes, if everyone received a superior education. For many families, this is not a reality. Some teenagers enter the work force early by necessity. Not all young adults face adulthood on a straight trajectory in a neat, government-sanctioned fashion.

As Mark and Helen Hegener comment, "This goal denies the fact that for many young people, better alternatives exist than continuing to attend a school that does not make sense for their lives, driving them toward a diploma that will not even solve their economic problems because a reasonable job is difficult to find even with a diploma. . . . This goal justifies tracking students in either vocational education or college preparatory programs, this perhaps increasing the likelihood of graduation but often not serving the needs or interests of the students. Also, this goal could be used to justify a myriad of punitive truancy measures."[22]

Part of this plan is the School-to-Work Act, which became law on May 4, 1994 (Public Law 103–239). Part of the plan provides money to schools that are willing to implement School-to-Work programs. Such programs allow a student to earn a Certificate of Initial Mastery by the end of tenth grade, from which point a student could move into a vocational or apprenticeship program. At the completion of twelfth grade, students earn a Certificate of Advanced Mastery. These portable credentials ideally would prepare students for a high-skill, high-wage first job or for entry into college. Many home educators believe this trend will reduce schools to job training centers that exist simply to meet the future needs of corporate America. We object to the narrowing of options this would represent for the average high school student. While it is true that students need to learn to make a living, schools are supposed to be the places where horizons are expanded and lives are enriched—not merely funneled into a mold for the consumption of big business.

Others, like Larry and Susan Kaseman, believe that these types of programs simply do not work. The Kasemans have been home schooling since 1979 and are the authors of *Taking Charge through Home Schooling*. They note, "They have not worked in the past. Predictions for what kinds of jobs will be available in the future have proven to be inaccurate, and our economy and technology are changing even more quickly now than they did in the past. People who have followed recommendations that they become trained for specific careers can easily find themselves out of work. For example, consider the push in the '60s and '70s to train more scientists and engineers. Many of these white collar professionals are now out of work because of downsizing and because the supply exceeds current demand."[23]

In addition, how many government job training programs have we seen in past generations? With regard to the passage of federal school-to-work legislation, Senator Nancy L. Kassenbaum notes: "My opposition is based on my conviction that it compounds rather than corrects the deficiencies of current federal job-training efforts. Just consider the fact that we already have 154 separate job-training programs on the books. By passing this bill, we will have 155."[24]

The issue is much deeper than job training. It is this: Should the government be allowed to decide what children learn, how they think, and what they believe? In our free marketplace, a student still has the option to major in philosophy or theology, despite poor job prospects for philosophers and theologians.

### 3. UNITED STATES STUDENTS WILL BE COMPETENT IN CORE SUBJECTS.

Few would disagree that children need to be competent in the basics—reading, math, writing, and spelling. Beyond that, variations in curriculum are wide. A core curriculum has a great deal of appeal, but it takes away individual choice. What is "core" in one segment of society may not matter in another segment. For example, an agricultural community would have a different opinion as to what is at its core than an industrial community.

Another issue is how competence in core subjects will be evaluated. Mark and Helen Hegener warn, "Here is the rationale for all kinds of standardized testing and assessment, possibly a uniform, standardized national testing program."[25]

In a very real sense, curriculum is determined by testing. If national tests to evaluate whether children have absorbed core knowledge become reality, the test will necessarily reflect the new educational agenda. Cathy Duffy notes, "This means that the curriculum of your local school will actually be determined by test writers in Washington, D.C., circumventing the constitutional prohibition of federal interference in local curriculum development."[26] This further removes the control of schools and their curriculum from the community and its standards.

In a way, this goal is an insult to generations of educators and students. If the same way of doing business has produced a nation of poorly schooled, even illiterate individuals, will yet another government program aimed at competence be of any value? We are throwing money at a problem that simply cannot be solved with money.

### 4. UNITED STATES STUDENTS WILL BE FIRST IN THE WORLD IN MATH AND SCIENCE.

There is an issue of national pride involved in this goal. We love our young Olympic gymnastic heroes. Yet behind their accomplishment is often a childhood sacrificed at the altar of a parent's or trainer's ego. The temptation might be too great for our teachers to become driven taskmasters, to be first in the world at all costs.

We each have unique gifts from our Lord and Creator. A child who is not gifted in math and science will receive disparate treatment in a school setting that values math and science above all other disciplines. The Hegeners warn, "Here is a blatant statement that schools are to serve the state and the economy rather than the needs of the students, their families, and their communities. Goals such as this can lead to unbalanced curriculums, and unreasonable rewards for students who happen to have technical ability."[27]

The pride of our country should remain our individual freedom and the greatness achieved by individuals exercising those freedoms in a wide area of disciplines.

*5. EVERY ADULT WILL BE LITERATE AND BE ABLE TO COMPETE IN A GLOBAL ECONOMY AND EXERCISE THE RIGHTS AND RESPONSIBILITIES OF CITIZENSHIP.*

Not only is the federal government seeking to regulate and rule your children, but they have plans for *you* as well. The Hegeners comment, "This opens the door for schools to extend their authority to adults. Everyone would have to serve the economy, demonstrate competence in required skills, and live up to a definition of 'citizenship' defined by those in power."[28] Another point that is missed by this goal is that every adult *now* has the option to be literate and to exercise the rights and responsibilities of citizenship.

*6. EVERY SCHOOL IN THE UNITED STATES WILL BE FREE OF DRUGS AND VIOLENCE.*

Every school *should* be free of drugs and violence. This initiative starts at home. It is the responsibility of individual parents to train their children in these matters. Children should learn about violence protection, drugs, and responsible sexual behavior from their parents. It is disheartening to think that because some parents don't or won't take the time to teach their children, the privacy rights of all families will be compromised.

With sweeping, across-the-board initiatives like this, "Civil liberties could be lost as strict behavior codes, drug testing, and search and seizures are instituted or strengthened," note the Hegeners.[29] With increased regulatory power comes increased abuses of that power. There was a story in the news recently of a student who was suspended from school because she gave another student a nonprescription aspirin. This is an example of anti-drug fervor taken to its extreme. But if administrators are given unlimited power to stem the drug problem, all students could have their rights and freedoms diminished.

### 7. TEACHERS WILL HAVE THE PROFESSIONAL DEVELOPMENT THEY NEED TO HELP STUDENTS REACH THE OTHER GOALS.

Will this development take the form of training teachers to be social engineers? It sounds as if teachers will be taught to serve as the middlemen between students and government purveyors of social restructuring. Presumably, teachers have learned to *teach* in teacher's college. I do not wish to have my tax dollars spent on the latest federal schemes for improving education. This is throwing more money at a problem that simply can't be solved with money.

### 8. ALL SCHOOLS WILL PROMOTE PARTNERSHIPS THAT WILL INCREASE PARENTAL INVOLVEMENT AND PARTICIPATION.

Would the achievement of this particular goal mean that schools would cooperate with home educators? Chances are that framers of Goals 2000 have not even considered such a possibility. Authors Terry Dorian and Zan Peters Tyler note, "Homeschooling is the epitome of parental involvement. . . . It is discouraging to note that many of the professional educators who are touting the 'new banner' of parental involvement are very much opposed to homeschooling."[30]

On March 31, 1994, Goals 2000 was signed into law (Public Law 103–227). Later that same year, the funding bill for Goals 2000 was passed. On October 20, 1994, Improving America's Schools Act (IASA) became law (Public Law 103–382). The purpose of IASA was to tie federal funding of schools to acceptable federal standards. While Goals 2000 may have been "voluntary" in its inception, a school wishing to opt out would lose precious funding.

The overall problem with Goals 2000 is that it increases the role of the federal government in education, an area that has traditionally been subject to state and local control. With Goals 2000 will come federal dollars—*a lot* of tax dollars. This will give the federal government greater control over where those dollars will be spent.

A commentator for Focus on the Family notes, "Goals 2000 is projected to cost more than $5 billion in its first five years. But what taxpayers will get for their money is precisely the kind of education reform that pro-family constituents do not want. . . . Those powers include the ability to implement national curriculum, national testing, uniform requirements for materials, and uniform instruction. . . . The Department of Education insists that Goals 2000 is strictly voluntary, yet states must produce plans that conform to the content and performance standards set out by national panels in order to qualify for the federal handout."[31]

It is clear that the voluntary nature of Goals 2000 is not voluntary at all. It is a political charade full of platitudes and false hope for education. It is not just a Band-Aid for our schools but an expensive, unnecessary full-body cast that will restrict and immobilize all of us. We may want to believe it will solve the problems, but it will only be a breath of political hot air.

Solutions lie within individual families and with individual initiative. The federal government will spend millions of dollars with few if any results. Individual home school families seek to be left alone to implement their highly individual initiatives for improving education. It is not my premise to suggest that home schooling can solve *all* of education's ills, but those who do choose this solution should be free from harassment and interference.

## Outcome Based Education

In a sense, when we teach our children, we are seeking a certain outcome, such as the ability to read, to recite multiplication tables, or to explain the circulatory system. Broadly defined, all education is outcome based in that it looks to some performance result. The government version of Outcome Based Education (with capital letters) is problematic for a variety of reasons.

Outcome Based Education is one component of Goals 2000. Although it has many different names and nuances, OBE is essentially a federal attempt to influence curriculum and culture. OBE is the brainchild of Dr. William Spadey. According to his original theory, OBE could take one of three forms: traditional, which uses the school's existing curriculum and alters the objectives to conform to OBE outcomes; transformational, which requires a complete restructuring of a school's faculty and curriculum; and transitional, which falls somewhere between the two.

Like many theories, OBE was not inherently flawed in its inception. Rather, the difficulty lies in the manner in which students will be evaluated as to whether they have met prescribed outcomes. Of greatest concern is a shift from emphasis on the cognitive domain to the affective domain, or a focus on attitudes, values, feelings, and emotions rather than pure subject matter.

The Christian Home Educators Coalition of Chicago expressed its concern as follows:

> In order for the Goals 2000 standards to be met, the U.S. Department of Education has authorized several publishers to develop a national curriculum. Although there are many labels for this new curriculum, educators call this new "high quality" curriculum Outcome Based Education (OBE) or Mastery Learning. Traditional standardized tests, which have long provided the academic benchmark for comparison between pupils, schools, and school districts, have been tar-

geted for obliteration. The presidents of the Educational Testing Service and the American Federation of Teachers revealed this information at a joint appearance in the 1990s. The presidents described the new tests as a mixture of essays, open-ended questions, demonstrations, and hands-on tasks. These tests will evaluate such intangible traits as "coping skills," "self-esteem," and "need for affiliation." Academic skill development will not be measured as much as attitudes and beliefs will be assessed. Students who are not taught with textbooks which coordinate with this nationalized curriculum are sure to perform at a lower level than those who have been taught the appropriate "outcomes" or "goals."[32]

In a position paper for Focus on the Family, Linda Page writes: "The bottom line is that OBE minimizes the consistent, proven components of successful education. Instead, it concentrates on feel good, sound good solutions which use laudable language, but which divert time in the educational program away from substantive academic goals and education results. OBE is open to abuse and mischief because it does not define specific student learning, but rather aims toward esoteric performance outcomes, values, and attitudes."[33]

OBE is more federal smoke and mirrors to try to fix education—or perhaps just to make us feel better about the awful state it is in. If we feel good about the miserable state of public education, then perhaps we will be willing to fork over our tax dollars to continue feeling good.

Jeff Hooten of Focus on the Family's *Citizen* magazine, a publication that examines political and societal happenings, comments, "In areas where parental opposition sidelined their plans, some 'OBEists' have adopted a fresh strategy: Give the educator some new clothes. Outcome-based education has taken on new life as 'World Class Education,' 'Performance-based Education,' 'Developmentally Appropriate Practice,' 'Total Quality Management' or 'Schools for the 21st Century,' to name a few."[34]

How can a parent detect OBE? Jeff Hooten suggests, "Parents [should] begin with a simple question: 'Is the outcome one that defines something we would expect a young person to do academically? Does it have something to do with arithmetic, science, English, history, geography or fine arts?' . . . The opposite question is, 'Does it have something to do with values, attitudes or social outcomes that require certain behaviors?'"[35]

The most complex OBE issue is this: How do you measure it? Does the government define those values, attitudes, or social outcomes, or is it a matter for individual families to imbue with their own values and faith?

Jeff Hooten warns:

> A shift toward subjective outcomes and away from traditional letter grades is but one hallmark of OBE. Other characteristics include:
>
> - Cooperative learning, which focuses on group projects at the expense of personal responsibility.
> - Downplaying standardized tests and other objective forms of assessment in favor of having students compile "portfolios" of their work.
> - A top-down approach—backed by state departments of education, teacher unions, education consultants, even the federal government—that undermines parental authority and diminishes local control.[36]

Outcome Based Education, by whatever name, is a dangerous tangent for public education. It will only serve to sacrifice academic achievement at the altar of high self-esteem.

As home schooling parents, we are confident that our children are receiving rigorous academic training that is within our budget, our value system, and our beliefs. They are receiving an education that is not subject to the latest social trend. We would not have this confidence if we had not taken them home.

_4_

# _Home Schooling Success_

**W**hat would you say if you were told that your child could receive a superior education, develop well socially, possess a positive self-concept, and be equipped with a passion for God—all for about five hundred dollars per year? Is this one of those television infomercials that appears too good to be true?

Not for home educators. Research in this field is impressive and will convince even the harshest critic of the successes of home education. The evidence, both anecdotal and scientific, proves that home education works. It is cost efficient and provides many benefits for the family in terms of increased closeness, family cohesion, and spiritual development. Dr. Brian Ray notes, "I know of no research showing problems with too much parental input in children's lives, but there's a huge amount showing that there's not enough."[1] Home educators will never look back in regret at time not spent with their children. Home teaching adds challenge, excitement, depth, and color to that time spent together.

Not all the benefits of home schooling are quantifiable, but many are. Home schooled families are successful academically, socially, and in character issues.

71

## Academic Success

Psychologists and academics have been studying home educators for years. The year 1995 was perhaps the most significant for research in home education. A large sample of home schooled students took the Iowa Tests of Basic Skills that year. This group consisted of 16,320 students in grades K–12 in all fifty states. Dr. Brian Ray of the National Home Education Research Institute reports: "These home-educated students scored, on average, at the 79th percentile in reading, the 73rd percentile in language and the 73rd percentile in mathematics." The basic battery report, a combination of these three skills, was in the 77th percentile. Note that the national average is the 50th percentile.[2] This report is especially significant because of the large number of students tested with this well-accepted standardized test.

In another 1995 study of students in Montana, Dr. Ray studied 367 home educated children in 207 families. The children scored in the 75th percentile for reading, 73rd percentile for listening, 63rd percentile for total language, 67th percentile for math, 77th for science, 75th for social studies. The complete battery, which was a measure of all subject areas in which students were tested, showed a score in the 73rd percentile. The national average is the 50th percentile.[3]

In the spring of 1994, hundreds of Illinois home educated students took the Iowa Tests of Basic Skills. The results show that "79.6% of home schooled children achieve[d] individual scores above the national average (compared to 50% of conventional school population)."[4]

Success in academics and critical thinking skills are closely allied. Dr. Ray reports the results of Bob Jones University researchers who sought to determine differences in selected critical thinking skills among freshman Christian college students, some of whom had come from home schools: "The researchers found that the students who were educated in home schools had a slightly higher overall mean critical thinking score than that of students who were from public schools, Christian schools, and A.C.E. (Accelerated Christian Education) schools."[5]

A 1990s study by Dr. Ray gathered test results from 1,500 families and 4,600 children. In this study, the students "averaged at or above the 80th percentile of standardized achievement tests in all subject areas. Scores in reading (84th percentile), language (80th percentile), and mathematics (81st percentile) were relatively high. . . . These students scored, on average, at the 84th percentile in science and the 83rd percentile in social studies."[6]

While billions of dollars are expended on public education, a mom at home spending a few hundred dollars a year can achieve outstanding academic results.

## Social Success

One of the main criticisms of home education is that children are denied a significant social experience. It is thought that they will forever be out of step in society because they have been sheltered by their parents.

Does it take a village to raise a child, as the African proverb says? David Wagner of the Family Research Council comments, "If you never take your kids outside, and you throw up a real or metaphorical wall, they can be isolated. But the 'village' concept is abused when used by the authorities to justify state power. A village can be one's parents and friends," notes Wagner. "There is socialization among home-schoolers; it's not just regimented by age group the way it is in [traditional] schools, which is unnatural. And it is not selfish to give kids the best education you can. What's good for kids is good for society."[7] Home school families are turning out good kids. That's good for the family, the neighborhood, and society.

Home schooled kids *are* out in the world—involved in their communities and with other children. This has been documented by solid research: "A 1988 study by Seattle University researcher Linda Montgomery found that home-schoolers were just as involved as conventional students in music and dance lessons, scouting and 4-H clubs, and were even more likely to have jobs such as delivering papers, mowing lawns or babysitting. In 1988, the Washington [state] Home School Research Project surveyed 219 home-schoolers and found that more than half spent 20–30 hours a month in community and volunteer activities. About 40 percent spent more than 30 hours a month with friends outside their families."[8]

There are many benefits to this selective socialization: "Dr. Mona Delahooke reported that the only significant difference she found between the home educated and the conventionally schooled was that the home educated were less influenced by peers and less peer-dependent."[9] It also appears that "the home educated children perceived their parents as primary authority figures more often than did the private school children."[10]

In an age in which there is enormous peer pressure to experiment with illicit drugs and sex, it is a comfort to know that home education increases the likelihood that my husband and I will retain our parental authority rather than giving it over to a band of teenage peers.

In yet another study, Dr. Larry Shyers observed free play and planned group activity by children. Dr. Brian Ray reports, "He [Shyers] concluded that conventional school children displayed significantly more problem behaviors than did the home educated. Shyers conjectured that the better behavior of the home educated might be due to the fact that their primary models are their parents, whereas conventionally schooled children spend much time with peers who might be their primary models."[11]

Another report described Dr. Shyers's findings as follows: "The traditionally schooled tended to be considerably more

aggressive, loud, and competitive than were the home educated. Dr. Shyers noted that his findings draw into question
the assumption made by many people that traditionally educated children are more socially well-adjusted than those who
are home educated."[12]

Researcher Thomas Smedley's 1992 master's thesis, "The
Socialization of Home School Children," used the Vineland
Adaptive Behavior Scale to evaluate the social maturity of a
sample of equally matched public school and home schooled
children. The score on this scale measures the general maturity of the subject. The results "demonstrated that the home-
schooled children were better socialized and more mature than
the children in the public school. The home-schooled children scored in the 84th percentile while the matched sample
of public school children only scored in the 27th percentile."[13]

Dr. Wesley Taylor studied self-concept in home educated
children. Utilizing the theory that positive self-concept is
related to positive socialization, he studied 224 home school
students throughout the United States in grades four through
twelve. He found that the "self-concept of home school students was significantly higher than that of public school students for the global scale and all six subscales of the Piers-
Harris Children's Self-Concept Scale (PHCSCS)."[14]

The Bible states, "He who walks with the wise grows wise,
but a companion of fools suffers harm" (Prov. 13:20). To your
children, you are very wise. The variety of people they will
meet through home education may be very wise. Home schooling allows them an opportunity to walk with the wise a bit
longer before venturing into the decaying and fallen world.

## Character Success

Many families home school primarily in order to develop
good character in their children. In this context, shaping char-

acter is shaping the will to be more like Christ. Researcher Dr. Tracy Romm was interested in the transmission of civic culture in home school families. He studied a broad range of families from different religious and racial backgrounds and found that home schooling parents "are concerned primarily with the character-building function of education . . . as well as mental abilities that serve to preserve the distinctive qualities of each individual child. Schools are rejected as the referent for this process; they are viewed as serving more as a force for social conformity than as a protector of individual integrity."[15]

Dr. Raymond and Dorothy Moore, the grandparents of the home schooling movement who have been writing and advocating on behalf of home schooling families for several decades, also believe in the importance of character formation.

> Character education is the missing link. The highest goal of teaching at its best is character education. It is bringing to our children/students lessons of love which breed concern for others—putting them ahead of ourselves. It is showing by example that honesty, dependability, neatness, order, industry, and initiative pay richly. It is teaching the equality of human beings by practicing the Golden Rule. It is demonstrating to children how to work and how to help, instead of waiting for things to be done for them. It is teaching them to feel needed and wanted and depended upon—in order to develop a sense of self-worth. The child who has this advantage generally becomes a self-directed leader in his society. He knows where he is going and is not easily pressured by his peers.[16]

With so much contemporary focus on family values and character education, one needs to realize the vital role home schooling can play in this equation. Researcher Jayn Carson examined the structure and function of home school families. Her findings suggested that "there are stabilizing forces within home school family systems which allow most of these families to accommodate higher levels of both adaptability and cohesion than the population of families whose children are more conventionally schooled. . . . Home schooling may be a stabilizing mechanism in the family as it increases the amount of control the family has over its life stage tasks which are related to the socialization and education of their children."[17]

Many parents count the days until their child becomes eligible for school, then they gleefully ship them off to the care of others. They are missing a golden opportunity for greater family cohesion and building their child's character.

Home schooling provides a superior academic opportunity, a sane socializing experience, and an opportunity to build character in a stable, yet adaptable environment. How do these children fare in college?

## Home Schoolers and College Admissions

Higher education institutions ranging from Adrian College in Michigan to York College in Pennsylvania have accepted home educated students, and the numbers are growing.

It is not necessary in all instances to take the GED high school diploma equivalency test to enter college, although a few colleges might require this. The admissions boards usually rely on a variety of materials, including portfolios of student work, SAT scores, grades from community college courses, and private recommendations.

The best advice for the college-bound student is to begin communicating with potential colleges early. Find out from the admissions office what documentation and course work are required, and plan your child's program accordingly. Another option is to enroll your child in an accredited correspondence or satellite program for high school. Not all programs are accredited, and if your program is not, your child may not be eligible for certain financial aid. Before signing on with any program, check carefully to see that it will meet your needs and expectations.

Mr. Dale Fenton of Wheaton College in Illinois notes, "Private colleges have admitted home educated applicants at a rate of nearly three to one compared to public institutions."[18] No matter which school your child applies to, admissions personnel need to be able to assess whether he or she fits the profile of students who succeed at their college and evaluate how your child compares to other applicants.

An article in *The Chronicle of Higher Education* notes: "Highly selective colleges with big admissions staffs may have the fewest adjustments to make in adapting to home-schooled applicants, because they routinely weigh all sorts of personal characteristics. 'We have always taken the time to evaluate students from unusual situations,' says David P. Illingworth, a senior admissions officer at Harvard University, which saw about 30 applications from people with at least some home schooling in their background this year, out of a total of 18,000."[19]

Fenton reports:

A survey conducted and published by the National Association for College Admission Counseling reports the following factors according to their influence in admission decisions. The percentage indicates the portion of surveyed colleges and universities who rated the criteria as having "considerable importance" in making admissions decisions.

1. Grades in college prep courses    82%
2. Class rank    49%
3. ACT/SAT test scores    47%
4. Grades in all subjects    36%
5. Counselor recommendation    21%
6. Teacher recommendation    18%
7. Essay    17%
8. Interview    12%
9. Work/Extracurricular activities    6%[20]

Fenton offers a few suggestions for home schoolers who plan to apply for college:

1. If you cannot provide a piece of requested information, always inform the college and ask if it can be waived or if something else may be substituted. An application file which is incomplete will not be given full consideration.
2. Plan to take both the SAT I and the ACT. Some students do considerably better on one or the other.
3. Be prepared to take the SAT II subject exams as well. Some colleges may require some of these because it is a good way to demonstrate competence when your curriculum is difficult to assess.
4. Take at least one traditional course at the college level (for many home schoolers a lab science is a good choice) and do well in it. This will alleviate questions about your ability to perform in a classroom and it validates your high school curriculum as being sufficient preparation for successful college studies. [Author's note: Many junior colleges allow high school age children to enroll in courses.]
5. If you have taken several college level courses ask about entering with advanced standing. While it generally sounds appealing to begin college "ahead of the game," if you are counted as a transfer applicant rather than a freshman, it may have undesirable results in regards to orientation, housing and roommate assignments, and scholarships. You may still transfer certain courses while maintaining freshman classification.[21]

With increasing numbers of home educated young adults attending college, the future for our young children looks promising. As home schoolers continue to refine their record-keeping and their ability to present their accomplishments to admissions boards, colleges will become more accustomed to this new breed of student. You can rest assured that your choice to home educate will not compromise college options for your child.

## Home Schoolers as Adults

In one of the first studies of adults who had been home
educated, a University of Michigan assistant professor of education studied a sample of fifty-three adults. A Home School
Legal Defense Association report discusses this work as follows: "Dr. J. Gary Knowles was the first to focus on adults
who were home educated. He collected extensive data from
a group who were home educated an average of about 6 years
before they were 17 years old. He found that they tended to
be involved in occupations that are entrepreneurial and professional, and that they were fiercely independent and strongly
emphasized the importance of family. Furthermore, they were
glad they had been home educated, and would recommend
it to others, and had no grossly negative perceptions of living
in a pluralistic society."[22]

It is interesting also to note, of this same study, that "two
thirds were married, which is the norm for adults their age.
None were unemployed or on welfare. . . . He found that more
than 40% had attended college and 15% of those had completed a graduate degree."[23]

Would you be pleased if your adult child was entrepreneurial, professional, fiercely independent, and strongly
emphasized the importance of family? I would count that as
a "success" in child rearing.

When all factors are balanced, the inescapable conclusion
remains: Home schooling your child, when done responsibly
and prayerfully, will do no harm and may reap great reward.
It could be the best thing you do for your child.

# 5

# *Approaches to Home Education*

$\mathscr{S}$ ome families have a classroom contained within their homes that mirrors the public school down the street. Others have "school" while cuddling on the couch, which is our family's favorite. There are various ways to approach the physical process of home schooling. Moreover, there are various ways to govern the overall philosophy of the home schooling family. This chapter will explore some of the major home schooling approaches.

## The Traditional Approach

In the traditional approach, textbooks and workbooks are used and many other classroom tools are transferred directly into the home. A graded textbook guides teaching, and subject matter is covered in increments over the course of a school year. Textbooks may be supplemented with skill development texts or books. There are many major Christian publishers who supply excellent traditional curricula, although they each may have varying doctrinal approaches.

This approach works very well for many home schooling families. Those who need a schedule and accountability will do well with this method. Those desirous of more flexibility may rebel against the regularity of the traditional approach. In reality, most home schoolers incorporate some form of traditional schooling in their home schools, usually in the subject areas requiring a systematic approach, such as math or phonics.

A few major suppliers of traditional texts are A Beka Books, Bob Jones University, Rod and Staff Publishers, Christian Liberty Academy, Alpha Omega, and Christian Light Education.

## The Classical Approach

In ancient Greece, emphasis was placed on learning the *tools* of learning. These tools could then be applied to the study of any subject. This so-called classical approach would have students study grammar, the dialectic or logic phase, and finally rhetoric. These tools were known as the "trivium." Following the study of these subjects were arithmetic, geometry, astronomy, and music—called the "quadrivium."

English writer and educator Dorothy Sayers (1893–1957) proposed that a modified version of this approach be used to educate contemporary scholars. In the grammar tool of learning, the student would focus on the mastery of facts in all subject areas. Thus, a student from ages six to ten would focus on reading, writing, spelling, Latin, basic math, and Bible memory work. In science, he would learn to classify plants and rocks and to collect specimens. In world geography and history, he would learn his way around the globe and some of the major historical events.

In the dialectic phase, the ten- to twelve-year-old child is taught the rules of logic and how to reason. He asks *how* and *why* things happen as his gateway to greater depth and understanding. The child engages in logical discussion and debate and learns to draw accurate conclusions. The goal of this stage is to equip the child with thinking and language skills.

Finally, the student enters the rhetoric phase at about age fifteen. In this stage, the student hones verbal and written language skills in order to be able to persuasively express himself. He will begin to channel his energy into a chosen branch of knowledge that could lead to his life's work. By use of this method, he will be on his way to becoming a student who can learn for himself. This was the true end of education, according to Dorothy Sayers.

If you are interested in this approach, consider reading *Rediscovering the Lost Tools of Learning* by Douglas Wilson. This book contains the text of the original article by Dorothy Sayers entitled, "The Lost Tools of Learning."

There is a home schooling family (Harvey and Laurie Bluedorn) who publish a quarterly magazine and sell resources relative to teaching the trivium:

Trivium Pursuit
c/o 139 Colorado Street, Suite 168
Muscatine, IA 52761
309-537-3641

## The Principle Approach

The Principle Approach is a way of life, not just a philosophy of education. It is based on three concepts: knowledge of our Christian history, our role in the spread of Christianity, and the ability to live according to the biblical principles upon which our country was founded. Any subject is approached with a focus upon the study of the four R's:

Researching God's Word
Reasoning from biblical principles

Relating the truths to the student's character
Recording the application of biblical principles to the
 subject

The concentration is always the relationship between Christianity and the American form of government.

This is not merely a history course but an approach to the study of all subjects. Followers of this approach hold that there are seven biblical principles upon which this country was founded that should govern all areas of life: (1) individuality, (2) self-government, (3) Christian character, (4) conscience, (5) the Christian form of government, (6) how the seed of local self-government is planted, and (7) the Christian principle of American political union.

The definitive work on this subject is *A Guide to American Christian Education for the Home and School: The Principle Approach* by James B. Rose. There also exists an audiocassette course called *The Principle Approach* by Stephen McDowell.

A group called the Foundation for American Christian Education (F.A.C.E.) has developed the Noah Plan, featuring principle approach educator guides and training for teachers, parents, and administrators. There are grade level guidelines for K–12 broken down into weekly summaries of content goals for each grade. These are available from:

F.A.C.E.
P.O. Box 9444
Chesapeake, VA 23321-9444
804-488-6601

## Charlotte Mason, Living Books, and Life Experiences

Charlotte Mason was a turn-of-the-century British educator whose approach was to teach children basic skills such

as reading, writing, and math, and then expo
best sources of knowledge for all other subjec
mean taking nature walks, visiting museums
close, or reading what she called "living boc
were dry and dull and to be avoided in favor or richer ___
of knowledge.

Her concern was more for the character and minds of children rather than the empty exercise of "getting an education." Children were to be given vast experience with the out-of-doors, allowed lots of time to play and create, and encouraged to narrate and dictate passages from the good books they had read.

Ms. Mason believed that education was a life process and a discipline. By learning throughout the entire day, children would become self-educated. Formal classroom work would last no longer than one-half day. The remainder of the time was for running and playing, exploring nature, doing crafts, or cooking. There was enough time left in the day after school for living.

Ms. Mason despised what she called educational twaddle—the time-wasting nonsense that takes up much of the traditional school day. Her concern was that children be exposed to a classical education, with vocational education to be addressed when they were more mature.

The curriculum suppliers who most closely follow this philosophy are the Calvert School and Sonlight Curriculum. For further reading about Charlotte Mason, you may wish to read *For the Children's Sake* by Susan Schaeffer Macaulay, *Books Children Love* by Edith Wilson, and *Teaching Children* by Diane Lopez. A home teacher could, theoretically, design a custom curriculum using these three books. The six-volume set of *The Original Home Schooling* series by Charlotte Mason is also available. They are wonderful books that provide a parent with a real grounding in the Charlotte Mason philosophy.

Finally, *Parents Review* magazine is a publication that reprints Ms. Mason's original work and also contains articles about the contemporary application of this philosophy. It is a thoughtful publication that can be very useful and encouraging. For subscription information, you may contact:

Charlotte Mason Research Institute
P.O. Box 172
Stanton, NJ 08885

## The Unit-Study Approach

A unit study takes a specific theme or topic and delves into it deeply over a period of time, integrating language arts, social studies, science, history, fine arts, and math as they apply. The unit-study philosophy emphasizes that all knowledge is interrelated and is learned more easily and remembered longer when taught in such an integrated fashion.

This method has several advantages: All ages can learn together to their level of ability. A young child can learn something about birds while his older sibling studies the mechanics of flight. Studying a unit can generate curiosity and independence, encourage intensity and depth of study, and is a more natural way to learn rather than artificially switching from one subject to another.

Primary resources for curriculum in this area are Alta Vista and Konos, as well as resources for do-it-yourself unit studies, such as *How to Create Your Own Unit Study* (Common Sense Press) by Valerie Bendt, and the Design a Study series by Katherine Stout (see appendix A). Remember, a packaged unit-study program generally does not include math, reading, phonics, spelling, or handwriting. They must be supplemented in these areas.

*Home Schooling Today* is a magazine that features unit studies and lesson plans. They may be contacted at:

*Home Schooling Today*
P.O. Box 1425
Melrose, FL 32666

## The Unschooling Approach

John Holt was a twentieth-century American educator who believed that children's natural curiosity and desire to learn were destroyed by traditional schooling. He is generally associated with the unschooling approach, which focuses on nonstructured learning that allows children to pursue their own interests and believes that children should be included in a meaningful way in the life of adults. The approach is very child-centered, and the child is exposed to a rich environment of resources, including an adult who models a lifestyle of curiosity and learning. Formal academics are pursued when the need arises or when the child indicates willingness.

In practice, a child will work harder and probe things more deeply when he is doing what he thinks is important, rather than what someone else has told him is important. When you force a topic or a skill on a child who is not ready, you are in danger of short-circuiting real learning.

Unschoolers may unschool to various degrees. Some have a life completely driven by the children's interests. Others take a more structured approach to the basics and unschool the rest of life. Their commonality is acknowledging the child's enthusiasm and spark as the most important factor in education.

The philosophy and heritage of John Holt is carried on by Holt Associates. Their magazine, *Growing without Schooling,* is a must for unschoolers and may be obtained at:

Holt Associates
2269 Massachusetts Avenue
Cambridge, MA 02140

Holt Associates offers a variety of other materials for sale, including a taped workshop given by Pat Farenga, president of Holt Associates, called "Unschooling." The unschooling experience of the Colfax family is chronicled in the fascinating book *Home Schooling for Excellence.* In addition, many of John Holt's books are still in print and available, such as *Teach Your Own* and *How Children Learn.*

## Delayed Academics

Dr. Raymond and Dorothy Moore are experienced educators and writers who believe that we rush children into formal academics far too quickly. The life of a child should be about practical living experiences and loving, warm, responsive parental involvement. They also believe that a young child should not spend too much time with peers lest he become peer-dependent. The Moores have been educating educators for decades and have much to teach home schoolers.

Their own report is called *The Moore Report International.* In addition to this quarterly magazine, they offer curriculum design services and accountability methods available through:

The Moore Foundation
Box 1
Camas, WA 98607

The Moores have written many books, including *Home Grown Kids, Home School Burnout, Minding Your Own Business,* and their most recent work, *Successful Home Schooling Family Handbook.*

In evaluating any curriculum, distinguish between the teaching approach and your child's learning style. They are distinct considerations and need to mesh if the home school is to be successful. Most people use a mixed approach. Beware of trying to mold your child to fit your chosen method. The learning styles of children will be discussed in more detail in the next chapter.

# 6

## *How Does Janey Learn?*

*D*o you have a Wiggly Willy or a Social Sue? Perhaps your child is a Perfect Paula or a Competent Carl. What is the difference and why does it matter?

One of the many beautiful aspects of home schooling is understanding how children learn. Instead of using traditional methods to teach mathematics, your child may learn to add by touching colorful cubes or counters or playing a game where he jumps while counting. Conversely, another child may enjoy math workbooks. Home schooling can accommodate—even capitalize on—different learning styles, a concept given little or no consideration in the structured public school environment. Research and commonsense observation can lead to a more fruitful learning experience for our children.

As parents, we might tend toward teaching methods used in our own academic experience. People tend to teach in a manner that makes the most sense to them. Our children may be different types of learners than we are, so we should guard against forcing personal preferences on our children.

This does not mean that home schooling must always be pleasing or fun for the child. I believe our children must learn that life involves hard work, dedication, and commitment. We must find a delicate balance in this process, helping them to identify and work with their own strengths and weaknesses.

One of the travesties of modern schooling is that learning has become entertainment, sometimes sacrificing quality for

90

quantity of learning. Our children must come to an early real-
ization that learning is hard work and involves a serious commitment to a *process*. In my opinion, that concept is diluted
by those who devalue the reality of true life experiences with
a solid diet of irrelevant videotapes, games, and field trips.
The child is entertained—but at his own long-term expense.

You know your child better than anyone else. Beware of
trying to pigeonhole your wonderful child of God into a structured classification system. Given that precaution, however,
you may see some of your child's strengths and weaknesses in
the following descriptions.

## Learning Styles

To more clearly understand learning theories, reflect for a
moment on the way God has made us—we can assimilate
information through eyes, ears, touch, or movement. A child's
strength may lie in one of these basic modalities.

### Visual Learners

Visual learners like to *see* what they are learning—or they
like to watch others do something so they can learn to do it
too. They immediately catch typographical errors and are
aware of minute visual details in their surroundings. They
remember words, facts, names, and numbers better when they
are able to see them. I knew my oldest daughter was visually
oriented when, at the age of three, she could recall for me the
details of clothing she had seen at the mall, including the color
of a scarf someone had been wearing. According to home
schooling author and expert Mary Pride, good materials to
use in teaching the visual learner are flash cards, matching
games, puzzles, instruction books, charts, pictures, posters,
wall strips, desk tapes, videos, or simulation software.[1]

## Auditory Learners

Auditory learners can hear a name or a song once and remember it. They may talk to themselves; in fact, they often talk incessantly. Following verbal directions is far easier for them than following written directions. They enjoy lectures, songs, and stories. Auditory learners may have trouble writing the answer to a question, but they can easily verbalize an answer if given the opportunity. Author Mary Pride notes, "They need to be told what to do. Auditory learners will listen to you reading for hours, but you may not think they are paying attention because they don't look at you. They like to memorize by ear and can easily develop a good sense of rhythm. Naturally, auditory learners have a head start when it comes to learning music."[2] Materials for working successfully with auditory learners are cassette tapes, educational songs, and rhythm instruments. Fortunately, there are many songs and tapes available for learning phonics, arithmetic, science, grammar, and a host of other subjects.

## Tactile/Kinesthetic Learners

Tactile/kinesthetic learners seem to be in constant motion. They have trouble sitting still and are always touching everything in sight. They like to tinker with things and take them apart. "Hands-on learning is a must for kinesthetic learners," says Mary Pride. "They need to mold or sculpt or whittle or bend, fold, and mutilate in order to express themselves. Kinesthetic learners learn to read best by learning to write. They like math manipulatives and sandpaper letters. Kinesthetic learners do not like sitting at a desk for hours staring at the blackboard—it's like blindfolding a visual learner to do this to a kinesthetic learner."[3] For these types of learners, long nature walks should be used to teach science. Let them assemble model kits; have them do yardwork and gardening. Textured puzzles of any sort also work well for them. You might allow them to type instead of writing longhand.

## Learning Personalities

Author Cathy Duffy expands on the learning styles and identifies four types of learning personalities. In her categories, she takes into account social characteristics and group functioning. Her four learning styles are Wiggly Willy, Perfect Paula, Competent Carl, and Sociable Sue.[4]

### Wiggly Willy

Wiggly Willies are hands-on learners. They are not deep thinkers but prefer to be free and spontaneous. Planning and organizing are not their strong points, but give them a hands-on project and they will perform beautifully. "They have short attention spans (unless doing a task of their choosing), are difficult to motivate, and can be disruptive in groups," says Cathy Duffy. "Sometimes these children are labeled as having attention deficit disorder, although the real problem is that, because of their age and temperament, they really need to be moving around more than is allowed in a typical classroom."[5] The best approach is a varied approach, with audio and visual aids, hands-on projects, physical involvement, and short, dynamic bursts of instruction.

### Perfect Paula

The Perfect Paula seems to be the ideal child. She likes to do everything correctly with clear structure, planning, and organization. She is disturbed by spontaneity or activities that are open-ended. Perfect Paulas like to follow rules and work well with a school-like curriculum and approach. These children thrive with workbooks, structure, and routine. They will learn from lectures, repetition, drill, and memorization. On the other hand, they may need assistance in developing more creative thinking skills to stretch the imagination.

### Competent Carl

Cathy Duffy's third learning style is that of Competent Carl. As his name implies, he likes to be in control of himself and his surroundings. He is continuously engaged in explanations, analysis, and problem-solving. Carls tend to be strong in math and science and like long-term, independent projects. They value wisdom and intelligence, yet they tend to be weak in the area of social skills and may have trouble relating to peers. This type likes logically organized lessons and tasks with a clear sense of purpose.

### Sociable Sue

Sociable Sue possesses a warm personality and is genuinely interested in people, ideas, principles, and values. She wants to see the meaning and significance in things and likes general concepts more than specific details. Although these children are initially excited about new projects, motivation tends to wane once the project is underway. Sociable Sues are often overachievers in an effort to impress others. They work well with small-group discussion, social interaction, creative writing, and role-playing, but require personal recognition and repetition for learning detailed information. Sociable Sue needs help in attending to detail and following through on projects.

## The Young Child

Young children—under the age of eight years—are still in the early stages of personality development. Perhaps that is what makes them so much fun. Trying to categorize the young child will only prove frustrating for both parent and child. The best learning method is to integrate all the approaches and attempt to achieve balance.

All home educators should pursue a broad approach to teaching. Use the opportunities presented by daily living to teach the child. Give your child hands-on learning, such as nature walks or working with tools, in addition to book learning. Engage your child in conversation and discussion, either in the form of a Charlotte Mason type of narration, wherein the child retells what she has heard, or just discussing the day's events. Ask many "why" and "what do you think" questions. Provide ample time for formulation of thoughts and opinions.

Use any opportunity for visual, auditory, or kinesthetic learning. Continuously seek to be creative! Our middle daughter experienced trouble with the concept of subtraction. We tried cubes; they didn't work. We tried counting sticks and other manipulatives; they didn't work. Success finally came when we put a long number line on the floor and had her jump forward or backward to illustrate the mechanics of addition and subtraction. Now the paper and pencil exercises make sense to her.

I explain to my children that God gives us the gift of passions—those interests that excite and sustain us. Regularly I will ask them, "What is your passion?" Then we indulge that passion—within reason. So far they have experimented with ballet, a dog, a rabbit, violin, karate, piano, and a host of interesting self-designed unit studies. Indulging their passions, to a reasonable extent, allows children to feel more invested in their own education.

Finally, don't neglect the imagination. If your child draws, writes stories, paints, or whatever, enjoy and encourage these creative outlets. Provide limited freedom within established boundaries and try to channel the child's interests. If she tells a great story, suggest, "How about writing that down?" If a child loves to dance, invite an aunt over for tea and an impromptu living room dance performance. Give substance and wings to a child's imagination, and then enjoy the ride!

## Choosing a Curriculum

Next to making the decision to home school, choosing a curriculum is probably the most difficult aspect of home education. Many dollars are spent on books that wind up gathering dust on the shelf. Christopher Klicka quips, "A Ph.D. in home schooling simply means that your unwanted stack of curriculum is 'piled higher and deeper.'"[6] With some observation and knowledge of your children and comparison shopping, you can make wiser, easier, and more economical choices for your family.

The first thing to remember is that there is no perfect curriculum. What works for one mom may not work for another because we have different children and our families face different challenges. As children mature, curriculum needs may change from year to year. One size does not fit all, especially in home schooling.

Remember that curriculum is only a tool. You are the parent/teacher. Don't abdicate your control to any curriculum. Mary Hood reminds us, "Most parents originally became home schoolers because they want to be the directing force behind their children's educations. Unfortunately, the first thing many of them do is to give their control away again. Some hand it over to curriculum suppliers or correspondence schools. Others defer to educational supervisors, evaluators, or 'homeschooling experts,' who claim to know what is right for their individual families."[7] God called *you* to teach your children. He doesn't make curriculum recommendations.

I like what Gregg Harris says: "I used to be really concerned about what they were putting into the curriculum in the public schools, but now I realize the kids aren't reading it anyway."[8] Your home educated children will *use* their curriculum. Don't allow it to use *you*.

Finally, a curriculum must not only meet your child's needs but yours as well. It should be compatible with your teaching style. If you hate it, you will not compel your child to love it. If the approach or anything about it doesn't ring true to you, it will be difficult for you to ignite your child's enthusiasm.

Clay and Sally Clarkson, authors of *Educating the Whole-Hearted Child*, offer these questions to consider when choosing a curriculum:

- Can I teach this subject naturally without a curriculum? What will this curriculum do for my children that I, or they, cannot do without it?
- What good books on the subject could I buy with the money it would take to buy this curriculum?
- Am I just attracted to its packaging and promotion? Am I judging the book "by its cover" or by its contents? Is it effective, or just clever?
- Do I know anyone personally who is using or recommending this curriculum? Have I read any good reviews on it?
- Does the tone of the writing appeal to my children's maturing appetites, or to their immaturity and childishness?[9]

In planning or purchasing your curriculum, remember you are focusing on skills as well as content. *Skills* are basic things like reading and writing, and generally need to be approached in a systematic manner. *Content* is what you cover and does not necessarily need to be in a specific order. If this is a concern, get a "scope and sequence" chart. This is a plot of what details of a subject are covered at each grade level. They are available from textbook publishers, such as Bob Jones University Press, Rod and Staff, Alpha Omega, and Accelerated Christian Education. An inexpensive one is available from World Book Educational Products (101 Northwest Point Blvd., Elk Grove Village, IL 60007).

With one child it is easier to experiment with styles and suppliers. If you are teaching multiple grades, it is beneficial to cover as much material in one setting as possible. Teach all you can at the same time. For example, *Learning Language*

*Arts through Literature* is an integrated program that covers phonics, reading, language arts, spelling, and handwriting.

Another approach to multiple grades or multiple children is to use unit studies, such as Konos or Alta Vista. Jessica Hulcey, cocreator of Konos, says unit studies are like a bus ride—the younger children can get off the bus earlier and the older children can take the ride much farther. In a study of birds, for example, a young child might learn the parts of a bird and learn to identify a few with a field guide. An older child might study the bird's anatomy and migration pattern. All the children are studying birds, but older children are doing so in greater depth. Most unit studies generally do not include a systematic study of phonics or math. If you choose unit studies as your primary method, you will need to supplement with a math and phonics program.

Correspondence schools such as Christian Liberty Academy, Alpha Omega, or Accelerated Christian Education can be completed with minimal supervision, especially in the upper grades.

Major curriculum suppliers offer services in a variety of formats. Again, you must closely examine and analyze what your own family needs. Do you basically want to be left alone? Then avoid signing on to a program that requires weekly papers be sent to a "real" school elsewhere. On the other hand, you may want the accountability of a correspondence program, especially if you are a new home schooler.

If you make a bad choice, try to alter the curriculum to fit your needs. If that is impossible, many materials may be sold or traded at a local support group curriculum sale.

There are entire books devoted to the selection and evaluation of curricula. Many of these books are available in public libraries. Mel and Norma Gabler, best known for their book *What Are They Teaching Our Children?* have been busy reviewing the content of textbooks for the past thirty-five years. If you are interested in their dedicated work in exposing the inadequacies and revisionism of textbooks used in public schools, you may wish to contact them:

Mel and Norma Gabler
Educational Research Analysts
P.O. Box 7518
Longview, TX 75607-7518
903-753-5993

Cathy Duffy has written the *Christian Home Educators' Curriculum Manual,* one for the elementary grades and one for junior and senior high school. They each contain detailed, in-depth information about the many curriculum choices available. Also, Mary Pride has written the multivolume *Big Book of Home Learning.* She discusses virtually every product available for home schoolers. Borrowing or buying these materials can help you to make wiser choices and save you money on your curriculum budget.

Curriculum decisions are important, but do not forget: "The most formative, most profound, and most lasting things in life, we will, without fail, learn not from books or videos or computers or classes, but from each other. In other words, it takes people to teach people to be people."[10]

# 7

# *Getting Started*

*L*ike life itself, education is a process. As a beginning home schooler, I was very intimidated by other home schooling moms who appeared confident of their role and seemed to have it all together. They could nurse a baby, teach phonics, bake bread, study ancient Egypt with their older children, and cook a month's worth of dinners in one day. Ultimately, I had to rely on God's strength to help me put one foot in front of the other and take it one day at a time. We have developed into a family lifestyle and an educational philosophy that make the most sense for us.

Our home school is unique. It does not resemble the schools of others in my support group. Exercise caution in comparing your efforts to that of another. Your children are unique; your home is special. You can tailor your home school to meet individual needs and goals. Your family may not look like the family on the cover of the latest home schooling magazine. The apostle Paul warns, "Each one should test his own actions. Then he can take pride in himself, without comparing himself to somebody else" (Gal. 6:4).

## Who Should Teach?

In most (but not all) families, a stay-at-home mom is the home teacher. Given the amount of preparation and teaching time required, this is the most viable arrangement for many families. Some single parents who work outside the home have been able to home school, but only with a great deal of help and support from grandparents and other relatives. Teaching is full-time work that must be done in addition to all the other work required in running a household.

Even in the early stages of considering home schooling, view home education as a lifestyle of learning, a logical extension of the nuclear family, instead of something set apart from everyday life. School isn't something you *do,* rather, education is something you *live.* Like life, it is a process, a journey. I am dismayed at some stories I hear about well-intentioned mothers who make their children wear uniforms or answer the call of a school bell for the beginning of a school day. If you truly intend to teach your children at home, it will demand dedicated blocks of time and will also entail looking at the things you do every day as educational experiences. Rather than an artificial attempt to copy traditional school methodology, a rich home life is, perhaps, the best education.

As a home teacher, make sure you are prepared for the sacrifice it will require on your part. I dearly miss women's Bible study at my church, but I cannot justify an entire Wednesday morning away from our work at home. Your lifestyle will have new limitations. Home schooling is not a hobby. It involves a commitment to minister to your children in a unique way. It will stretch you in ways you cannot imagine.

Home schooling requires you to spend lots of time in one-on-one tutoring. First graders take the most instruction time. Their reading skills are still emerging and they are only able to work independently for short periods of time. They require a great deal of one-on-one contact in the beginning. As children mature, they are able to handle increasingly independent work. Most parents find, however, that their preparation time increases as their children mature. This will cut considerably into your free time. If you are not ready to commit the

effort and do what it takes, you may grow weary and resent-
ful of your task.

People often ask us, "How long will you continue to home
school?" We don't know. We *do* know we will continue to step
out in obedience until God shows us another direction.

Pray as a couple *before* making any home school decision.
If you are certain it is God's will for your family, then step out
in obedience and faith. Allow ample time to make decisions
and consider all the consequences. Yet don't give yourself so
much time that you wake up to realize that your child has
already finished grammar school while you are still considering home schooling. Don't pull your children out of school
on impulse or a whim, but don't wait for the perfect time
either, because it may never arrive.

When our oldest child spent her one and only semester
in public school, the two and one-half hours she was gone
each day were challenging and convicting. I knew she was
safe, but I felt that I was disobeying God's will for our family and taking the path of least resistance by sending her to
school. Those brief months strengthened my resolve. Whenever home schooling becomes troublesome and public
school looks tempting, I recall that unsettled feeling. Things
may change for us in the future, but for now our path is
clear.

In the early stages, be clear about why you are home schooling. A former astronaut turned home schooler, writing in *The
Successful Homeschool Family Handbook,* asks, "Most funda-
mentally, who or what is your motivator? Why do you home-
school your children? God is my motivator, my lamp, the One
who convicted me with this mandate for change. I home-
school, for it is better spiritually, socially, and academically.
But when God guides our convictions, only he tells us when
to quit. Better academics and socialization are just by-prod-
ucts of a very critical task he has endowed us with. I personally cannot separate my homeschool stand from him, the

Source of my strength and blessings."[1] The carefully thought-out decision to home school will lay the foundation for your entire experience. If home schooling is a matter of obedience, persevering in your decision through rough times will be a test of that obedience.

Be confident in your decision. Don't be blown about like a leaf or "like a wave of the sea, blown and tossed by the wind" (James 1:6). You will hear many opinions from others, most of them negative. Remember that as parents, you know your child better than anyone else. Rely on the promise that "all things are possible with God" (Mark 10:27)—even home schooling. If you believe that God has called your family to home school, he—*not you*—will provide the confidence, patience, resources, and anything else you may be lacking.

As home schooling experts Raymond and Dorothy Moore remind us, "Remember that you are the greatest gifts you can ever give to your children. And your best for your children under your circumstances will likely be far superior to the preschool teacher's best with nineteen other children under her circumstances."[2]

A final suggestion for the beginning home schooler is to learn the state law and comply fully with each caveat and requirement. Consider joining the Home School Legal Defense Association (P.O. Box 159, Paeonian Springs, VA 22129, 540-338-5600). They are a legal services organization devoted to serving the needs of home schooling families. They will be your strongest advocate and ally in court should your decision to home school ever be legally challenged.

## Setting Goals

In the classic tale of *Alice in Wonderland,* Alice inquires of the Cheshire cat:

"Would you tell me, please, which way I ought to walk from here?"

"That depends a good deal on where you want to get to," said the Cat.

"I don't much care where," said Alice.

"Then it doesn't matter which way you walk," said the Cat.[3]

If you don't know what you want for your family, chances are you will not feel fulfilled by the end result of your parenting. Better to establish a philosophy and goals for your home school from the start. Know what you believe about faith and family values. Know why you hold these beliefs. Brainstorm with your spouse and place your ideas in writing. If you have a clear handle on some of these difficult questions from the beginning, your journey will be easier in the long run.

Author Mary Hood sees four benefits to establishing beliefs, setting goals, and planning your materials. First, it eliminates many unnecessary activities. With identified goals, you can choose the most productive path. Second, you will save money on unused curriculum supplies. Third, "Your approach to education will become more consistent, and you will be equipped to defend that approach to others." Finally, you will become more discerning. "When you know more about educational philosophy, it will help you to recognize and understand alternate points of view, and 'sift the wheat from the chaff' when deciding whether to listen to the advice of others."[4]

Jackie Wellwood, home schooling author and mother of seven, sets yearly goals for each of her children in six specific areas: spiritual, academic, character, work skills, physical skills, and life principles. If we have written goals, we will be able to evaluate what we do in light of these goals. Mrs. Wellwood reminds us, "Rather than being irritated by a child's behavior, look at it as a training opportunity to train in character or some other goal." Some goals might be to develop godly character, achieve academic excellence, and develop an independent learner with a love of learning.

With written goals for each area, you can evaluate the activity or opportunity to see if it will further that child's goals. For example, a spiritual goal for a child might be to have a daily devotional time alone, with a sibling, or with mom. Academic goals might be to eliminate careless work and to work on typing skills. Character goals (which are often carried over from year to year) might be prompt obedience, learning to wait patiently, and taming the tongue. For work skills, a young child might have a goal of making her bed each day. A suitable goal for an older child might be to finish chores without being asked or reminded. For physical skills, a young child might be learning to shower or brush her teeth alone. An older child might be expected to emerge from the bedroom dressed and ready for the day. Finally, for a life principle, a yearly goal might be speaking to one another in love—a challenge for all families.

For older children, Bill and Cindy Short list fifteen areas in which young adults need to set goals: spiritual life, scriptural knowledge, character, habits, following instructions, love of work, love of knowledge, reading, communication skills, liberal arts, math and science, sex education, social skills, independence, and occupation.[5] If this sounds like an ominous task, recall that you have been working with your child on many of these skills all along.

There is an old expression: "If you don't know what you stand for, you'll fall for anything." By giving some consideration to these complicated areas, especially as your child approaches the teen years, you will help your child develop goals and a vision for the future.

Ted Wade, in his book *The Home School Manual,* submits a sample of general beliefs and goals for home educators. We have personalized these for our family and copied them into

a planning notebook. It is very helpful to review them periodically to keep on track.

We believe

- That our children do not belong to the state; that it is the responsibility of parents to properly direct the needs of their children
  mentally, emotionally, spiritually, socially and physically.
- That parents have the constitutional right to choose the best
  method of providing for each of these needs, including the
  child's formal education.
- That the learning process begins at home from the moment of
  birth, and parents are the prime educators of their children.
- That conscientious parents can provide in the home a very adequate and often superior comprehensive program for their children's education.
- That home schools offer the very best method of teaching: one-
  to-one tutoring.
- That a child's educational needs can be met on a more individual basis in a home environment; that the flexible nature of
  a home school program allows each child to progress at his own
  ideal pace in every subject, without stressful competition or
  pressure.
- That the home school atmosphere encourages an intensive
  adventure into learning through natural self-discovery; this
  builds self-confidence and individual thinking rather than peer
  dependence.
- That home education encourages valuable social interaction
  with people of all ages, in the home and in the community.
  This helps the child learn to relate well to people outside his
  own peer group.
- That the family is the basic link in the structure of any society, and that America has seen a definite weakening of the family unit in recent years. Home schoolers have found that the
  relaxed, intimate interaction between parent and child in the
  home school serves to strengthen the family unit as well as providing the best possible alternative for education.[6]

It is helpful to ask yourself these questions: For what am I
preparing my children? to make money in the future? to serve

God? to be a faithful spouse? Perhaps you are concerned with all of these things, including wanting your child to have an appreciation of fine arts and excellent computer skills. Having a sense of direction will help you come closer to the mark.

There is a wonderful book by Borg Hendrickson that addresses many of these early goal-setting tasks: *Home School: Taking the First Step.* This book is a handbook to help you plan your home school from top to bottom. Ms. Hendrickson guides you through the drafting of documents of rights and reasons, lesson plans, schedules, and calendars. If you are seeking to build your own plan from scratch, this is an excellent resource. If you use an established curriculum supplier, much of this work is already done. Whatever approach you use, spend some preparatory time outlining your philosophy, goals, and beliefs and much of the rest will fall into place.

## Ordering Your Home School

### Schedules

Maybe you are a highly structured person. You have future oil changes noted on the calendar and never miss an appointment with the dental hygienist. Or maybe you are a little more free-flowing—you have noble goals and fabulous ideas but no clue as to how to proceed.

Home schooling challenges us to be a bit of both. To accomplish sequential learning, like phonics and math, there must be some structure and planning. But home schooling is not always about phonics and math. It's about living and learning in an unpredictable world where babies get sick, the phone rings with people asking for help, and friends from church experience crises.

With these thoughts in mind, here are some factors to consider in home school scheduling.

*SELECT A BASIC STRUCTURE OR SCHEDULE FOR YOUR
HOME SCHOOL.*

How many days a week will you work, how many hours a day, how many days a year? What vacations and holidays will you plan? There is no ideal schedule for every family.

*PREPARE A SKELETAL YEAR-LONG SCHEDULE.*

Develop a month-by-month plan. Target what weaknesses you will focus on during each segment.

*DEVISE A ROUGH DAILY SCHEDULE.*

It doesn't have to be as rigid as "math from 9:00 to 9:30." Rather, it can be a loosely followed flow of activities. First we eat breakfast, then we do chores. Then we have devotional time, then we start on math. This is your basic schedule, devised in blocks of time. It will change with the seasons and your child's skills and interests. Most families find that academics are best tackled in the morning, when both mother and children are at their best. This leaves the afternoon for projects, reading, trips, play, or chores.

*DO A GENERAL CLEANING OF THE HOUSE IN THE MORNING.*

Once things are picked up, then it feels like you are ready to work. Schedule a quiet time at midday. Even if you don't have nappers, your children can read, write letters, or play computer games during this time. It also gives you a break to relax or do catch-up work and chores. Remember, you are not your children's cruise director! They do not have to be engaged and entertained twenty-four hours each day. They can (and should!) learn to be delighted with their own minds, ideas, and projects.

*KNOW WHAT YOU WANT TO TEACH.*

With a packaged curriculum, your teaching subjects will be well defined and outlined. If you are designing your own curriculum, do so with wise guidance, such as a good scope and sequence chart and other books that are discussed in this book.

*HAVE AN APPROACH TO THE ACADEMIC YEAR.*

Not everyone goes to school eight or nine months a year. This is a carryover from the time when children were needed on the farm and were only available for school during certain months. There are advantages to having a year-round schedule. For one, mom gets more frequent breaks. Yes, the breaks are shorter, but they are more frequent and can give everyone some much-needed breathing space. Second, the children remember more of what they learn without a three- or four-month gap between sessions.

Even if your state requires somewhere around 180 days of instruction, any one of these variations would be in compliance:

Teach twelve weeks, take four weeks off—or three months on, one month off. The most popular months to take off are April, August, and December.

Teach six weeks, take two weeks off, giving you a year with six two-month blocks in it.

Teach three weeks, take one week off—one week off each month. This works well for those with lots of young children and for new home schoolers because it gives you the chance to regroup, clean your house, plan some more lessons, and adjust your attitude.

Teach forty-five four-day weeks, with seven weeks off per year when desired. A four-day week works well for many people. This provides a weekday for running errands, attending planned activities, and going to the library.

Remember that one size does not fit all, especially in home schooling. Do not discount Saturday as a teaching day. Many dads appreciate the opportunity to take part in a real school day. They often are not otherwise available. Weekends can be a time of family learning, which is just as legitimate as a structured phonics lesson. In fact, these times of family learning will often be the most memorable moments of home schooling.

### Character Training and Discipline

Develop and implement a character training and discipline plan. Establish rules and order. Children like structure; they need to know what is expected of them in this new venture. While a military-like academy structure is not needed or preferred, your children must have established parameters for behavior and conduct.

J. Richard Fugate says, "There are two facets of child training, controlling and teaching. . . . You cannot teach children who are not under control."[7] Teaching is easier than discipline, but you cannot teach a child who will not obey. Your job is compounded if your child is adjusting to your new role as teacher as well as parent.

If you feel that you need to get a system of discipline in place, there are several resources to help. You can start with any of the books written by Dr. James Dobson of Focus on the Family such as *Dare to Discipline* or *The Strong-Willed Child*. Michael and Debi Pearl have written a very helpful book called *To Train Up a Child*, which deals with the training of children by God's principles. It is available through them directly (1010 Pearl Road, Pleasantville, TN 37147) or may be ordered through An Encouraging Word (see appendix A).

*Proverbs for Parenting* is a very popular topical guide for child-raising from the Book of Proverbs. It is available through Lynn's Bookshelf (P.O. Box 2224, Boise, ID 83701) along with *A Coloring Book of Bible Verses from the Epistles* and *A Coloring Book of Bible Proverbs*.

Many home schoolers believe that character training is more important than anything else. Your child may be a math genius, but if he doesn't love God and have his heart in order, then his math skills are meaningless. There are many ideas for training character. Any approach is better than leaving this important aspect of training to chance.

Your foremost resource for character training is the Bible. The wisdom contained therein is sufficient for a lifetime. The lives of Abraham, Daniel, or many other heroes of the Bible are the most inspiring biographies available. The Book of Proverbs contains more wisdom than we can digest. Can you imagine how wise your children (and you) would be if you spent a couple of years studying Proverbs? Let the Bible be your first resource in character training.

### Ten Steps to Training Character

Kathie Morrissey of the Courtship Connection, speaking at the May 1996 Illinois Christian Home Educators (ICHE) Convention, described ten steps for training character.

#### 1. WATCH THE CHILDREN'S EXAMPLES AND SOCIAL EXPOSURE.

Watch whom your children play with. Especially while they are young, you are in control of their social lives. Teach them discernment early and they will make good choices later on.

#### 2. PUT GOD'S WORD INTO THEIR MINDS THROUGH SINGING AND MEMORIZING.

Any Christian bookstore has tapes by Keith Green called "Hide 'Em in Your Heart" in which Bible verses are set to music with an accompanying activity booklet. Even my two-year-old has a few verses memorized from these tapes. It warms my heart to hear her little voice sing, "I can do all things through Christ who strengthens me."

Many churches offer AWANA clubs. These are fun-oriented groups in which scriptural memorization is encouraged. Children memorize verses from handbooks and earn special awards for their achievements. To find a club near you, contact AWANA Clubs International, One East Bode Road, Streamwood, IL 60107.

Memlock is a picture-based Scripture memorization system. Memorization cards offer a word-picture for the first key words of Scripture verses to jog your memory. The whole family can use this system to memorize many, many verses each year. They may be contacted at: Memlock, 420 E. Montwood Ave., LaHabra, CA 90631, 1-800-373-1947.

The most cost-effective way to memorize Scripture is to write verses out and hang them up where you will look at them several times a day. I hang many things over the kitchen sink. We don't have a dishwasher, so I spend a fair amount of time at the sink. This can be a productive, meditative time in your busy day.

### 3. CHOOSE SPECIFIC GOALS OR TRAITS FOR EACH CHILD TO WORK ON.

You know what each child needs to improve. One child may need to work on initiative, another on kindness. Let them focus on behaviors and attitudes they can change or develop. We have used Kathie Morrissey's idea of a Kindness Cup from the 1995 Illinois Christian Home Educator's Convention. Each child gets twenty nickels in a paper cup. When they are unkind to one another, they lose a nickel. The child who was wronged gets the nickel. We did this for two weeks and saw a marked improvement in behavior. At the end of this experiment, we went to the candy store and spent the remaining nickels. When this becomes a problem again, we will once more fill the cups. Find a fun, creative way to increase your child's awareness of their character issues.

### 4. FOCUS ON ONE TRAIT PER WEEK OR MONTH.

Don't overwhelm your kids. Jackie Wellwood says, "If your husband came home with a list of your character faults and wanted them corrected within 30 days, how would you feel?"

If you assault your children with your assessment that they're inattentive, lack patience, and aren't respectful, they will become discouraged. If you choose one area, encourage them, and give them ideas to help them, they will show improvement.

### 5. PRAY THAT YOU EXEMPLIFY THESE TRAITS.

Children learn more by your example than any other method. You can memorize the Book of Proverbs, but if you don't live it, your children will never catch your vision for their future.

### 6. CORRECT CONSISTENTLY.

A child left to himself brings parents to shame. On a trying day, it seems easier to let minor matters slide, but your child learns that sometimes he can get away with a behavior and other times he will be punished for the same infraction. Such inconsistency is not healthy and causes confusion and insecurity.

### 7. MEASURE AND CHECK THEIR PROGRESS.

Kathy Morrissey, through her business, The Courtship Connection, has several ideas (see appendix A). She has checklists, special certificates, and ribbons for excellence in character. You can order these through her or adapt these ideas for use in your own family.

### 8. ENCOURAGEMENT MAKES THEM WANT TO DO IT.

Celebrate both small and momentous victories. The encouragement doesn't have to be a monetary reward. It can be in the form of time spent together—a simple trip to the candy store or a special bike ride. Children love to hear feedback that they are improving. I often turn to one of my daughters and say something like, "You've really been doing well on being kind to the baby. I really appreciate that." When you are tempted to nag your child to change and grow, remember that the Bible tells us that encouragement is much more effective: "Therefore, encourage one another and build each other up" (1 Thess. 5:11).

### 9. *GIVE THEM A CHANCE TO CHANGE.*

Look at how much we struggle with our own weaknesses. Don't expect perfection, but rejoice in each small bit of progress.

### 10. *KEEP YOURSELF MOTIVATED, ENCOURAGED, AND ENTHUSIASTIC.*

Make sure you are reading your Bible or some devotional material each day to keep your spirit refreshed. Perhaps the biggest encouragement for parents is seeing positive character traits develop in their children.

One mom quoted in *The Successful Homeschool Family Handbook* says, "Argumentative and rebellious or self-centered children dishearten and burn out parents far faster than the mechanics of teaching. We found it a good tradeoff to work more on character building and less on academic education."[8]

Some other materials we have used for character training have been William J. Bennett's *The Book of Virtues;* a series of books by Ron and Rebekah Coriell called *Character Builders;* any of the products from Doorposts (5840 SW Old Hwy 47, Gaston, OR 97119) such as their topical child-training reference guide, *For Instruction in Righteousness;* and any of the materials available from Pearables (P.O. Box 9887, Colorado Springs, CO 80932), such as *The Narrow Way* character curriculum or *Pearables Character Building Kingdom Stories,* vols. 1–3.

An approach we have taken with our children is to choose a character trait, find a definition of that trait, find Bible verses related to that trait, and brainstorm for examples of that trait in action. The children have notebooks into which they copy the definition and some other notes. As they get older, these notebooks will expand with their greater understanding of true Christian character.

Children may not be the only ones who need to overcome stumbling blocks. Mr. Fugate reminds us, "One obstacle to overcome in home schooling is ourselves. If we are undisciplined, we will not be very successful in teaching our children."[9] Home schooling has forced me to increase in patience, self-discipline, and perseverance. I can improve on these traits even as I help my children learn them.

## Your Physical Environment

### ORGANIZE YOUR HOME SCHOOL ENVIRONMENT.

Many successful home schools are at kitchen tables, like mine. This is perhaps the most important location in any home for significant conversations and time together as a family. Other families have a separate room or section of the house devoted to the school area. What physical changes are required to accommodate home schooling? You don't need to build an addition on your house or finish off your basement. Home schooling doesn't have to be elaborate or fancy. It just has to be organized and it has to be *done*.

### CREATE LEARNING CENTERS.

Shelves and used desks are prime components of a home school, especially for older children. They need a place where they can sit and work. My older girls have desks in their rooms where they can do their work and store supplies. They also have a comfy reading chair with a light.

When children are young, they don't need desks. Instead, give them low shelves so they can have access to their toys and books. Have art supplies and paper readily available.

### THERE SHOULD BE A PLACE FOR EVERYTHING.

Take one room at a time, starting with the kitchen. De-junk ruthlessly. Everything has to have a place; if it doesn't, get rid of it. Home schooling complicates your life and your time. Dealing with clutter distracts from that time. Simplify now and *maintain* that simplicity. Review every few weeks to make sure things aren't cluttering up again. I used to resent having to sort through my daughters' junk. Then I realized they are busy, productive little people. They create things and they draw incessantly; these are messy but valuable activities.

Home schooler Annette Vittetoe writes, "Many of our frustrations in organizing our homes and lives stem, I think, from the mistaken idea that getting organized is something you do. Instead, it is something you become. . . . Getting rid of clutter is not enough. We must allow the Lord to free us from our bondage to attractive things as well."[10]

Terry Dorian and Zan Peters Tyler say we must first find the will to organize time and possessions. They note, "There are a number of very good books on the market which can enhance our lives by helping us to declutter our homes and manage our time. But, overcoming a lack of knowledge is not the first challenge we face; the first obstacle which many of us have encountered, at one time or another, is an unwillingness to become faithful stewards of all that God has given us. Only by his grace can we find the will to organize our time and material possessions in ways which minister to those around us and allow us to fulfill our life purpose in him."[11]

God has given me so much. I need to regularly weed through everything (especially books and papers) to keep my focus on the best things and the most important things in my life. If not, my blessings will overwhelm me.

### Keeping Records

As part of your recordkeeping, your home school notebook might include your family goals, the purpose of your home school, your course of study, a school calendar, a monthly calendar, and weekly lessons. You can keep it simple, like I do, but you should have some sort of plan for recordkeeping and documentation. This can be a formal lesson plan book or simply a journal. Many parents use a spiral notebook to record the day's accomplishments. Write down page numbers covered per subject, books read, or trips taken. In a separate folder, keep a portfolio of sample papers. Have a separate file for each child's work. We buy folders and have the girls decorate their covers each month. Then their papers are placed in the folder. The children actually enjoy looking them over during the month, thereby reviewing the month's work.

Many children keep their own journals as well. Some write daily, some less often. They can choose what they want to record or they can be given an assignment to write about (e.g., "What is your favorite book and why?").

If you are required to keep attendance records, a simple check mark in your journal indicating that you "did school" that day might be enough. If you need to track hours, you can also do that in a spiral journal. Other records you may want to keep are field trip records, reading lists, lending and borrowing lists, or Scripture memory records.

We keep a portfolio of artwork and put it on display every few months. We put up a sign that says, "Clare's Art Gallery," and this encourages her and lets her see how her technique and interests have changed over the months.

Whatever approach you use to teaching, you must come up with a recordkeeping system you can live with. Raymond and Dorothy Moore suggest, "Let your children share in the planning. And when you write in your daily log at the end of the day, include their stories about their experiences, poems they have written, flowers they have pressed and catalogued, collections of rocks, shells and other of their laboratory experiences."[12]

### Children and Chores

Children can do a lot to help with the maintenance of the house. When you send your children to school, your house stays cleaner because it is not constantly occupied. When you home school, you make a lot more messes. The earlier your children can help clean up those messes, the more time you will have for school and fun.

Even small children, two or three years of age, can do things to help. They can pull the covers up on their bed, carry their dishes from the table, pick up their toys, and put their dirty laundry away. Children of four or five can make their beds, set and clear the table, dust, water plants, stir ingredients, help carry groceries, and pick up their rooms. Six- to ten-year-olds can do even more. They can feed pets, do yard work, wash the car, wash and dry dishes, clean the bathroom, and much more.

Come up with a chore chart so your children can track their progress. This can also help them to remember so they don't have to be constantly reminded. It also helps them know what you expect. We have written chore standard charts, such as: "When Mommy or Daddy says to clean my room, I must make the bed, put dirty clothes in the basket, put clean clothes in the drawers, close all the drawers, put toys where they belong, and keep the dresser and shelves neat." I laminated these charts and hung them on the wall so the children could have a checklist of what was expected of them. We also have chore charts for cleaning the living room, being a kitchen helper, helping with the baby, and helping with the laundry.

We want our children to be able to do things around the house, but we must take the time to train them to do so. It might seem easier to do the job yourself, but if your children are going to learn to help, you must take the time to train them.

Organize a daily chore routine. In their book *A Survivor's Guide to Home Schooling,* Luanne Shackelford and Susan White say, "Realize that home teaching is a job. You are now employed at least part-time away from your usual household routines. It will be harder to get the other stuff done."[13]

You might want to make a checklist of things that need to be done each morning, noon, and night. This gives the whole family the big picture of what is involved in family mainte-nance and allows you to delegate the jobs as children mature. With adequate planning, prioritizing, and organization, suc-cess is attainable.

## Using Technology Wisely

### Taming the Television

"It has been called the God with the Glass Face," notes Rick Boyer.[14] It robs families of precious time. It steals the ability to effectively communicate with others. It robs critical edu-cational encounters. It plays on psychological weaknesses by creating meaningless needs.

Ray Ballman notes, "Between the ages of six and eighteen, the average American child views 15 to 16,000 hours of tele-vision, compared to 13,000 hours spent in school. According to a *Nielson Report of Television,* children watch thirty to thirty-one hours of television weekly, more time than any other activ-ity except sleeping."[15]

The cognitive, physical, and emotional effects of TV are indeed fascinating. Cognitively, it increases sensory awareness but decreases intellectual ability. Physically, it leads children away from their natural propensity for play and increases with-drawal behavior. Emotionally, the visual violence is damag-ing to children. Cartoons are often the most violent form of television, especially for a young child who cannot discern between "pretend" and real violence.[16]

Children who are constantly stimulated from the outside (by TV or video games) become addicted to this type of stim-ulation. It limits their attention span and decreases their motivation. They learn to depend on this stimulation, rather than learning to amuse themselves.

Television leaves children with the impression that "learning" is something someone else does for you. My husband and I have each taught at the junior college and college level. Our observation is that the students expect school to be entertaining. They have been raised on entertainment and so they expect it at every turn. They want school to be peppered with tricks and attention-grabbers—just like television.

The younger your children are when you gain control of this stimulus, the healthier their educational environment will be. Some alternatives for dealing with television are:

> Get rid of it. If it breaks, consider yourself blessed. If it still works, put it away in the garage.
>
> Limit viewing to certain hours or days.
>
> Have a television budget. Each week, your children get a certain number of chips, each worth one-half hour of television time. They have to choose on which shows and at what times to "spend" their chips.
>
> Review the television listings each week and decide what you will view as a family. Otherwise, the television stays off.

We have lived both with and without a television. I believe the quality of our family life improves without it.

It should be noted, however, that valuable programming does exist, especially on cable television. Your local public television station, the Discovery Channel, and the History Channel, to name a few educational stations, offer a broad range of educational fare. *Cable in the Classroom* is a monthly magazine for educators that categorizes and discusses the educational material available. We have been able to tape some wonderful series for our home school.

*Cable in the Classroom* may be contacted at:

*Cable in the Classroom*
1900 N. Beauregard Street, Suite 108
Alexandria, VA 22311
703-845-1400
http://www.ciconline.com

## *Computers and the Home School*

Are computers important for home schoolers? Maybe. They must be used wisely, like any other technical resource. Abe Lincoln didn't need the Internet to rise to greatness. Neither do your children. Certain aspects of computers can be useful in motivating children, however, particularly in the areas of math and phonics. And some learning styles are very compatible with computer learning. In addition, everyone needs some computer skills in our society today. If your child is interested, computers can provide a great training ground.

The resources available for computer learning are very, very good, or very, very bad. Programs are expensive. Try them out in a store before buying, or ask for referrals from other parents. Better yet, experiment with some shareware before investing in expensive resources.

When using shareware, you pay a small fee for a disk of software. If you like the software, you send the author an additional payment for which you may receive a bonus program or a manual. Public domain software is free. It has either been donated or is otherwise not subject to copyright restrictions. The small fee you pay is for duplication of the disk.

A good source for shareware, which costs only a few dollars per disk, is M & M Software. They are very helpful and friendly to home schoolers and are listed in appendix A. We have tried and enjoyed many of their offerings.

The Internet can be a significant tool for home schoolers. As a parent/teacher, I like to use it for sharing with others and learning new teaching ideas. I have found many great lesson plans and ideas on the Internet. I have also wasted a lot of time fiddling around with it. Like any other tool, it must be used wisely, and children's use of the Internet needs to be supervised carefully.

Some of the best Internet sites for home schoolers are listed below. While these predominantly provide information and inspiration for home schoolers, many also have extensive links to educational sites.

Christian Interactive Network's Homeschool Forum
http://www.gocin.com/homeschool

Homeschool World
http://www.home-school.com

Home Education Magazine
http://www.home-ed-press.com

If you don't have a home computer, many libraries have computers available for use by the public. They often have state-of-the-art programs and CDs. Generally, you need to reserve a time for their use.

Dr. Arthur Robinson has developed a high-tech solution to the single parent/individual instruction time crunch. He is the father of six whose wife died suddenly when the children were ages twelve, ten, nine, seven, seven, and seventeen months. Based on his wife's detailed preparatory work in planning curriculum for their children prior to her death, he developed a set of twenty-two CD-ROMs that contain a complete curriculum (supplemented only by Saxon Math) for grades one through twelve. The curriculum includes a program of self-study, using high quality books and materials that may be printed out for use (for information, see appendix A).

With the increasing popularity of home schooling and developments in technology, home schooling families will continue to see innovations emerge that seek to make schooling easier, faster, and more efficient. These methods, however, can never be considered a substitute for the deep relationships that develop between members of a home schooling family. Those close relationships are at the heart of home schooling.

## Taking Them Home

If your child has spent time in a public school, there may be an adjustment period when he first comes home. Often the major problem is peer dependency. When your child has been absorbed with school friends, he may resist home schooling and may even tell you that you have "ruined his life." These can be hard times for both parent and child alike. If you are firm in your resolve, you can weather difficult times and look forward to a brighter future. Understand and empathize with your children, but reassure them that this is in their best interest. I have told my own children, "Someday, you will appreciate this."

If your child has had a difficult time in school or has the misfortune of being labeled with a learning problem, he may require nursing of self-esteem and mending of a wounded heart. We focus on our children's worth in the eyes of God. How others view us is of little consequence.

If your child has placed a high value on being popular in school, he may react adversely to being removed from the limelight. This is a good time to foster *accurate* self-esteem, as opposed to the perhaps overinflated self-esteem enjoyed in school.

School may have caused "learning burnout." The children's love of learning may have been extinguished. Allow them time to explore *their* interests in a relaxed setting. Soon, they will become excited about learning again.

## Staying Flexible and Focused

Flexibility is the real beauty of home schooling. My children will always know that relationships and people are more important than lesson plans, that compassion and love are to be valued above any and all structure and accomplishments. It is indeed exciting and freeing to be available to deal with illness and family emergencies. It is exhilarating to have the freedom to take advantage of opportunities that occur on the spur of the moment—a beautiful sunset, free tickets to a concert, or an unplanned outing to a museum. Public schools do not offer such flexibility and freedom.

Be enthusiastic. It is contagious. If you view your new responsibility as drudgery, your children will too. If you are excited, your children will be too. You will learn as much as them.

Lest you be overwhelmed at the task at hand, remember to keep to the basics and keep your focus clear. Many people who begin home schooling become disillusioned: "They miss the blessing of teaching their children because they will not eliminate the distractions. They cannot delight in the tasks at hand because they are consumed by the unnecessaries which they are determined to lug about."[17] What are your "unnecessaries"—time commitments, distractions, clutter? Resolve to have a plan to deal with such issues before you start home schooling.

I have the problem of being distracted with too many good things. I have to constantly reevaluate my priorities and time commitments. Our family motto is "Simplify, simplify, simplify." In an era of unlimited opportunities, we must exercise wisdom to have time and energy for the best things in life.

### Seven Habits of Effective Home Schooling

Stephen Covey's book *The Seven Habits of Highly Effective People* has influenced many people to look at the way they live their lives. Llewellyn Davis of Elijah Company, a home school book distributor, has adapted these habits for effective home schooling. They are helpful to consider here as a way to stay focused.

### FIRST, "PICTURE EACH CHILD'S FUTURE."

Stephen Covey calls this beginning with the end in mind. What kind of person do you want to see when your home schooler graduates from high school? What skills should she have, what will her relationship with God look like, what kind of relationship would you like to have with this child? When your child is young and still under your influence, you can begin to work on these end goals *now.* "What would it take for the Lord to say, 'Well done, good and faithful parents!'"[18]

### SECOND, "FOCUS ON RELATIONSHIPS FIRST, SKILLS SECOND, AND INFORMATION LAST."

Our primary relationship is with God, then with ourselves, then with others, then with things or events in our environment. If God were really first in your life, what would it look like? For most of us, our lives would look remarkably different from the way they are now.

What skills are really needed for life? I believe in the three R's, but Llewellyn Davis reminds us there are also relationship skills, character education, social skills, business skills, thinking skills, gender skills, aptitude/interest/gifting skills, and academic skills.

The gathering of information should be our last priority in this category. Davis notes: "There is no question that the 3-Rs are foundational to all further learning, so they must be mastered. However, we believe that once our children are rightly related to God, self, others, and created things and once they acquire the life skills mentioned above, they can pick up any other information they need when it becomes useful."[19]

*THIRD, "PUT IN THE BIG ROCKS FIRST."*

If we are giving sufficient attention to the big things in our lives, the little things will fall into place. This is illustrated by Mr. Covey with a jar, large rocks, and small pebbles. He challenges his audience to put all the rocks and pebbles into the jar. The only way they will fit is if the big rocks are placed in first. Then the pebbles will nestle in and fit themselves around the big rocks.

What are the big rocks in your life? Are you putting them in first or trying to jam them in with all the small stuff? The only way we will know balance is through tending to our "big rocks" first.

Our focus should be on things that are important, such as: crisis prevention, building relationships, reflective time, renewal of vision, learning new skills, planning, studying, recreation, and moving toward goals. These are the only things that contribute to long-term success.

*FOURTH, "ALWAYS MOVE TOWARD THE CONTEXT THAT NURTURES YOUR GOALS."*

Look at your physical and emotional environment. Think of your children as plants and your home as a garden. Does your home—your garden—nurture growth in your children? Does it nurture the relationships, skills, and values you are developing in your children? If not, what changes can you implement? Perhaps you need to order your physical environment, improve your time management, and find a stress-free recordkeeping system.

*FIFTH, "FIND A BALANCE BETWEEN THE PROCESS AND THE PRODUCT."*

We should be interested in the long-term result of home education—a godly, educated person. But we must enjoy and savor the process along the way. The type of learning we seek cannot be mass produced; it is the individual crafts-manship of the home schooling family. Take time to savor that process.

### SIXTH, "KEEP DAD INVOLVED."

Dad is the one who makes a home school hum. If he approves and is actively involved, children will think it's important, instead of just "Mom's thing."

### SEVENTH, "CARVE OUT MARGIN."

We need to leave spaces in our lives between where we are and where our limits are: "Margin is having time, energy, and money to spare. It is having physical, emotional, and spiritual reserves. Margin is living within our limits."[20]

We need to make sure we have reserves of emotional margin by refreshing ourselves spiritually and emotionally; of physical margin by proper nutrition, exercise, and rest; of time margin with our time priorities in order; and financial margin by wise use of our resources.

Author, public school teacher, and home schooling parent David Guterson writes, "Although home schooling may work, it is by no means easy. Most American adults are fully competent, of course, to learn whatever they have to learn—facts, skills, methods, strategies—in order to teach their children. But should they want to do it, they should strive to be good at it, and they should face the endeavor seriously. It should bring them satisfaction; it should feel like important work. No one should undertake to homeschool without coming to terms with this fundamental truth: It is the fabric of your own life you are deciding about, not just your child's education." He concludes his article by saying, "Teaching is an act of love before it is anything else."[21]

Home schooling is not easy. Most people don't talk about the difficult aspects of this lifestyle. Home schoolers are often pictured in an idyllic rural setting, with the children working on the farm and Mom always finding time to sew quilts. This is not the reality for many home schoolers. Many are in cities. Many are tired and pray for strength to make it through this adventure. But we have a peace in our hearts that cannot be matched by any other choice.

# 8

# Positive Relationships with the Public Schools and Community

*A* trend is developing for cooperation between home schoolers and public schools. Potential services to be shared might include achievement testing, selected classes, textbooks, libraries, sports activities, field trips, health screening, counseling and psychological services, and special education resources.

The interest is particularly strong in the area of sports. "That's because competitive sports is the one activity families can't easily duplicate as their children reach high-school age," notes Scott Somerville, a lawyer with the Home School Legal Defense Association.[1] In addition, for talented athletes, sports may provide an economic advantage for potential college scholarships. In 1996, the National College Athletic Association established guidelines to deal with home educated students:

> According to the guidelines, home-schooled athletes who have sufficiently high standardized-test scores and proof that they took at least 13 courses that meet the association's core-course standards may be automatically awarded freshman eligibility. . . . The National Association of Intercollegiate Athletics and the National Christian College Athletic Association also have policies, put on the books two years ago, to govern the eligi-

bility of home-schooled athletes. The rules in both organizations state that home-schooled students may meet the requirement that athletes earn at least a 2.0 grade point average in
high school either by earning a General Education Development diploma or by receiving state certification that they have
achieved the equivalent of a high-school diploma.[2]

According to *The Chronicle of Higher Education,* "In 1985,
Washington and Oregon became the first states to allow home-
schooled athletes who meet certain academic standards to participate in sports at public schools. Now, eight states in all
have such legislation. Similar measures are pending in five
more. In nine other states, sports-governing bodies or state
education agencies allow school districts to decide whether to
allow home schoolers to participate in high-school activities."[3]
Officially, this arrangement is called "shared time" and refers
to an arrangement in which students enrolled in nonpublic
schools can attend public schools for instruction in certain
areas, usually laboratory science or home economics, and to
attend extracurricular activities. The law among states is far
from uniform.

A case in point is Idaho. The law, sponsored by Representative Fred Tilmen (whose own children are home schooled),
"allows Idaho's estimated 4,000 home-schooled students (as
well as those in private schools) to attend regular public school
classes, as well as compete in extracurricular activities."[4] The
law also contains a safeguard against abuse. An athlete receiving failing grades may not transfer to home-schooled status
to circumvent the law and continue to play sports.

It has long been argued that education is a fundamental
right and home schoolers should not be forbidden from par-
taking of portions of the public school curriculum. In places
such as North Dakota where the state constitution creates a
fundamental right to a public school education, it is more
likely that home schoolers would be allowed free access. Leg-
islating this fundamental right means that a home schooler's

exclusion from public school activities must withstand a legal test called "strict scrutiny."

If you reside in a state in which your state constitution views education as a fundamental right, this provides a strong foundation for attempting to access public school services. If your state does not consider education to be a fundamental right, you may experience impediments in this battle. It should be noted that there is no *federal* fundamental right to an education. Thus, the issue is relegated to individual states.

In the paper "Access of Home Schooled Children to Public School Activities," the Rutherford Institute notes: "Case law regarding parochial school students has clearly established no constitutional right exists to access extra-curricular sports activities, and any right to participate in such activities must arise from some administrative or statutory entitlement."[5]

As with any other aspect of home schooling law, check your statutes. Several states have specific provisions for access to public school activities. Some states provide full access, including all courses and activities. Other states allow dual enrollment, wherein a student can take courses from both private and public schools. Check the laws of your state carefully before inquiring with your superintendent of schools.

## Home School/School District Cooperation

Many home schoolers simply wish to be left alone. They do not want to be studied, scrutinized, subsidized, or counted. Others prefer to have a more cooperative relationship with the local school. Home school families can experience benefits from limited participation in the public school, as we have already noted. Conversely, public schools can benefit from the presence of home educated children. Mike Shepherd, a Dallas teacher, regularly uses home schooled kids to tutor public school students. He notes these mutual gains:

1. Older home schooled students can tutor public elementary schoolers.
2. Older home schoolers can teach minicourses in art or other specialties.
3. Home schoolers can attend music classes offered at the public schools and pay any fees necessary.
4. Home-taught students can enroll in school but use the school's curriculum for home study.
5. Schools can test home taught students using nationally formed tests.
6. Home-taught kids can be allowed to compete in science fairs and spelling bees along with public school students.
7. Home-taught students can be invited to special school events and field trips.[6]

A willingness to meet one another halfway is the starting point.

In Ames, Iowa, home schoolers and public school students join together daily to reach the goal of educational excellence. Legislation enacted in 1991 paved the way for dual enrollment for Iowa students. This allows—but does not require—enrollment for academic or instructional programs, participation in any extracurricular activity offered by the district, and use of services of an appropriate area education agency. "What that means for families and school districts," notes Mary Terpstra, coordinator of the Home-Based Education Program, "is that home education can be a team effort in alternative education."[7] While recognizing the problems and challenges presented by such an arrangement, she envisions a future in which public schools may serve as an umbrella for some types of alternative schooling. Schools benefit from increased state aid and home school families benefit by having an emotional connection to their local school.

An attitude of cooperation by both parties could potentially pave the way for a satisfactory and successful arrangement. Regrettably, as recently as the early 1990s, Thomas Shannon, executive director of the National School Boards Association, termed home schooling, "a giant step backward into the 17th century," adding, "the youngsters are getting shortchanged. Society ultimately has to pay for any mistakes, not to mention the loss of a child who might otherwise have made a maximum contribution." His sentiments are echoed by the National Education Association (NEA), which passed a resolution in the early 1990s declaring, "Home-schooling parents cannot provide the child with a comprehensive education experience."[8]

Kathy Collins, former legal counsel to the Iowa Department of Education, calls home schooling either a public relations asset or disaster: "The opportunity is there for school administrators to make the public schools look like the most open-minded and accepting of alternatives just by the way they treat home-schooling families. But the potential is greater for a public relations nightmare, for an administrator to be caught in an inflexible position, to be involved in a lawsuit, to have some parents take the whole thing to the media. In the end, it's up to school administrators to decide."[9]

A different approach was taken in a recent *Education Week* commentary. The author noted,

> The issue for public education is not whether, as some opponents claim, home-schooled children have an unfair advantage because they receive such prime pedagogical fare as one-to-one instruction. Rather, it is whether and how such an advantage can be gained for all children. By studying home schools, reformers perhaps could find something in how children engage in out-of-school experiences that could work inside the education system as well. The home-school phenomenon provides an opportunity for reformers to strengthen their case for greater parental involvement and the use of diverse schooling approaches matched with individual learning styles. . . . With education rapidly being reshaped by technological advances and efforts to foster diverse and personalized approaches to schooling, schools of the future may look more like home schools look today. For the good of Amer-

ica's children, maybe it is time for us to understand what is
happening in home schools and acknowledge that movement's
momentum.[10]

The impressive results obtained by home schooling families are the results sought by all parents. Yet an antagonism
remains between the school establishment and the family.
Each could make great gains with a spirit of cooperation and
respect. The future might look something like this, as reported
in the *Education Digest:*

> At least one California school district, in an attempt to keep
> home schoolers linked with public schools, gives a sort of cur-
> riculum subsidy to home-schooling families: $1,000 per child
> per year to purchase district approved textbooks and other
> teaching tools. Under a provision of California law, the Cuper-
> tine Union School District allows home-schooled children to
> "enroll" in—without being required to attend—one of the
> district's alternative schools. If they do, both the district and
> parent benefit. The district gets nearly $3,000 in state aid for
> the child and maintains a line with the home-schooled stu-
> dent. And the home-schooling parent receives the $1,000
> toward costs, plus optional testing for the child, access to a
> teacher available specifically to help with home-schooling
> concerns, and the chance to participate free of charge in any
> staff-training program open to district teachers.[11]

Many families would reject the offer of the California
school district noted above. The thousand dollars they receive would not be worth the independence they sacrifice
by being required to use district-approved textbooks. One
of the beauties of home schooling is its flexibility to accommodate the philosophies of all dedicated parents. Perhaps
this is the future vision for home education: cooperation
*without* loss of control. There is a long road to travel in most
states.

## Dealing with School Authorities

Researchers Mayberry, Knowles, Ray, and Marlow surveyed school superintendents and noted that across states, "they did not appear to have a clear and consistent understanding of home education law."[12] The majority ranked their public schools as far superior to home schools. Survey results clearly ignore previous research on the positive outcomes of home schooled children. This raises the question of where and how school officials receive their information about home schooling. What, if any, obligation do home schooling parents have to educate the administrators?

It is clear, given the growth of the home schooling movement and continuing exodus from public education, that superintendents and school boards will have to become more directly involved in home school policy-making. Educators must have a deeper understanding of the laws, issues, and motivations of home schooling families: "Given the current political tenor emphasizing school choice issues and taxpayer revolt, parent educators who feel they are not being accommodated by local school officials could prove to be a substantial force toward requiring full consideration of home educators by the professional education community. They represent a potentially active constituency that superintendents would be ill-advised to ignore or inadvertently misjudge."[13]

School board member and associate professor of education Betty Jo Simmons, writing in *The American School Board Journal,* comments:

> Instead of becoming alarmed each time a parent applies for home schooling, school leaders would do well to cooperate and inform parents about such matters as curriculum options, testing procedures, teaching qualifications and opportunities for socialization. When a school district answers parents' questions honestly, parents are better prepared to made a decision in their children's best educational interest. For your part, it is

also in the children's best interest to allow home-schooled children to participate in as many of the regular school offerings as the family desires and the schools can legitimately accommodate. Parents have the right to find the best education for their children. If it happens to be home schooling, so be it. After all, home schooling is not a subversive activity.[14]

There is an obligation, as home schoolers, to comply with laws and to cooperate to the extent that individual consciences will allow. The best approach is to do the job well. Give your children the finest education possible; if it is ever called into question, your actions and results will speak for themselves.

What about requirements that children have five-hour school days or the equivalent? Read each state statute very carefully. Many of the requirements apply to the administration of public schools. In other words, they legally establish the dimensions of a school day or school year for a public school. Remember that in a home school, learning can take many forms and dimensions. If you were to keep a record of all the educational activities in your home, you would probably withstand even the most stringent state requirements.

Cooperate to the maximum extent possible with school authorities. Do not consider it unreasonable to request that all communications be reduced to writing, both those given to and received from school authorities. Should a phone call be received from any school authority, it is well within your legal rights to request written communication. A record will then be created documenting that actions and activities are legitimate.

The Home School Legal Defense Association (HSLDA) is worth investigating. It is a group legal services program providing legal representation to home school families for a nominal yearly fee (see appendix B).

## A Guide to Vouchers and Tax Credits

Another heated issue in the home schooling community is that of taxes and vouchers. Many parents argue that state or federal governments should issue tax credits or tuition vouchers for home education.

A tuition tax credit is an indirect transfer of funds to parents who send their children to private schools; it gives them an income tax credit or deduction. A voucher is a more direct transfer, a type of grant from the state government that parents can then use to apply to tuition. It is a direct payment of funds to parents, even those whose incomes are so low that they would receive no benefit from a tax credit.

The issue of vouchers is seductive. Home schoolers pay taxes for education and realize no resultant benefit. In fact, most families pay extra for the privilege of teaching their own children. They buy their own curriculum and also relieve the teacher-student ratio within the public school classroom. A payment to make up for the money the government would have spent on a public school education for the child sounds very appealing. Parents might be eligible to receive vouchers for private school enrollment and, presumably, for home schooling. The rationale is that privatization of educational services will spur competition and encourage excellence.

Authors Larry and Susan Kaseman have written extensively on the many legal issues related to home schooling. They observe: "In reality it is clear that vouchers would not be allowed to be used for home schooling unless the government had strong control over home schools, unless there were strong regulations being enforced, unless home schoolers could prove that their children were really getting a good education. Therefore home schoolers are forced to conclude that the only way we could participate in a voucher system would be to pay for it with our freedom."[15]

The Christian Home Educators Coalition forewarns, "As a result, all 'choices' will become eventually reduced to government-regulated schools. Finally, all differences between public and private schools disappear. These reform policies will eliminate true competition in educational choices within a matter of years."[16]

Government money never comes without strings attached. Vouchers would be payable only to qualifying schools. What criteria would home schoolers need to possess to be considered a qualifying school? The Christian Home Educators Coalition couches it in these terms: "The funding provided in the scholarship program for private/home schools will be sweet in its first taste, but then will quickly turn bitter as the consequences become clear."[17]

The Rutherford Institute, in their position paper titled "School Choice and Tax Credits for Home Education," reminds us: "Studies have shown that the majority of families have chosen home schooling because they hold certain religious beliefs that influence their conceptions of education, and the morals and character-building that it should entail. For many of these, no amount of choice among public schools will matter."[18]

The main concern of home schooling parents should be to protect the autonomy and independence of their respective home schools. Becoming involved in a cooperative effort to accept financial incentives may compromise continuing independence.

## Standardized Testing

Individual states require periodic standardized testing for home schooled students. In some states, the children must score above an arbitrary point in order to continue home schooling.

If you are forced to test your children, attempt to prepare them for the testing situation. You might procure an old test through a support group, school district, or public school teacher. At the very least, review test-taking procedures, such as introducing your child to multiple-choice, true-false, and fill-in-the-blank questions.

Usually, this is not a problem since home schooled children do perform exceptionally well on tests. Typically, the thresholds are ridiculously low. Should the child score below the required threshold, he may not be allowed to continue to home school. For example, in Colorado, the threshold is the 13th percentile. Home schoolers consistently have been found to score above the 80th percentile.

One alternative to testing is a portfolio review or progress report. The parent/teacher presents a representative sample of work to school officials. This procedure is not without drawbacks, as attorney Christopher Klicka notes: "Requirements of evaluations, portfolio reviews, or progress reports are much more risky since you are opening yourself up to much greater scrutiny and arbitrary discretion of the public school officials. . . . The legal advantage of test scores over portfolios or evaluations is that they cannot be subjected to arbitrary interpretation by the school officials or the judges."[19]

Be cautious of which standard of comparison is used in testing. Criterion-referenced tests are designed by school systems and may be a problem for home schoolers. Such tests measure student achievement against a given standard, such as a set of reading skills for a particular school district. "The more popular and safer testing for home schoolers is the norm-referenced testing," says Christopher Klicka. "The Stanford Achievement and Iowa Basic Skills test are norm-referenced. These tests tend to have less value-laden questions and are not designed to fit any certain public school curriculum."[20] Rather, they measure the student's achievement against a group of students perceived to be typical of the nation as a whole.

Even with the slightly more acceptable norm-referenced test, what is being measured is how the child performed on the test in relation to other children. The goal is to assess what the child has learned. Most home schoolers believe they are in the best position to evaluate their child's progress.

Christopher Klicka believes, "We should oppose a nationally mandated test for all children because there is strong evidence that such a pervasive system of testing could easily be abused to conform the values of the children to something contrary to Christianity."[21]

Testing can, however, become an assurance for parents that they are doing an adequate job. If that is a private motivation for testing, then it can be very reassuring. In addition, the home schooler's willingness to be tested says something to the education establishment. Authors Terry Dorian and Zan Peters Tyler note, "We need to strive to present educators, legislators, and the community around us with unbiased evidence that homeschooling works. Even though many people do not understand homeschooling, they understand test scores."[22]

It is interesting to note the consequences for testing when school systems are involved. In the report, "Use of Standardized Tests to Measure Home Schooling Success," the Rutherford Institute concludes: "When a home schooled child 'fails' a standardized test, it is assumed the parents, for one reason or another, did not do, or were incapable of doing, an adequate job of teaching. . . . Yet when a child fails in public or private school, most often specified as culpable in the blame-affixing process are the child's motivation, the child's lack of prerequisites, or—most ironically—the parents' socioeconomic status, the parents' lack of involvement, or the home environment and not the teacher."[23]

It seems that parents take the blame either way. Conversely, home schoolers can rightfully take the praise when their students excel.

## Social Service Workers

Social service workers or child protection workers can sometimes be intrusive. They might seek to find ways to get into your home to close down your home school.

Anonymous tip lines can sometimes be a problem for home schoolers. A disgruntled neighbor might complain that your children are playing outside during school hours or that the children are poorly dressed or lacking supervision. Social workers may attempt bullying their way into your house on a "fishing expedition" to look for potential problems, although this is occurring less frequently as home schooling gains more acceptance.

Parents who voluntarily allow entry to such social service workers may be hurting themselves. An overzealous worker may find something he doesn't approve of and use that situation to cause you trouble. These workers, whether they be truant officers, public school officials, social service workers, or police officers, should not be admitted into your home unless they have a search warrant or an arrest warrant signed by a judge. Insist on a phone call to your lawyer first, even if there is a police officer present. The best policy is to politely refuse entry and assert your legal rights. You might respond: "I respect the job you have to do, however . . ." Don't be belligerent or uncooperative. It will hurt you in the long run. It is also extremely dangerous to allow workers to talk to your children, especially alone. Children, mine included, can be persuaded to say nearly anything.

The Rutherford Institute position paper on "Administrative Searches and Home School Visits," notes, "Although the government interest in protecting children is substantial, home visits have not been shown to be necessary for the advancement of the regulatory scheme: There are other less restrictive means of ensuring the proper education of children, such as with standardized test scores."[24]

The government, through programs such as Goals 2000 and Parents as Teachers, is seeking greater input into our families. The more we allow the government into our homes under the guise of educational reform, the more freedom we forfeit.

Compliance with the law is required, but we do not need to unnecessarily invite trouble into our homes. Christopher Klicka reminds us, "A school official can only inspect a home schooler's home if the family voluntarily allows them to come in or if the state official has a warrant or court order signed by a judge. Any home school family who does not want to voluntarily participate in home visits cannot be required to do so without violating their Fourth Amendment and privacy rights."[25]

## Home School Bill of Rights

With rights come responsibilities. Home schoolers will continue to expand their rights in our traditional school society. Our duty is to home educate responsibly—to teach our children diligently, faithfully, and within the bounds of the law. As we are responsible with this task, we can begin to claim the rights delineated in the following Home School Bill of Rights, proposed by the Rutherford Institute:

> The right to free exercise of religion. You are allowed to home school for religious reasons.
> The right to family self-determination. Parents have the authority to select children's education.
> The right to privacy. You have the right to be left alone. This includes family relationships and child rearing.
> The right to due process. The state cannot make a vague law regarding home schooling.

The right from burdensome state regulation. The state cannot force your children to go to public school or require a state teaching certificate if you are home schooling.

The right to freedom of thought and belief. Parents are the most aware of their children's needs and are best qualified to teach them according to the family's beliefs.

The right to teach children from a religious viewpoint. You can teach your children from a religious viewpoint rather than a vocational or cultural one.

The right to alternative education. Parents do not have to send their children to public or private school if they believe the schools do not teach the correct values.

The right to decide policy in public education. Even if a parent home schools, the parent can have a say in how the public schools operate.

The right to take certain public school courses. If you pay taxes and home school, your children should be able to take selective classes at the public school.[26]

# 9

# *The Question of Socialization*

"Your children need to be with other children," I am often informed by friends and relatives. The implication is that we are huddled in our home learning the three R's and Bible verses and that my children never see the light of day or have normal social experiences.

I love the analogy of a greenhouse. Our children are tender seedlings; to set them out before they were ready would signal sure crop failure. Rather, they are nurtured and sheltered in a protective environment until they are ready to be hardened in the garden outside.

Linda Dobson says, "Off the top of my head, I can't think of another species besides human beings that separates a child from its parents when she's ready to acquire life skills."[1] Most home schoolers believe that those life skills are best learned in the home rather than in a school environment.

Too often, people assume that the public school environment is more "normal" than that of the home school—but is it really? When again in their lives will our children be completely surrounded by people their own age? When they report to their first job, will they be assigned to a specific unit because that's where all the twenty-two-year-olds work? Of course not. They will require the ability to interact with people of all ages. Even at fast food restaurants, teenagers work alongside housewives and retirees.

144

Schools promote multiculturalism and tolerance, yet they insist that age segregation is the healthiest setting for children. They imply that children in home schooling families have an emotionally unhealthy experience because siblings of all ages learn together. The schools want our children to embrace all cultures, creeds, and orientations, but not necessarily their own siblings, who are kept in separate classrooms. Which approach could be more accurately defined as "normal"?

One of the many things that gives me great joy is to see my children playing together. They vary in ages, but in our everyday life, they are comfortable with older or younger people. We view this interaction as normal and healthy—not the public school cliques of young girls or boys relating to one another within a narrow frame of reference. Our children's lives are much broader and richer than that.

## Problems with Peer Dependency

Too much time spent within age groups is not the healthiest of situations for our children. In fact, "Dr. Urie Bronfenbrenner and his Cornell teams found that children who spend more elective time with their peers than with their parents until the fifth or sixth grades—about ages eleven or twelve—will become peer dependent. Such knuckling under to peer values incurs four losses crucial to sound mental health and positive sociability. These losses, stated in lay terms, are self-worth, optimism, respect for parents, and trust in peers."[2]

Dr. Raymond Moore calls this a "desocializing phenomenon," and cautions, "Every child needs an adult or adults to whom he can consistently relate over the long term of his development, who models the right values and who cares enough about him to guide him by precept and example into adopting these values."[3] This adult is not likely to be the day-care provider or the teacher at school who can only provide a few minutes of one-to-one time each day. This adult is *you*.

Home schooling father and author Rick Boyer notes, "School children in America spend between thirty and forty hours per week with their age peers in large groups and the 'well-rounded' ones more than that through extra-curricular activities. This has been common practice for decades and we are now conditioned to think of it as normal. Kids need lots of time with kids their own age. We don't know just why, but we assume it's so. After all, that's the way the government school professionals do it and the government would never deceive us, would they?"[4]

Age segregation is the way school professionals *have* to do it; they have no choice. They deal with volumes of children each day. As a home schooling family, you can choose to opt out of this factory form of socialization and education and teach one-on-one in the beautiful, natural, healthy setting of the home. This is the best preparation for the real world because the real world has all ages worshiping, working, living, and playing together.

My oldest daughter came dangerously close to being peer addicted. She lived and breathed for her friends. The few months she attended school included a series of social activities. She reflected the views of the other little girls in how she thought about herself. If she was viewed positively by them, she had a good day. If one of them made a cutting remark, she was crushed. As Linda Dobson quips, "The old cliche about the blind leading the blind was written, I suspect, by an elementary school teacher eavesdropping on student conversations on the playground."[5] My impressionable daughter was basing her self-worth on the opinions of immature and inexperienced young people. None of them, including my daughter, had learned to "encourage one another and build each other up" (1 Thess. 5:11).

Since my daughter has been home, the addiction has been tamed. It is still a battle, but she is less peer dependent. She is better at making her own choices and forms her opinion of herself through a variety of life experiences rather than through the narrow focus of her peers.

## Cruel Social Games

The way for our children to have a life of success and a life that makes sense is, for many of us, to refuse to participate in the cruel social and segregating games of the school system. Instead, our children are taught in an environment of love and acceptance. When problems arise, as they inevitably will, they can be dealt with, rather than being the cause for a child's ostracism.

The social benefits of home schooling are often misunderstood. A writer for the *New York Times Magazine* notes: "When I described unschooling, or at least my understanding of it, to Kathleen Lyons, a spokeswoman for the National Education Association, she didn't pause. 'I wouldn't want my child educated like that,' she said. 'Or to grow up in a society where the majority were educated like that. Our society is loose enough as it is. The thing that binds us together in this country is public education.' [John] Holt wrote that schools don't really provide that kind of glue and can't, 'Not as long as they also have the job of sorting out the young into winners and losers, and preparing the losers for a lifetime of losing.'"[6]

## Rebellious Behavior

In the past, I viewed school as a break for Mom from the challenges of parenting. Some days I wish I had not taken the road I have taken. Then I read what Christopher Klicka says: "Schools function like an anesthetic for many parents. They won't endure the discomfort of having to deal with an unruly child and so they send him off to school under the misguided notion that somehow the school will be able to straighten him out."[7] This strategy works for a little while, but soon the child has emotional support from his peers for his rebellion and disrespect for his parents.

Dealing with the problems and challenges of parenting yourself, rather than sweeping them under the public school carpet, is a much better way. The Book of Proverbs instructs us: "Discipline your son, for in that there is hope" (Prov. 19:18). While it may seem easier to delegate this chore to someone else, the ultimate responsibility rests on the parents' shoulders. An extremely difficult task in the short run will reap tremendous blessings in the long run.

David Guterson, author of *Family Matters,* says this about children spending their lives surrounded by other children: "Their need for adults, unfulfilled and frustrated, urges them to grasp even more obsessively—this a staple of psychological theory about adolescent peer dependency—at what their peers have to offer in consolation. . . . Homeschooling, when practiced carefully, allows children to develop a more balanced set of relationships not only with peers and with adults in their communities but with their families and parents as well."[8]

In thinking of the social woes we face today—divorce, drug abuse, AIDS, suicide, and other problems—Rick Boyer says, "I am hard pressed to think of any that seem to result from children spending too much time at home."[9] Many problems can be traced to a deficit of time and attention in the home.

It is the duty and the desire of most parents to protect their children from societal ills. Yet we knowingly and enthusiastically allow them to attend government schools where we know that God is not welcome, where all forms of tolerance are praised, where drug education and sex education are part of the curriculum. What is the message we are sending to our children? The message is that the world is a rotten place, that God doesn't exist, that they should do what they can to pleasure themselves while they are on this planet. We have by default delegated our responsibility for values education to the schools; how can we then complain that children have no values?

We believe, as home schoolers, that the highest aim of humankind is to glorify God. The training of our children seeks to reflect this truth, not some politically correct rhetoric. With strong faith training, they will be better prepared to deal with any social issues when they arise.

## Negative Socialization

Rick Boyer describes the negative socialization that can happen in peer groups.[10]

> PEER GROUP SOCIALIZATION TENDS TO MAKE CHILDREN DEPENDENT ON THEIR PEERS.

When children are with other children, they seek to be popular. Scoring well in math may not be popular. The really popular kids may be the ones who smoke cigarettes and show blatant disregard for adults.

Children want to be like everyone else. This pressure to conform causes them to lose their uniqueness, their individuality. They are precious gifts from God, not mere clones of their contemporaries.

> PEER SOCIALIZATION SUBJECTS CHILDREN TO CONSTANT ATTACKS ON THEIR SELF-ESTEEM.

Spend a few minutes at your local schoolyard listening closely. Do the children build one another up and speak words of love and encouragement? You are more likely to hear them calling one another "stupid" or some more offensive epithet.

As children advance to middle school, every day becomes a battle. They have to ward off teasing and negativity. If your child is the least bit different—overweight, tall, short, or a glasses wearer—then the battle will be intensified. With so much time spent dealing with the preservation of self-esteem, little energy is left for learning.

### PEER SOCIALIZATION CREATES NEGATIVE ATTITUDES TOWARD OTHER AGE GROUPS.

Show me an eighth grader speaking kindly to his third grade brother and, in all probability, I'll show you two kids who are home schooled. In most age-segregated settings, those younger than a child are considered to be a nuisance and those older are perceived to be members of the Stone Age. The older the children, the narrower their social abilities become. A junior high student may have no concept of how to relate to others outside of his class. Yet this socialization is considered normal and healthy. Conversely, a home schooled child who is regularly exposed to people of all age groups will easily relate to both old and young alike.

### PEER SOCIALIZATION BREAKS DOWN FAMILY RELATIONSHIPS.

One of the primary reasons we home school is to foster a relationship with our children. We want to have an integral part in their development, not just the remains of their day after school.

Some parents actually worry that their children will be too dependent on them. So they ship them off to other adults to raise. A woman spoke to me once about how independent her first-grader seemed: "Between school and playing with friends after school, she hardly needs me at all," the mother noted sadly. The truth is that this precious six-year-old needs her mother more than anything. Instead, she gets the cheap substitute of school socialization.

God puts people in families, not in institutions. His Word tells us: "Listen to your father, who gave you life, and do not despise your mother when she is old" (Prov. 23:22). If peer socialization in schools breaks down family relationships, we can choose a better way—a way that celebrates and strengthens families: home schooling.

> *PEER SOCIALIZATION ISOLATES CHILDREN FROM THE REAL*
> *"ADULT" WORLD.*

It is ironic that we send our children to an age-segregated setting in order to prepare them for an adult society. With separation from adults being the norm, how can we expect them to be prepared for adulthood? Home schooling can give our children a broad exposure to many age groups and types of people.

## Is the Home School Too Sheltered?

What's so bad about sheltering our children? Admittedly, our world is not a safe place. Shouldn't we do everything we can do to ensure the safety and security of our children?

Llewellyn Davis, in the book *Going Home to School,* explains the benefits of sheltering children: "Children who are allowed to mature and achieve in secure, non-threatening environments are more capable of handling life's problems because they have developed a strong sense of identity. Much of modern man's inability to cope is a result of what psychiatrists have called an 'identity crisis' resulting from feelings of meaninglessness and lack of purpose. Christian home education, properly applied, should impart self-confidence, self-motivation, and a sense of destiny to children."[11] If we have the opportunity to shape destiny, how can we delegate that to a school system? It's about more than getting a good job or getting into a good college; it goes to the essence of who we are as human beings—creatures of a great God.

Linda Dobson says, "When we pass responsibility for educating our children to others, and send them all off to an institution to do it, we place Life in an artificial context."[12] We believe that faith, family, life, and education are interchangeable. School is the artificial context into which we entrust our children. Home schooling is the natural, sensible alternative.

Jonathan Lindvall, a home schooling speaker, notes: "God gave children parents to shelter them. My challenge to us is: Dare to shelter. Be bold. Shelter your children from those things that would cause them to stumble."[13]

If parents, those who love their children the most, do not dare to shelter them, who will? Many temptations of this world would cause our children to stumble and fall. We believe it is best to wait until they have the strength of character and spiritual maturity to deal with the world before releasing them into it. Home schooling gives us the opportunity to shelter our children from a valueless society while they are becoming strong in their own values. When their belief system is formed, then they will be able to deal with anything the world throws their way.

## Socialization

First and foremost, one must ask the purpose of social interaction. Cheryl Gorder says, "One of the criticisms of home schools is that people believe these children won't have enough time to be around other kids so that they can learn how to be a kid. However, it's not important to teach a kid how to be a kid. They already know that. It's important to teach a kid how to be a good person."[14] Home schoolers believe a child becomes a good person by focusing on vertical relationships (with God and adults) rather than horizontal relationships with peers.

Yet many would level criticism that home schoolers are overprotective, sheltering children from the real world. In a growing body of studies, several academic researchers have investigated this issue with surprising results. Home schooling is *not* a negative factor in healthy socialization. Indeed, it may be the healthiest way to raise our children.

Researcher Lee Stough studied some thirty home schooling families and thirty-two conventionally schooled families with children seven to fourteen years of age. He employed several measures to compare groups, such as the Vineland Adaptive Behavior Scale and the Piers-Harris Children's Self-Concept Scale. According to his findings, children who were educated at home "gained the necessary skills, knowledge and attitudes needed to function in society . . . at a rate similar to that of conventionally schooled children." He also found no difference in self-concept between the two groups of children, concluding, "insofar as self concept is a reflector of socialization, it would appear that few home-schooled children are socially deprived, and that there may be sufficient evidence to indicate that some home-schooled children have a *higher* self concept than conventionally schooled children."[15]

The bogeyman of a socialization deficit in home educated children is being blown out of the water. Consider the research of Larry Shyers reported in the well-known *National Review:* "In his study, eight to ten year old children were videotaped at play. Their behavior was observed by trained counselors who did not know which children went to regular schools and which were home schooled. The conclusion: 'The study found no big difference between the two groups of children in self-concept of assertiveness, which was measured by their social development tests. But the videotapes showed that youngsters who were taught at home by their parents had consistently fewer behavioral problems.'"[16]

More recently, Dr. Brian Ray reported the findings of researcher Steven W. Kelley. Kelley studied students in grades two through ten in the Los Angeles area. He carefully matched home educated and conventionally educated students using demographic criteria to achieve a meaningful comparison. "Kelley found that 50 percent of the home-schooled children were at or above the 80th percentile of the PHCSCS (Piers-Harris Children's Self-Concept Scale) global scale. This was significantly more positive than scores for the conventionally schooled students. . . . Kelley suggested that a low anxiety level, more contact with significant others, peer independence, a sense of responsibility and self-worth, and parental love, support, and involvement may be the factors contributing to these home-educated children's positive self-concepts."[17]

How do the home educated fare as adults? Julie Webb, one of the few researchers who has studied adult lives of the home educated, reports that "all who had attempted higher education were successful and that their socialization was often better than that of their schooled peers."[18]

### Violence

Home schoolers seek to shelter their children from unwholesome influences such as outright violence. In my own research, I discovered a shocking and disconcerting book entitled *Safe at School*. I presumed it would contain information about safely crossing streets, avoiding playground accidents, and keeping box lunches fresh until noon. Apparently, our society is far removed from such trivial concerns. As Saunders reports,

The National School Safety Center (NSSC) has been able to document from surveys and studies that over three million crimes occur in schools each year, and the number is rising. . . . Consider the following:

- More than one million students report that they have avoided some part of their school building out of fear of an attack at least once during the school year.
- Approximately 90,000 guns and 600,000 knives are taken to school every day.
- Over one-third of all students know someone personally who has either been killed or injured from gunfire.

- 11% of teachers and 23% of students have been victims of violence in or near their public schools.[19]

It's not just the inner-city schools—statistics are comparable for suburban schools as well: "A 1989 Justice Department survey showed that 3% of urban students had taken a weapon to school, as had 2% of suburban students. Twenty-four percent of urban students were afraid of attacks at school, as were 20% of suburban schools."[20] How are students to concentrate on achieving the goals of education if they fear for their physical safety?

Watching the news reports of yet another shooting near a school, you can feel the fear within students and parents. In many schools, the problem is weapons being carried to school. In 1990, the Center to Prevent Handgun Violence (CPHV) issued a report which found that, over the previous four years, "71 people had been killed with guns in school, 201 had been wounded, and at least 242 had been held hostage by gun wielding assailants. The incidents occurred in over 35 states. . . . high schools (63%) were not the only schools affected—junior high/middle schools (24%) and elementary schools (12%) were affected as well."[21]

Yet there are those who would condemn home schoolers for sheltering their children. We all need to learn to deal with the problems of society, but is this so-called socialization to take precedence over our children's very lives? Not in our family.

## Overstimulation

The busy-ness of the socialization scene at school is a strain on our children. They become overstimulated and accustomed to constant activity. Author Donna Carroll notes, "When it is time to come home they are listless, dull-eyed, over stimulated, and unable to think of anything to do with themselves.

They mope around the house and crab at each other. It makes me wonder if 'socialization' isn't overrated and that to thrive, children must be given huge chunks of time alone in which to dream and to become."[22]

We are programming, scheduling, and schooling our children right out of creativity and self-directed learning. In attempting to provide our children with "edutainment," we have made sure that learning is easy, fun, and always enjoyable. This does not teach children about real life. Life isn't always fun and entertaining. Sometimes it is just plain hard work. Raymond and Dorothy Moore note this recipe for genius or high achievement: "1) Much time spent with warm, responsive parents and other adults; 2) Very little time spent with peers; and 3) A great deal of free exploration under parental guidance."[23] This is precisely the diet received by most home schooled children. The results indicate that the recipe is a huge success.

## Not Being "Salt and Light"

Is it realistic to expect that a six-year-old, immature in his faith, can bring the power of God's love into his classroom? While we might touch the lives of others on an individual basis, our young children are not ready or able to change the world. Author Mary Hood notes, "Several people have told me they would like to be home schoolers, but they believed that their children could do more good by going to public school and witnessing to the other students. That sounds good on the surface, but young children are much more likely to be swayed themselves than to serve as a 'point of light' for others to follow."[24]

What is our fundamental responsibility as parents in this arena? J. Richard Fugate says, "Children are not soldiers to be thrown into battle unarmed and untrained against an enemy they do not know. They are little ones to be protected from harm."[25] As Jesus told us, "But if anyone causes one of these little ones who believe in me to sin, it would be better for him to have a large millstone hung around his neck and to be drowned in the depths of the sea" (Matt. 18:6).

It is the mature believers—*you and I*—who are called to be salt and light; it is not our children. If we send our children into a setting that corrupts them, we are cheating our children out of their childhood and possibly much worse. As Fugate notes, "To throw young untrained children into the world to be 'lights of the world' before the eyes of their souls have even opened is throwing these children into satan's hands to confuse or even to destroy."[26]

## Public Schools—A Healthy Socialization?

Going to school, particularly in middle childhood and adolescence, is a game of comparisons—who is the prettiest, the most handsome, who has the best clothes, the coolest computer, and so on. A student is daily forced to take an accounting of herself to see if she measures up to the external standard of school culture.

One of the more beautiful benefits of home schooling is the chance to discard this unhealthy comparison system. Research has shown that this can be particularly helpful for home schooled girls. Author Susannah Sheffer, an extensive researcher of home schooled adolescent girls found, "They made the connection between their trust as home schoolers in internal sources of knowledge and the way that they could extend this same trust as girls to issues such as preoccupations with weight and appearance. This is an important connection to make, and home schooled girls who can make it are also better off in areas that have nothing to do with home schooling."[27] She concludes the discussion: "The more power each individual girl feels, and the greater her sense that she does not have to give up any significant part of herself in order to exist in the world of others, the less likely she is to need to organize her social life by cliques and cruelty."[28]

I would have deep regrets if my children suffered damage to their self-concept because of a school exposure I willingly allowed for them. I want them to be strong, independent thinkers who love God and love their lives. I believe the best way to achieve this goal is to teach them at home.

J. Richard Fugate reminds us, "Parents should ask themselves if they ever learned a healthy self-concept by being exposed to childhood peers. Usually only the extroverts, bullies, clowns and popular thrive in this atmosphere. Many sensitive children are damaged for life."[29]

All children can thrive and flourish in a home environment that is loving and supportive and accommodates their individual needs.

### Little Boys and Maturity

Raymond and Dorothy Moore have a passion for young children. They believe that we force them to perform tasks they are not yet ready to perform at too early an age. Their concern is especially intense for little boys. The earlier that children go to school, they note, the greater the likelihood for dropouts and delinquency: More little boys were admitted early to school than little girls, and twice as many boys as girls were suspended during elementary school and four and a half times as many boys were suspended during high school.[30]

The Moores believe that the optimum time for normal children to start school in a formal setting is between the ages of eight and ten: "We call this chronological age period the Integrated Maturity Level or IML—the optimum time for most normal children to start school entering at the level of their agemates at grade three, four, or five. . . . Although little girls usually enjoy an advantage, even they do not bring all their learning tools together before age eight. And when little boys are allowed to start at nine or ten in grades three or four or five, they have no trouble keeping up with girls of the same age."[31]

Some families view a home schooling commitment as one lasting from birth to college. Others choose to home educate through grammar school and still others just through third grade, a popular age for school reentry. Whatever time, great or small, you can give your child at home will be a blessing and a benefit to them.

### Little Girls and School Bias

Much recent attention has been given to the short shrift little girls receive in school. "Girls are the majority of our nation's schoolchildren," note authors Myra and David Sadker, "yet they are second-class educational citizens. The problems they face—loss of self-esteem, decline in achievement, and elimination of career options—are at the heart of the educational process. Until educational sexism is eradicated, more than half of our children will be shortchanged and their gifts lost to society."[32]

Much of this theorizing is attributed to a 1990 study by the American Association of University Women, which sought to learn how boys and girls from ages nine to fifteen viewed themselves. The greatest gap was in self-esteem, particularly between the elementary and middle school years. The perceived self-esteem of girls plummeted during this time. "While 60 percent of girls said they were happy about themselves in elementary school, 37 percent answered affirmatively in middle school, and only 29 percent in high school."[33] The correlation between a growing dislike of self, loss of confidence, and the length of time in school is unmistakable. The longer girls are in school, it seems, the greater their loss of potential.

The Sadkers conclude that institutionalized sexism is "like a thief in school . . . twisting it into a system of socialization that robs potential." They ask us to consider this record of losses to girls:

- In the early grades, girls are ahead of or equal to boys on almost every standardized measure of achievement and psychological well-being. By the time they graduate from high school or college, they have fallen back. Girls enter school ahead but leave behind.
- In high school, girls score lower on the SAT and ACT tests, which are critical for college admission. The greatest gender gap is in the crucial areas of science and math.
- Girls score far lower on College Board Achievement tests, which are required by most of the highly selective colleges.
- Boys are much more likely to be awarded state and national college scholarships.
- The gap (between boys and girls) does not narrow in college. Women score lower on all sections of the Graduate Record Exam, which is necessary to enter many graduate programs.
- Women also trail on most tests needed to enter professional schools: the GMAT for business school, the LSAT for law school, and the MCAT for medical school.
- From elementary school through higher education, female students receive less active instruction, both in the quantity and the quality of teacher time and attention.[34]

Even the federal government is concerned about this trend. The United States Department of Health and Human Services, under the leadership of Donna Shalala, has launched a program called "Girl Power!" to encourage and empower nine- to fourteen-year-old girls to make the most of their lives. Ms. Shalala comments: "What we know is this: Between ages 9 and 14, too many girls, once full of resilience, somehow lose their very selves and enter the second decade of their lives without the strength that got them there. . . . We want to tell every girl, 'You are unique, you are valuable, and if you put your mind to it, you can succeed.' We want to tell every parent and every other adult, 'By listening to your girls, encouraging them, by setting high standards, and by providing opportunity, you can help your child not only survive—but thrive—through this difficult period of adolescence.'"[35]

Doesn't this sound like the dream of all home schooling parents for their daughters? Home schooling, without requiring yet another federally funded self-esteem program, can help young girls to grow up strong, confident, and grounded in faith. When all is said and done, I don't want my daughters to be denied personal dreams predicated upon some disparate treatment received in school. They deserve the chance to use their God-given talents to the fullest extent.

Women have made much progress in achieving equality in the eyes of the world. When I was in my first year of law school in the early 1980s, a professor informed a fellow female student that she would be better suited to raising babies than lawyering. These days, he would have been served legal notice in due course. Whether my colleague might have chosen mothering, lawyering, or both, she deserved fair access to academic and career opportunities. Thankfully, the attitudes my own daughters will confront have improved to some degree.

Adolescence is tumultuous. Yet I believe that girls can grow through this time and keep their self-respect, love their families, and serve their God. Perhaps they are freer to develop into godly women without the school peer pressures. One young girl said of her public school friends, "They cannot understand the freedom."[36] It is parents who hold the key to that freedom.

## What's the Solution?

One solution to the academic crisis that is being chosen by more and more families is the biblically sound, academically effective option of home schooling. It works.

What's the solution to the socialization problem? The question assumes there *is* a problem with the socialization of home schooled children. Perhaps you have been convinced that such concerns are overstated. Still, children require social training and home schoolers believe the home to be the best arena in which to receive that training.

Home is the best place in which to learn social skills, academic skills, and spiritual maturity. Yet there is still the stereotype of the home schooled child as a social nerd. The misconception is that he cannot function in a normal social setting and thus possesses a low self-esteem. Research would seem to indicate a result to the contrary.

Several studies have been done to measure self-concept in home educated children. Self-esteem is correlated with the ability to interact on a social level. In one study, the home schooled kids did great: "The study found [using the Piers-Harris Children's Self-Concept Scale] that one half of the children score above the 90th percentile and only 10.3% scored below the national average," notes attorney and researcher Christopher Klicka.[37]

Another 1992 study is similarly encouraging. Using the Vineland Adaptive Behavior Scale, researcher Thomas Smedley sought to evaluate the maturity of home schooled children as compared to demographically matched public school children. Among skills measured were communication, socialization, and daily living skills. Home schooled kids did amazingly well, scoring in the 84th percentile while the matched sample of public school children scored only in the 27th percentile. The researcher noted, "In the public school system, children are socialized horizontally, and temporarily, into conformity with their immediate peers. Home educators seek to socialize their children vertically, toward responsibility, service, and adulthood, with an eye on eternity."[38]

Another 1992 study by Dr. Larry Shyers compared behaviors and social development test scores of two groups of children and discovered that the home schooled children had consistently fewer behavioral problems. He noted, "The results seem to show that a child's social development depends more on adult contact and less on contact with other children as previously thought."[39]

Not only does home schooling provide that essential adult contact, but it also serves to protect our children from the negative socialization of the schools, such as the peer pressure toward the use of drugs, sexuality, and rebelliousness.

Parents who send children to private schools feel that in some way they are protecting their children from many of the ills of the public school setting. In one sense, perhaps they are, but they might be fostering the same peer dependence that many home schoolers see as unhealthy. Christopher Klicka notes, "Another researcher compared private school nine-year olds with home-school nine-year olds and found no significant differences in the groups in virtually all psychosocial areas. However, in the area of social adjustment, a significant difference was discovered: 'private school subjects appeared to be *more* concerned with peers that the home-educated group.' This is certainly an advantage for home schooled children who can avoid negative peer influence."[40] Paying the cost of private school tuition may only buy greater peer dependence for your child.

There is an alternative. At the dawn of a new century of choices and challenges, parents can choose the exciting challenge of teaching their own children at home and showing them a better vision for the future.

Gregg Harris notes, "The biblical solution to providing social training for children is practicing hospitality."[41] Friend and fellow author Jackie Wellwood has "M.U.G." nights in her home. These "Monthly Uplifting Get-togethers" are a chance for women to come to her home and either hear her teach about a topic related to homemaking or simply to share tea and relax. Her two oldest daughters, ages nine and eleven, greet visitors, serve refreshments, and make sure everyone is taken care of. Her daughters made the entire presentation on the topic of home schooling. They are learning many socialization skills with this enterprise. Do you think these kids really need to go to school to study manners in social studies class?

Another suggestion from Gregg Harris is to foster international friendships, perhaps by entertaining foreign students and missionaries. If you are fortunate enough to have a nearby college, contact the dean of students to inquire about such a possibility. If your church is missions-oriented, consider getting actively involved in that ministry. With an extra room in your home, you can serve as host to international missionaries.

One cannot deny that children love to be with other children. We cannot isolate them, but we must be wise about their social contacts. Gregg Harris explains: "It is never wise to leave a group of children to pool their inexperience alone for long periods of time. Better to allow children to become friends of your entire family."[42]

Other socialization activities might include church groups, support group activities, and field trips. Our local area has science clubs, 4-H, scout groups, and much, much more. The possibilities are only limited by the imagination of home schooling parents.

# 10

# *Positively Promoting Home Schooling*

*I*f you want to know if someone is a genuine Christian, don't merely ask them; look at how they live their lives. Their actions will speak louder than church attendance or doctrinal correctness.

What others see within your family will do more to help (or harm) the cause of home education than anything you can verbalize. Be conscientious, considerate, and caring and you will win converts to your choice of home education.

"Many educators see an inherent, if unintended, arrogance among home-schoolers," notes writer Lynn Schnaiberg. "We, the untrained, can do as good or better a job teaching our children than you can. But, in fact, many home-schoolers view traditional, state-run, compulsory schools as the blip in education history—a brief interruption in what for centuries was the norm. From their vantage point, it is the children in the public schools who are part of some experiment. And it's not a very promising one at that."[1]

I have been guilty, on occasion, of that arrogance. Unintentional, perhaps, but a note of self-satisfaction sometimes creeps into my voice when I say, "We home school." When I am able to catch myself, I usually say, "We home school because it is the right thing for us to do." That softens the message a bit.

The *Congressional Quarterly Researcher* reports, "Among the general public, only 28 percent favor home schooling over traditional schools, according to a June NBC News–*Wall Street Journal* poll. A September 1993 poll asked whether home-schooled children learn as well as children educated at public schools and found 44 percent agreed and 44 percent disagreed, according to the conservative Family Research Council."[2]

It is clear that the educational establishment and public at large are misinformed about home schooling. They have not studied the benefits or seen the results. Like any other unknown phenomenon, most people are ready to dismiss it as too bizarre or too conservative or too radical. Some people will think you are some kind of supermom. Others will think you are just weird. Most people will secretly believe your children will turn out to be oddballs.

Don't argue when someone expresses disapproval about your choice to home school. A tone of moral superiority will turn people off. In the great spirit of American education, both home schoolers and traditional schoolers simply need to remain open-minded.

Beware of making statements that you may regret later, such as, "I could never send my kids to public school!" What if you or your husband died? What if some other unforeseen circumstance removed your ability to choose home education for your child? Some families cannot home school. One need not risk such alienation by making sweeping proclamations.

A similar statement to avoid is, "I don't like my kids playing with those kids." Those other kids are likely to be children of the adults you are addressing. You're not only insulting them but their children as well. If you practice selective socialization with your children, just practice it—don't talk about it.

Do not attempt to try to convince anyone that they should home school. Leave that job up to the Holy Spirit. For me, the mere idea of home schooling was so overwhelming that ultimately it was the Holy Spirit that brought decision. I read extensively and talked to many people, but no one tried to force their beliefs down my throat.

Luanne Shackelford and Susan White write in their *Survivor's Guide to Home Schooling*, "We are usually not persecuted for our faith so much as for the failure to live out our faith. Let your decision to home teach motivate you to become more like the Lord Jesus. Are there attitudes and habits that others see, or even that they don't see, which are inconsistent with the character of Christ? Be willing to confess these as sin and ask the Lord to help you as you purpose to change."[3]

"To put home schooling in a better light [Dr. Brian] Ray recommends that proponents try to highlight the advantages to public educators by asking, 'How would you like to have just five pupils in your class, or just one, and be flexible so that when a red double-crested booby suddenly alights on the window sill, you can stop the lesson and show the children how to look it up in the bird field guide?' Home-schoolers need to better explain this, not necessarily to criticize the public schools, but to show what can be done."[4]

The approach I prefer is to express my enthusiasm for home schooling. I like to talk about the fun projects we are able to do and the freedom we experience. I try to express the deep satisfaction and awe that I feel at being able to watch my children grow and learn on a daily basis.

While you should not try to convince others to home school, do try to educate them. Recounting personal experiences in a nonthreatening way is a good start. If the person you are speaking with appears interested, gently talk about the biblical basis for home schooling and the impressive results obtained by home schooling families.

The whole world does not need to understand and respect what you do in your family. Even those closest to you, such as your extended family, may not approve of your choices. Many parents find that grandpa and grandma question the wisdom of their decision. Although they can be your greatest source of support, perhaps they do not understand home schooling. You can enlighten them by lending them this book or any of the other fine books available about home schooling. In dealing with disapproving relatives, sometimes all you can do is love and pray for them and then go back to work.

## Dealing with the Media

If you have the opportunity to represent home schooling to the media, attorney and author Christopher Klicka suggests focusing on three main points: (1) Home schoolers are a minority. The media seems to love stories of the little guy fighting the big bureaucracies. (2) Second, emphasize that home schooling works. Have some statistics readily available, such as the fact that home schoolers consistently score in the 80th percentile on standardized achievement tests. (3) Finally, highlight that home schooling is a right guaranteed by the First and Fourteenth Amendments, not merely a crazy experiment or a fad. Mention some of the great names in history who were home educated, such as Albert Einstein and John Quincy Adams. All of these points provide a greater sense of legitimacy for your activity. Klicka concludes: "The Home School Legal Defense Association (HSLDA) has found that home schoolers who are more public through the media and who are members of the HSLDA will be more likely to be left alone by the school district. The school district figures that it is much easier to try to pick on a lonely home school family without media contacts or legal counsel because they can quietly close them down without public embarrassment."[5]

Your position as a home schooler exists well within biblical principles, has academic validity, and makes sense socially.

## Home Schooling and the Community

There are many ways in which to take a proactive approach to promoting home schooling in the community. These not only serve to portray home schooling in a positive light but can also be an encouragement for families who have not yet made a commitment to home education.

Each year, a local group in my area sponsors a "Home Schooling Information Day" at the local library. They promote the event through flyers and press releases. On the day itself, a speaker gives a short presentation, the resources of the library are highlighted, and several home schooling families are available for questions. This is always very well attended. It promotes the cause of home education and, without fail, increases the membership of this particular group.

Finally, if your home school group has a project fair, science fair, or geography fair, invite the media and public. Some well-placed notices or press releases could win some supporters to home schooling. In addition, most children love to have their work displayed and noticed. This collaborative approach is good for your child, your group, and your community. It can be a shining moment for all.

# 11

# *The Home School Support Group*

*I*n the earliest days of home schooling, families functioned on their own. There were no national support organizations or monthly magazines for encouragement. It was the networking of these early pioneers that caused the home schooling movement to grow. Networking helps families to keep going, day after day. Support groups help families stay informed, stay enthused, and stay connected with others. Groups exist on the local, state, national, and international levels.

Networking brings strength to the home schooling community. A case in point is the story of House Resolution 6 (H.R. 6). In 1994, an amendment to a pending bill posed a possible threat to home schoolers. H.R. 6 was the $12.7 billion Elementary and Secondary Education Act (ESEA). Contained within it was an amendment mandating that all school districts seeking federal funding require all teachers to be certified by 1998. One possible interpretation of this bill was to require teacher certification for all parents who teach their children at home.

Shortly after learning about this bill, Representative Dick Armey (R-Tex.) offered an amendment to exempt home schoolers from this requirement. Within days, the Home School Legal Defense Association (HSLDA) mobilized its forces. A record eight hundred thousand calls flooded Congress. Michael Farris of the HSLDA made numerous national radio appearances. The end result was that the Armey Amendment to protect the rights of home educators passed by a vote of 374 to 53.

Commentator Grover G. Norquist said of this series of events: "In secular Washington, their [home schoolers'] affiliation with born-again Christianity has led allies and adversaries alike to underestimate the home-schoolers' political sophistication. But the most powerful union in the country (the NEA) recently tried to pull a fast one on them and got burned."[1]

This showing of legislative and legal muscle indicates that home schoolers have considerable political clout and can lobby for favorable legislation. The success of the Home School Legal Defense Association and other similar special interest groups shows that home schoolers can influence those in power and win court battles favorable to home educators.

Rapid growth in the total numbers of home schoolers has also lead to divisions. Secular groups prefer not to associate with Christian groups and vice versa. Moreover, many disagreements exist over methods and philosophies. Your decision-making process about home schooling should include a thorough and exhaustive search for resources in your area. You should find a number of support or networking groups, of which you should join at least one Christian group. There are also many other wonderful opportunities offered by groups of unschoolers or those who are not overtly religious. You can share enthusiasm for home schooling with these families, even if you don't share the same creed.

This is a broad picture of support groups across the nation. But how does this speak to you as someone considering home education or is new to the practice? The beginning of home schooling can be completely overwhelming. Decisions must be made. Curriculum must be designed or chosen. Intentional social interaction must be arranged. The choices are numerous and can be mind-boggling.

The Johnson family was amazed at the available home schooling resources: "The Johnsons soon found home-schoolers in their community who were trading skill, expertise, and resources and bringing their children together in small groups for both academic and social purposes. 'There were all kinds of opportunities we hadn't even known were out there,' says Karen. 'Once we got away from the schools, we hooked into this other world.'"[2] There is a whole other world outside of the traditional school. You and your children can participate in it on a significant level.

While our children were still at the preschool stage, I joined our local Christian support group. For a modest fee (twelve dollars a year at the time), I received a no-risk education in home schooling. I met and chatted with the real experts—other home schooling moms. I attended presentations and lectures intended to both educate and encourage. Prior to this, I had no idea of the services and resources specifically developed for home schoolers, many of which may be available in your own community. I had access to a library that was well stocked with reading material, videos, audiotapes, and supplementary curriculum materials. I attended curriculum fairs and spoke with parents who were actually using various programs. I got to view the materials and meet home educated children.

If your children are preschool age and you are even remotely considering home schooling, you have nothing to lose by joining a support group. If you have already jumped into the water of home education, a support group can be a lifeline for you *and* your children.

Contained in appendix B is a list of statewide home school organizations. These contacts will refer you to local groups within your area. In many areas, there are groups to suit every style of home educator, from the Christian to the unschooler.

## Support Group Services

Some services provided by support groups are:

*Emotional support.* You don't have to feel like the Lone
Ranger home schooling family. Support groups provide
a forum to share similar situations, trade war stories,
and gain from the knowledge and experience of more
experienced home schoolers. Many times we need
encouragement to see the work through to completion.
Friends within a support group can encourage stead-
fastness, as exemplified in 1 Thessalonians 5:11: "Therefore encourage one another and build each other up."

*A monthly newsletter.* These focus on distributing timely
information to members, such as upcoming meetings
or field trips. It can also alert members to potential legislative actions (of both positive and negative impact for
home schoolers), highlight news from the state level,
and provide a forum for members and their children to
contribute articles or artwork. A good monthly newsletter provides news, ideas, and encouragement.

*Monthly meetings.* Some groups have featured speakers and
agenda, while others have simple announcements and
play time for the children. This provides a great opportunity to meet and connect with parents who share similar educational views and who have children around
the same age as your own.

*Major yearly conferences and/or curriculum fairs.* Smaller
groups might feature local talent while larger groups
will attract national speakers on the topic of home
schooling. Some also feature used book and curriculum
exchanges. These are a great way to keep encouraged,
focused, and enthused.

*Field trips and activities.* By pooling resources, a support group
qualifies for special trip or subscription rates. Organized

co-op activities, science labs, art lessons, or team sports
can be facilitated by a support group. They can participate in programs like "Book-It" through Pizza Hut, which
offers pizza incentives to children for meeting reading
goals. Holiday parties and performances are a special treat
your children can enjoy with other home schooled friends.

In many ways, children in your support group are the equivalent of classmates. These are the children who will share
socialization experiences with yours and who will share the
mysteries and secrets of childhood.

Many talents and gifts are represented in support groups.
Different parents may bring a wealth of knowledge or expertise in areas such as physical education, organized sports, or
camping. Spelling bees, science fairs, and geography fairs can
also be organized through a support group. Many national
versions of these events actively encourage the participation
of home schooled children. Choirs, bands, bowling leagues,
and activity clubs are only some of the many other ideas that
have been initiated by support groups.

"What types of social activities do home schooled children
engage in?" asks author Cheryl Gorder. "Church-related activities, community groups, Girl Scouts, Boy Scouts, and 4-H
are high on their list. Unlike schools, community groups do
not deny their activities to children just because they are home
schooled. The types of activities chosen have a high correlation to the types of values that parents wish their children to
develop, and also provide the types of activities children need
in order to develop their own unique talents and interests,
such as music and drama groups. Home schooled children
tend to join groups for the involvement in special projects,
not just because 'all of my friends are doing it.'"[3] In my own
support group, I have participated in or organized a girl's math
and science club and a home school Girl Scout troop.

Another vitally important function for support groups is
to provide fellowship for parents and their families. Some

groups have smaller groups that allow communication on a more in-depth level. A "buddy system" for new home school families has met with great success. Within this arrangement, a new home schooler is matched with a veteran through the support group. Those more experienced can then share, on an intimate level, both the joys and frustrations of beginnings. Here are some other possibilities for support groups:

- Standardized testing is offered at a discount rate through some support groups.
- Graduation ceremonies, "school" pictures, yearbooks, and play performances are all projects available through some support groups.
- At the beginning of each school year, most home school support groups provide a new member packet with information about home education in the state, brochures from publications such as *The Teaching Home,* and information about local groups and the Home School Legal Defense Association. Many include a suggested reading list and copies of relevant local laws.
- Some groups have extensive lending libraries with general home schooling books, children's books, and curriculum. Videos or audiotapes that are otherwise unaffordable for the average family may be available.
- Support groups provide a liaison with state and national home school organizations. They provide information on the activities of these groups.
- A good group will keep members informed of legislation and lobbying information and opportunities.

As important as external support may be, authors Terry Dorian and Zan Peters Tyler remind us that another kind of support is most important: "External support is important, but it may not always be there. . . . When the trials come, I can persevere because I know it is God who has called me."[4]

# 12

# *Home Schooling Parents*

On a good day of home schooling in our house, breakfast happens without a major mishap. The two older kids help, then they go off to wash up and get dressed. They also pick up their room and gather their things for school.

While they are doing that, I dress Grace, our two-year-old, and start out engaging her in some activity. Puzzles, books, pictures, safety scissors, blocks, cubes, and many other items fill her "school" box. We also have a list of seasonal art projects we might do, as well as materials for nursery rhymes and learning colors and numbers. When the two older girls are dressed, they will join us in "Grace's Nursery School," as we call it.

Soon enough, Grace will tire of all this and wander off. Then Clare and Caitlin and I go to the table to begin our work. They both still need a lot of individual attention, so I take turns working with each of them individually. Before we know it, it is about 11:30 A.M. and we break for lunch. The older girls help me get it ready and then we eat.

After lunch, I rock Grace and she goes down for a nap. This is usually the first time I have sat still since 5:00 A.M. or so. While Grace is asleep, Clare and Caitlin finish up their work from the morning, read library books, and work on any special projects we might have. For example, each year we hatch chicken eggs and do a unit study on embryology. We've also studied a variety of other subjects such as Native Americans, rocks, bugs, and weather.

176

Later in the afternoon, I might let them watch a little public television, and they help me with dinner. In the evenings, we read, watch a little TV, or work on projects. We all go to bed thanking God for a good day together.

On a bad day, the baby whines from the time she awakens. The two older kids don't feel like doing school and have found the remote control and are watching TV when I emerge from the shower. They sulk and complain, but I turn off the TV and we fight our way through breakfast, eventually arriving at the table for school time.

Meanwhile, the baby is still crying.

My older daughter says she is too tired to do school, and my middle, strong-willed child will inform me that she WILL NOT do school today. We struggle through each assignment, and by 10:30, we are all exhausted. These days usually happen in February.

We painfully get through the rest of the morning and lunch. I rock the baby and put her down for her nap and go back to finish up with the girls. I hear some noises from the baby's room. I go in there to check on her and find that she has taken off all her clothes and her diaper, has gone to the bathroom all over her bed, has strewn clothes and toys around the room . . . and she's still whining.

The afternoon is a blur. My husband arrives home and I greet him by saying, "What could be so bad about sending them to school?"

In our home school, we have both good days and bad days. If I were not psychologically and mentally prepared for the bad days, I doubt I could survive. Knowing that they come, and knowing that they pass, makes the job easier.

## What Does It Take?

Many people think it takes some kind of superhuman effort or perfect parenting to home school. Luanne Shackelford and

Susan White, authors of *A Survivor's Guide to Home Schooling*, remind us that "You don't have to be perfect to home school . . . you just must be willing to improve."[1] Most home schoolers begin the process with some trepidation. They feel inadequate for the task, either emotionally or academically.

The desire to home school does not arrive as a fleeting idea. Most parents feel a deep-seated conviction that home education is the right choice for their family. That conviction, along with a healthy reliance on the power of the Holy Spirit, can lend confidence to do the job.

As for academics, the resources available to home schoolers are incredible. The materials range from preschool to higher level math. Teacher's manuals are well written and complete. When subjects of great difficulty are encountered, the home teacher can tap into networks where other parents share their expertise and teaching skills in areas such as math workshops or chemistry labs. There are also many fine video instruction programs available where an expert teacher on tape can instruct the student in more difficult areas.

Are you organizationally challenged? Home schooling not only requires a steady commitment, but it also requires good organizational skills. In addition to the already demanding jobs of homemaker and wife, the home schooling mom must take on the equivalent of another full-time job. The home school—indeed, the home itself—simply cannot run without some heavy-duty organization.

If you are seriously disorganized, I recommend that you research home organization and give yourself time to get your house in order before beginning a home school year. (Check out the organization books written by Deniece Schofield, *Confessions of a Happily Organized Family* and *Confessions of an Organized Housewife,* and Don Aslett, *Clutter's Last Stand.* You will be inspired to de-junk!) In addition, you will need time to review curriculum and plan lessons. If at all possible, dedicate the summer before the beginning of the school year to household organization and planning for school.

Some parents feel that another adult will be better able to teach their child to obey. They believe that the school atmosphere, with its schedules and enforced behaviors, will be a more appropriate place for their child. It is true that sometimes children will give more credence to an adult who is not their parent. But in most cases, the parents can take steps to reestablish their authority in the home so that home schooling can proceed.

What if you can't stand being with your children for long periods of time? I believe everyone goes through phases where this is true. Yet something amazing happens when we keep our children at home and away from negative influences that would distance them from us: In the love and acceptance of a home environment, children can become more likeable and more enjoyable to be with. When they know that they are genuinely loved and accepted, they become better behaved and easier to be with. When the fragmented family is able to refocus on home life, child teaching, and character development, they can actually begin to enjoy being a family again.

In choosing to home school, by default, I am choosing *not* to do other things I want to do. Those things can wait. Time with my children will not wait. While I am busy chasing other dreams, they are busy growing up. J. Richard Fugate reminds us, "Therefore, one obstacle to overcome in home schooling is ourselves. If we are undisciplined, we will not be very successful in teaching our children. However, any parent can be more successful in home schooling by setting up a few simple external controls over themselves and their children. Joining a good support group could help. . . . Most importantly, you should work on the root of the problem—your own character."[2]

I have struggled mightily with these issues. I was extremely organized in my profession but always believed that home should be a place where one could relax and let it all hang out.

When children came along, I thought the most important thing was that they were happy.

It has been a battle to discipline myself to organize my mind and my home. A major stumbling block for me was to embrace the commandments to teach and train our children. Loving them is not enough. We are called to do much more. The hard work of properly raising children takes self-disciplined parents who have prayed earnestly for God's guidance, researched home schooling, understand the organizational skills required to teach children and run a household, and who have resolved some of their own character issues.

## Mommy Burnout

Many home schoolers suffer from burnout. More often, the parents burn out before the children. They try to do too much and don't care enough for their own needs. Mothers in particular carry the heaviest burden with home schooling. Added to the responsibilities of child rearing, housekeeping, and church and community involvement is the responsibility for your child's entire education! It is not an easy load. Yet it provides a sense of satisfaction and balance in life that cannot be matched by any other endeavor.

Michael Farris, president of Home School Legal Defense Association, paid tribute to his wife in an article called "Who Thanks the Real Heroes?" He said, "Thanks for being willing to sacrifice the minutes, hours, days, months, and years of your lives so that your children will have the opportunity to grow up godly, mature, wise, intelligent, and loving. . . . Your true reward—at least the one you will see here on earth—will be children who rise up (while the rest of the world is stooping in compromise) and call you blessed with their lives, their words, and their deeds. It is your legacy of love."[3]

On a discouraging day or at the end of a dreadful week, it can be of enormous help to remember why you are doing what you are doing. You are acting with a servant's heart to leave your children a legacy of faith and love.

Remember, you are balancing many roles. You cannot have a stellar performance in all of them—wife, mother, teacher, friend, sibling, Sunday school teacher, homemaker, cook, and cleaner. Have realistic expectations for yourself. Perhaps you will earn a great grade in teaching this week and a really lousy grade in cooking. Which is of more importance to you? Your family will live through a dinner of canned soup and grilled cheese sandwiches. Establish your priorities firmly in your heart.

Do you have to do things the way you are doing things? Could you step back and take a fresh look at your methods? Never forget to look at home schooling through God's eyes: He is more concerned with the hearts of our children than with their transcripts. The true teaching we are doing is the spiritual and character training.

Don't compare yourself to other moms, even home schooling ones. All have different ways. And don't compare your household to the one in this month's *Better Homes and Gardens*. In fact, I have stopped buying some of my old favorite magazines because I felt some subtle guilt that I wasn't doing all the cool crafts and decorating things they suggested. Instead, I now read magazines that support my chosen lifestyle and mission, such as *The Teaching Home*.

It is extremely important to attend to Mom's needs first. A martyr is not a good role model. You need to rest, keep a decent diet, do some exercise, and get some quiet time for yourself. Hire a mother's helper and have an arrangement with your husband for you to get away. Mary Hood reminds us, "Making the decision to take control over your children's education does not necessarily require that you become a total martyr to your family. If you fail to pay attention to your own needs, you will probably wind up burning out."[4] Make some time for yourself.

Laugh with your children and find all you can to enjoy about each day. Share your passion with your children, be it crafts, art, or writing. They will be excited about it because you are excited. My friend Jackie Wellwood sews at night with her daughters. They have acquired extra sewing machines at garage sales, and her two older girls each have their own machines. Don't give up your hobbies just because you home school.

Learn to let go. There are things that can be done by others (like chores and shopping), and there are things that don't need to be done by anyone (like dusting). Jackie Wellwood suggests giving yourself a time deadline, such as no chores after 7:00 P.M. If you don't, the chores will consume all the time you have. There will always be laundry to do and rooms to clean, especially with little ones in the home all day long.

Communicate with your husband about burnout. Fellow home schooling mom Jackie Wellwood says: "While I have learned where to go to keep my enthusiasm high (after seven years of home schooling), I have not learned how to avoid burnout. I do get burned out and find myself responding to a situation rather than preventing it. I believe a less demanding school schedule or structure would be helpful, but I have no clue how to do that with six children. I'm not sure that we can actually prevent burnout. I think it may be more important to learn what the warning signals are and have a system in place for your family to implement when the telltale signs appear. Short temper, impatience with everyone, loss of enthusiasm for anything but sleep, overeating, preoccupation with talking about what it will be like to be a grandmother, and inability to remember anything are all examples of some of my warning signs. They will be unique for each person. Wise is the husband who knows these signs and does whatever it takes to keep the wife going. Home schooling is *not* easy!"

Make time with God. Meditate on his Word. Be thankful that God has called you to this difficult, rewarding job. He will equip you to do it. Find a quiet time to reconnect with him. If you are having trouble finding the time, ask him to help you find the time to spend with him. He will show you if you will listen. Keep up with your Bible study. You will be refreshing your spirit as well as setting a lifelong example for your children.

When things are getting dull for everyone, think of some changes you can try with your children. If you use a regular curriculum, try a unit study that you all do together. If you do unit studies all the time, it won't kill your kids to do some straight academic reading while you regroup.

Have a game day. Schedule one day, or afternoon, when you just play games. There's a lot children can learn from Monopoly, or you can play strictly educational games. Some great educational games are available from Aristoplay or Bealls' Learning Games. Peggy Kaye has written a series of books detailing games you can make to teach your child. The titles are *Games for Reading, Games for Math,* and *Games for Learning.* We have used these, particularly when we hit a problem area. We try to find a game to teach a difficult concept. Usually we have so much fun playing the game that we scarcely notice that the concept is being mastered as well.

Study something that your children have chosen. Have them choose the books, projects, and writings for a unit that they direct. Mine have chosen the study of fish, weather, ants, princesses, butterflies, the hatching of chicks, and more.

The Lord gives us each the same twenty-four hours. How we spend them is our choice. If we have chosen home schooling, everything else must fall in line with that priority. If God has put home schooling on your heart, keep it up even if you don't feel like it. Deuteronomy 33:25 promises, "Your strength will equal your days."

## The Home Schooling Dad

How do fathers make their special contribution to home schooling? This note from my husband hangs on my refrigerator:

> I'm both proud and appreciative of your work with the girls at school. It's hard sometimes, but God will bless it for us.
>
> Love, Mark

A faithful husband is a special blessing. A cheerful and willing father who assumes the role of spiritual leader is an essential to the home schooling family.

The Bible is not a book of practical suggestions. It is not a guide to 365 easy ways to live the Christian life. Rather, it is full of wisdom and commandments. Commandments are not just suggestions or nice ideas. They must be obeyed. Here are some of God's commandments for fathers:

> Ephesians 6:4 commands fathers to: "Bring [children] up in the training and instruction of the Lord." For some fathers, this obligation is fulfilled by bringing their children to Sunday school. For the home schooling family, however, the admonition is much broader and fuller.
>
> Deuteronomy 6:5–9 instructs: "Love the LORD your God with all your heart and with all your soul and with all your strength. These commandments that I give you today are to be upon your hearts. Impress them on your children. Talk about them when you sit at home and when you walk along the road, when you lie down and when you get up. Tie them as symbols on your hands and bind them on your foreheads. Write them on the doorframes of your houses and on your gates." As a Christian home schooling family, we believe that we are called to bring God's Word and his love into every aspect

of our lives. For us, the best way to fulfill this commandment is to educate our children at home.

## Faithful Fathers in the Bible

The faithful fathers in the Bible are perfect examples for the home schooling father. The Bible gives a study in contrasts between faithful fathers and those who failed. The chief priest Eli was charged with the upbringing of Hannah's son, Samuel. Samuel became a man of God who spoke God's words. However, Eli's own sons, Hophni and Phinehas, were a grave disappointment to him.

Eli realized too late that he had failed his own sons. Their inherent lack of character was caused by his own indulgence and lack of discipline in their early lives. Too late he said to them, "'Why do you do such things?' . . . His sons, however, did not listen to their father's rebuke, for it was the LORD's will to put them to death" (1 Sam. 2:23, 25).

Samuel's sons followed a similar path. Because he was so busy attending to his duties as judge and prophet, he neglected his duty to train his own sons, Joel and Abijah. Blind to their weaknesses, Samuel made his sons judges over Israel. "But his sons did not walk in his ways. They turned aside after dishonest gain and accepted bribes and perverted justice" (1 Sam. 8:3).

King David had a tragic relationship with his rebellious son Absalom. David had four sons. One son, Amnon, raped his half-sister Tamar. King David did nothing to punish or discipline Amnon for this transgression. This infuriated Absalom, who took justice into his own hands and ordered the murder of his brother Amnon.

When King David learned of this, he was also unwilling to punish Absalom. Even after Absalom's plot of treachery, King David still worried for the life of his son on the battlefield. He said, "Be gentle with the young man Absalom for my sake" (2 Sam. 18:5).

A father's failings harm his children, sometimes for generations. Success in the business world does not guarantee success in parenting. Moody Bible Institute president Joseph Stowell once said, "It is not what I do or who I am that is as important to my children as how much time I spend with them."[5] It takes the prayers and perseverance of a faithful father to raise faithful children who know and love the Lord. That is true success.

One such faithful father in the Bible was Abraham. Abraham knew he had to teach his descendants to follow God. It was essential that he do what was right in order for the nation to prosper. He knew, from God, that the real strength of a family was the strength of its spiritual values. He also knew that it was a father's duty to pass these values on from generation to generation.

Throughout the Bible, fathers are the teachers of succeeding generations and the purveyors of spiritual values. This is precisely the role of the contemporary home schooling father.

## Duties of the Faithful Father

What are the many mandated duties of a faithful father? The Bible provides specific instruction.

### A FATHER INSTRUCTS.

Proverbs 1:8 says, "Listen my son, to your father's instruction and do not forsake your mother's teaching." Home schooling fathers instruct in many ways. In our home, my husband studies Bible verses and character traits with our children. We work on one trait at a time, learning and copying a definition and studying illustrations of that trait in the Bible and other literature. My husband also finishes work remaining from the school day. As time permits, we may have a special project to work on in the evenings. Each family member partakes in reading a chapter from a book, truly a special time.

Some home schooling fathers assume specific areas of the curriculum. One dad may be the designated math teacher for his family; another may take all science lessons and experiments. If these areas are his passion, this is a tremendous manner in which he may personally experience the true fulfillment of home school family life.

Charlotte Mason's original publications contained an article entitled "A Father's Place in Home Training," which viewed the father's role this way: "It is not necessary for the father to do much of the training himself, during the greater part of the day, he may be away from home, but he should know all that is being done, he should be thoroughly posted, so that the children see and feel that their parents are completely one."[6]

### A FATHER GUIDES.

Jeremiah 3:4 asks, "Have you not just called to me: 'My Father, my friend from my youth.'" From birth to youth to adulthood, a home schooling father guides. He realizes that the time spent working on a relationship with his children yields invaluable eternal dividends. If that relationship is cultivated at an early age, it will endure most of life's stormy tempests.

### A FATHER EXHORTS AND COMFORTS.

In 1 Thessalonians 1:11–12 it is written, "For you know that we dealt with each of you as a father deals with his own children, encouraging, comforting and urging you to live lives worthy of God who calls you into his kingdom and glory." To attain true success, a father cannot be a silent partner in a family. He has many active roles, including learning some skills that might be new for him, such as comforting and encouraging. A ready ear to listen and a spoken "Well done!" or "Good job!" can mean everything to a child. Make a list of encouraging words and hang them on your refrigerator. If you want something good to say, consult your list.

*A FATHER GIVES HIS CHILDREN A PROPER UPBRINGING.*

Ephesians 6:4 charges, "Fathers, do not exasperate your children; instead bring them up in the training and instruction of the Lord." To fail to train is to exasperate a young child seeking guidance and limits. To fail to instruct is to miss a golden opportunity of parenthood.

Proverbs 3:12 says, "The LORD disciplines those he loves, as a father the son he delights in." For many parents, discipline is unpleasant. We would like to ignore bad behavior and hope that it will magically improve. This wishful thinking is a grave disservice to our children. God, who loves us, disciplines us. To fail to do so with our own children exhibits a lack of love.

*A FATHER MUST BE ABLE TO MANAGE AND CONTROL*
*HIS CHILDREN.*

First Timothy 3:12 says this of a deacon (or any man of God): "A deacon must be the husband of but one wife and must manage his children and his household well." Managing your children and your household are prerequisites for surviving home schooling. They are also the mark of a father acting as the spiritual leader of his family.

*A FATHER KNOWS HOW TO GIVE HIS CHILDREN GOOD GIFTS,*
*USUALLY TRANSLATED AS HIS TIME AND ATTENTION.*

In Matthew 7:11, we see the analogy to the good gifts we receive from our heavenly Father: "If you, then, though you are evil, know how to give good gifts to your children, how much more will your Father in heaven give good gifts to those who ask him!" The best gifts our children can receive are gifts of ourselves. Fathers, no matter how busy, must give this gift to their children. They need to know that they are loved freely and completely. The best way to convey this love is to spend time with them. Home schooling adds a whole new dimension to spending family time together.

*A FATHER IS A BLESSING TO HIS CHILDREN.*

Proverbs 20:7 says, "The righteous man leads a blameless life; blessed are his children after him." One of the greatest blessings we have received from our fathers is a heritage of faith. Mark's father is still with us, and we are so grateful to him for raising a Christian son and for being a strong example to us. This is the blessing you can be to your children as well.

## How to Be a Faithful Home Schooling Father

*REALIZE YOUR VITALLY IMPORTANT ROLE AS FAMILY SPIRITUAL LEADER.*

If your role is clear and your own spiritual life in order, you will contribute more to the training of your children than even the most superlative curriculum. Be the driving force behind church attendance, family devotions, and special religious celebrations. This is your highest family duty. God has set you as the spiritual steward of your family. Be faithful in that task. Pray for your family constantly. Set spiritual goals for your children, perhaps getting actively involved in religious education programs such as AWANA, Pioneer Girls, or Sunday school. Do you regret not having received better training in what it means to be a mature Christian? Don't leave your children with the same spiritual deficit.

*LOVE YOUR WIFE AND LISTEN TO HER.*

Encourage her in the work she is doing and realize what a difficult task she is undertaking. Part of a successful marriage is for both partners to anticipate and fulfill each other's needs in order to avoid unnecessary conflicts and breakdowns in communication. For the mother or father who is the primary home schooler, this is even more important. Spending intense educational time with children who may at times be uncooperative, inattentive, or unwilling can be a stressful and unnerving experience. It goes without saying that parents, while attending to their child's basic security and emotional needs, should not sacrifice their own spousal relationship. Home schooling spouses are subject to additional stresses that are placed on the marriage relationship and must always make time for each other. Fathers should take the initiative to arrange for surprise dates and special events alone with their spouses to help alleviate some of the additional and sometimes awesome responsibilities associated with home schooling.

*SET FAMILY GOALS AND BE THE GOALKEEPER.*

Participate in a system of accountability for your children, yourself, and your wife. There is no reason why mothers and fathers cannot set goals in the same areas that goals are set for their children—spiritual, academic, character, work skills, physical skills, and life principles. I have had the goals of rereading the Old Testament, learning to speak Spanish, working on patience, learning to type, exercising regularly, and keeping my family priorities in order. Unlike vague New Year's resolutions, setting solid goals ensures that you will grow along with your children.

*ASSIST IN PLANNING THE SCHOOL YEAR, BECOME INVOLVED IN SUPPORT GROUPS, AND ATTEND CONVENTIONS WITH YOUR SPOUSE.*

The cost of a baby-sitter for a weekend might seem economically prohibitive, but the quality of education within your home will reap yearlong benefits from such a simple investment. If Dad attends conventions or meetings along with the primary teacher, he will have a deeper understanding of home schooling and a greater appreciation for his wife's work.

*ACCEPT YOUR ROLE AS CHIEF DISCIPLINARIAN/SCHOOL
PRINCIPAL.*

While parenting is a team effort, fathers possess the biblical final authority. Your wife must know she can rely upon you for support and assume responsibility for some of the difficult and beleaguering battles often experienced in the home, as prescribed in Proverbs 3:12: "The LORD disciplines those he loves, as a father the son he delights in."

*IF YOU ARE ABLE TO DO SO, TAKE ON A SUBJECT.*

In our home, Dad does character readings with the children. At the very least, a father can participate by reading quality books with his children and helping with their assignments.

*BE INFORMED ABOUT LEGAL ISSUES.*

Both parents can be scrutinized for home schooling at any given point in time. Both must be equally prepared for unexpected and unanticipated telephone calls, visits, or challenges that might be lodged at any time.

In the unfortunate event that the primary home schooling parent should become disabled, gravely ill, or even prematurely die, a decision must be made whether to continue home schooling or place the child into a public, private, or parochial school setting. Have a plan in place to deal with the unthinkable and know the legal issues involved.

*KEEP YOUR LIFE AND THAT OF YOUR FAMILY IN BALANCE.*

As a child, my husband recalls watching a man on the *Ed Sullivan Show* who would attempt to spin plates on the top of a number of sticks located around the stage. In order to be successful, not only did he have to start the plate spinning, but he had to return to each one periodically and give it another spin to keep it from crashing to the floor. In many respects, home schooling is like balancing a number of different spinning plates on sticks.

The traditional household is filled with routine chores that are periodically interrupted by unexpected surprises including, but not limited to, appliance breakdowns, plumbing emergencies, and remodeling projects. To that add the normal stresses and strains of marriage relationships, finances, communication, church commitments, social engagements, and recreation. Then include home school preparation, instruction, and testing time, and there is a potential for high plate breakage.

While your children must learn the value of a firm work ethic from you, they must also clearly comprehend the value you place upon family and broader interests. Your work is important, but your family is God's gift to you. There is a great premium to be paid for imbalance. There is, however, a great benefit to be reaped by periodic reality checks to assess, reassess, and rebalance priorities. In order to succeed, there must be an intentional process of evaluation to clearly understand which plate needs a new spin.

*INCORPORATE LEARNING INTO EVERYTHING YOU DO.*

Holding a flashlight while Dad repairs the plumbing or handing him tools on a carpentry job can be a learning experience and a time to draw the bonds of love closer between father and child. Trips to the hardware store can teach basic home repair skills and the value of money to boys and girls alike. Building something together can be a treasured experience for children, whether it's a wooden marionette or a miniature dollhouse.

For our family, this is the magic of home schooling. If we stop to think about it, every action and behavior in life is a series of learning events. One way in which we assimilate this into every aspect of our family life is to regularly ask our children questions such as, "What makes that work like that?" "Why does that happen?" or, "What can you learn from this?"

Sacrifice for home schoolers involves time, focus, commitment, and energy. Christ's life was one of selfless service to others; as home schooling parents, nothing less is expected of us. For fathers, this might mean focusing your limited time and energy at home. It may mean cheerfully washing dishes, doing chores, changing a baby, or folding clothes. When these things are done out of a spirit of love and not in a patronizing or obligatory manner, they speak volumes to your family of your love and commitment.

Clay and Sally Clarkson suggest a variety of interesting "Do-Dads." These are activities that Dad can do with kids to give Mom solitude—something she desperately needs. "Take them to the park, take them to a nature center, take them to a lake or beach area, take them to a museum, ride bikes in the country with them, take them on a mini field trip, go on a hike with them, go swimming with them, take them to the library reading time, play tennis with them, take them to special events, take them to seasonal activities. Read books to them, play a game with them, throw a ball or shoot baskets with them, take a walk around the block with them, teach them something, clean up the yard together, make a tent with them, build something with them."[7]

Fathers should remember that research shows that even on mother's "days off" (Saturday and Sunday), she still spends four to five hours a day on household-related activities. Parenting, for moms, can be a veritable pressure cooker. Without a safety release valve, danger can loom on the horizon for marriage, family, and children.

If you can model your love for your children by demonstrating enthusiasm and love for learning, they will follow your example and become enthusiastic learners themselves.

When Dad is intimately involved in the home education adventure, he experiences great satisfaction. Gary Wyatt, writing in *Home Education Magazine*, says, "Unfortunately, for fathers to deny themselves full involvement in the lives of their children is to cut themselves off from something elemental and soul-sustaining, something vital for both themselves and their children."[8]

Home schooling is *good* for families. When it is done with intelligence and heart, with humanity and integrity, then there is nothing more exciting and there is no greater blessing for your family.

# *Appendix A*

# *Home School Resources*

ther writers and educators have done an effective job of creating home school resources. I would be remiss in a book about home schooling if I did not mention some of the best of the best and give you an idea of where to begin looking.

Keep in mind that home schooling families are now officially considered a market: "They are a market publishers and retailers of religion materials are beginning to discover," notes one writer in *Publishers Weekly.*[1] As a market, we should carefully weigh our options and be discerning about which products earn our hard-earned dollars.

Real education doesn't have to cost a lot—although it can. A free library card opens up a world of education. Don't sell the freedom you have as a home schooler. If you don't fit into a planned package or an expert's view of things, rejoice in your freedom to tailor your educational plan.

Cathy Duffy and Mary Pride have written the definitive guidebooks to curriculum choices. Cathy Duffy's books are called the *Christian Home Educators' Curriculum Manual,* published by Home Run Enterprises. One is for the elementary grades and the other covers junior/senior high. Mary Pride has written four volumes of *The New Big Book of Home Learning,* published by Crossway Books. Volume one covers getting started, volume two is for preschool and elementary, volume three is for teens and adults, and volume four is on the subject of after schooling, or activities that take place after school. Both of these writers have extensively reviewed resources. Many libraries have these guides available for loan. They are worth seeking out before spending lots of money on a curriculum.

What follows are some leads for getting started in home schooling.

## Information for Getting Started

Education Services
8825 Blue Mountain Drive
Golden, CO 80403
800-421-6645

This is the source for the wise writings of Ruth Beechick. She is one of the revered grandmothers of home schooling. She is a former teacher and professor of education and is a prolific writer on the subjects of teaching methods, Bible, and home education. You can order these Ruth Beechick titles from Education Services: *The Three R's* (for grades K–3), *You CAN Teach Your Child Successfully* (for grades 4–8), *A Biblical Psychology of Learning, Teaching Preschoolers, Teaching Kindergartners, Teaching Primaries, Teaching Juniors, The Language Wars and Other Writings for Home Schoolers,* and *Adam and His Kin: The Lost History of Their Lives and Times.* Whether you are a beginning home schooler or a veteran, you will find information and encouragement in the writings of Ruth Beechick.

The Elijah Company
Route 2, Box 100-B
Crossville, TN 38555
615-456-6284

This wonderful catalog is an education in home education! The company is run by a seasoned home schooling family that takes a thoughtful approach to home education. They carry books on every subject and make their own loose recommendations for building your own curriculum. They carry the usual stuff and a *lot* of the unusual stuff. I read every catalog cover to cover and learn something every time.

Mary Hood
Ambleside Educational Press
P.O. Box 2524
Cartersville, GA 30120
770-917-9141

Mrs. Hood is a veteran home schooling mother with five children who also happens to have a Ph.D. in education. She is a workshop speaker and publishes a newsletter called "The Relaxed Home Schooler." She has a variety of other publications available. Her two full-length books, *The Relaxed Home School* and *Onto the Yellow School Bus,* provide us with her educational approaches as well as encouragement. Her booklet publications can be quite helpful to the new home schooler. "Countdown to Consistency: A Workbook for Home Educators" and "Relaxed Record Keeping" are excellent resources for getting started. The first workbook takes parents through specific steps to identify their educational approaches and plan for successful home schooling. The book on recordkeeping is a great guide for those of us who have a loose curriculum and worry about documentation.

If you are interested in research or want a good resource guide, Mary Hood also offers a booklet called "The Home Schooling Resource Guide and Directory of Organizations." This is great to dip into and send for a variety of information to get educated and informed. Finally, there is "Taking the Frustration out of Math," which is a great booklet for those of us who worry about whether we are doing the right things in math. Mrs. Hood explains abilities and teaching techniques for each age level. Very informative for the math-serious student.

## Curriculum Suppliers

A Beka Book Publications
Box 18000
Pensacola, FL 32532
800-874-2352

This company provides a complete curriculum for preschool through grade twelve. You may order books and workbooks or their complete Video Home School. Textbooks are well written, colorful, and appealing. Publications are part of the publishing arm of Pensacola Christian College, and the books seek to reflect "the very best in scholarship, design, practicality, and scriptural fidelity." In the Video Home School, daily instruction is provided with regular staff evaluation of children's work.

Alpha Omega Publications
300 North McKemy
Chandler, AZ 85226-2618
800-622-3070

This curriculum is a self-explanatory, partially self-instructional program. By the use of a mastery learning, worktext approach, the student completes sequential texts punctuated by teacher-given tests and checkpoints. The program is not just workbooks, however. It also builds in projects, compositions, and other creative assignments. The worktexts are called LifePacs. There are LifePacs for five subjects each year: language arts, math, Bible, science, and social studies (including history and geography). Materials are available for kindergarten through grade twelve.

The company was recently purchased by Bridgestone Multimedia Group and now also offers a variety of audio, video, and software titles.

Alta Vista Homeschool Curriculum
Alta Vista College
P.O. Box 55535
Seattle, WA 98155
800-544-1397

Alta Vista offers a spiffy unit-study approach for multilevel teaching. The titles of units available are: *Plants, Animals, Earth and Space, People in Ethnic Groups, People in Political Groups,* and *People as Individuals.* Each unit has fifteen lessons—six lessons on math and science, five lessons on social sciences, three lessons on language and fine arts, and one summary lesson that fits the rest together in a biblical format. Student texts and worksheets are provided for each subject. The lesson plans are intellectually challenging and hands-on. They are very balanced and thorough.

The curriculum could also be considered economical when used for multiple family members. They offer a sample lesson packet for your review.

Bob Jones University Press
Greenville, SC 29614-0062
800-845-5731

This evangelical Christian publisher produces a complete curriculum for grades K–12. They have textbooks and teacher's editions for all subjects and grade levels. They also offer phone consultations on curriculum and an academic skill evaluation program. Their catalog is beautiful, with all materials eloquently explained. The textbooks themselves are excellent. While everything is written from a Christian perspective, this is meaty academic material. Their prices to home schoolers are wholesale—that is, the same price a school would be charged. Some of the prices of the teacher's editions may seem a bit high, but they contain material that is necessary for the complete utilization of the student book, and they can be used again with subsequent children. You may buy an entire curriculum or just selected texts.

Calvert School
105 Tuscany Road
Baltimore, MD 21210-9988
410-243-6030

Calvert School home education courses have been used to educate children at home since 1906. They are approved by the Maryland State Department of Education. When enrolled in the "Advisory Teaching Service," your child's grades will be monitored and available for transfer to other schools. The materials provide day-by-day teaching materials with little preparation required by the parent. The course manuals are thoughtfully written with respect for the child. This is the curriculum we use in our family, and we have been extremely pleased. In addition to their K–8 regular course of study, several enrichment options are also offered: *Discovering Art* (grades 4–8), *Come Read with Me* (for emerging readers), *Beatrix Potter: Her Life and Her Little Books* (grades K–3), The *Little House* book series (approximately ages 8–11), *Melody Lane* (music experiences for K–3), *Beginning French* levels one and two, *Beginning Spanish* levels one and two, and a new CD-ROM product called *King Arthur through the Ages.*

Carden Educational Foundation
P.O. Box 659
Brookfield, CT 06804-0659
860-350-9885

This foundation provides a complete private school curriculum based on the insights and theory of Miss Mae Carden. She ran a private school in New York, where she developed these materials based on her own classical approach to education. This is an incremental program in which students are introduced to new concepts with gentle, thorough questioning. All the materials are infused with a great deal of respect and love for children. The purpose of the method is to develop adjusted, capable, confident, eager, alert, courageous, generous, just, self-critical, compassionate, courteous, happy children who have a sense of humor, will be able to develop their native ingenuity, base their actions on the idea that we came to life to make contributions to the welfare of the human race, realize that happiness is a by-product of doing for others, and realize that the goal of living is not the amassing of money or possessions but the attainment of the desires of the heart.

Theoretically, you may only purchase the curriculum after you have taken Carden training. If this is not practical for you, you may request a waiver of this requirement.

Christ-Centered Publications
12500 N.E. Bernie Road
Claremore, OK 74017
800-778-4318 or 918-343-9292

Are you looking for a curriculum for your major subjects that truly has Christ at its center? God's Word is at the very center of all of Christ-Centered Publications. As fundamental skills are learned, the child's mind is saturated with the Word of God, encouraging him to view everything from God's perspective. What a heritage to give to our children!

The basics of this approach are detailed in Doreen Claggett's book *Never Too Early.* This is an inspiring volume to encourage home schoolers to begin the faith training of their children at the earliest opportunity. Mrs. Claggett uses her wisdom, experience, and maturity to address many of the issues and concerns of home schooling families. Following her philosophy, she then makes available to us the tools to provide our young ones with a Christ-centered foundation.

Mrs. Claggett's materials are for ages three through seven, and cover basic phonics and math, using many visual aids and manipulatives. What makes these materials so special is the care taken to encourage you as your child's teacher that this is a job you are uniquely qualified to perform. Mrs. Claggett gently leads your children through the basic material, which is refreshingly imbued with the love of God. You can cover the basics with your children at a very reasonable cost and be assured that your work is built upon a solid rock—the Word of God.

Christian Liberty Academy
502 W. Euclid Avenue
Arlington Heights, IL 60004
847-259-8736

Christian Liberty Press publishes a full line of resources for grades K–12. The curriculum for Christian Liberty Academy includes books from their own press as well as a broad range of other sources. Parents can choose from a variety of services. Christian Liberty Academy Satellite Schools (CLASS) offers families either the "CLASS Administration Plan," in which the academy grades the students' tests, issues report cards, and keeps records, or the "Family Administration Plan," in which the parents do the grading, issue their own report cards, keep their own records, and issue their own diplomas. Other services for independent home schoolers include independent achievement testing and independent curriculum recommendation. Parents may also purchase books from Christian Liberty Press to use as they please. This is a full-service organization with professional advising and very reasonable rates. If you are looking for a traditional approach to home education, make sure you check them out.

Christian Light Education
P.O. Box 1212
Harrisonburg, VA 22801-1212
540-434-0750

Christian Light Education provides a worktext curriculum for grades 1–12. They are a Mennonite publishing company that also provides tracts, books, and other materials. Their home schooling materials are divided into Lightunits, which cover five core subjects: Bible, language arts, math, science, and social studies. Their services are available at three levels: The full program provides recordkeeping and transcripts from the C.L.E. office based on your monthly progress report; C.L.E. will also provide training for the home teacher without these additional services; or the home teacher may purchase curriculum and diagnostic tests only. The materials are well organized, Bible-based, and thorough.

Clonlara School Home Based Education Program
1289 Jewett
Ann Arbor, MI 48104
313-769-4515

Clonlara offers a unique combination of support and flexibility. Students who enroll have the best of both worlds: home education and private school enrollment. Families are assigned their own contact teacher. Clonlara deals with all outside officials and maintains all student records. A private school diploma is offered to those who complete the program. Pat Montgomery, the school's director, is available as a witness in court proceedings. Upon enrollment, the family is sent an enrollment binder, which contains the step-by-step process for establishing a home education approach tailored to the family's needs. A curriculum is provided for your particular child along with math and communication skills guidebooks. Achievement tests are available each year. They also offer a unique high school program, including Compuhigh, which provides instruction via a computer network.

Covenant Home Curriculum
17700 W. Capitol Drive

Brookfield, WI 53045
414-781-2171

Covenant Home provides an academically solid K–12 program. Administrator Dale K. Dykema says in their brochure, "Our curriculum is aimed at serious Christian families who want to educate their children from a biblical and classical perspective. We concentrate on a modified development of the trivium and make extensive use of substantial literature, not current fads." Covenant Home stresses classical literature and the development of a Christian worldview. They include materials from many other publishers. Other services include diagnostic testing, tailoring of curriculum, and a grade auditing program. If you are interested in a classical approach to home schooling from a Reformed perspective, this is a curriculum supplier you would be comfortable with.

Critical Thinking Books and Software
P.O. Box 448
Pacific Grove, CA 93950-0448
408-393-3288

Do you firmly believe that a child who can think logically and critically can have better performance in all content areas of curriculum? If you are willing to spend a few extra minutes a day with your children, you can raise their critical-thinking abilities with these materials. *Building Thinking Skills* (for ages K–adult) is a series of simple activities designed to improve verbal and figural skills in four important areas: similarities and differences, sequences, classifications, and analogies.

This exciting company offers so much more as well. *Editor in Chief: Grammar Disasters and Punctuation Faux Pas* contains content-oriented exercises to make editing for content, grammar, punctuation, and usage fun and interesting. *Mathematical Reasoning through Verbal Analysis* are some of the finest materials I have seen to help the student bridge the gap from fundamental operations to abstract generalizations. Just think about it—a little extra time doing some fun exercises starting in grade two could lay the foundation for superior understanding of higher math.

This company also offers *Developing Critical Thinking through Science*. The two volumes cover grades one through eight and present a hands-on, interactive approach to scientific concepts covered during these years. The activities require little preparation or equipment and suggest critical-thinking questioning to use with the students in a learning dialogue.

Another resource offered by this interesting company is *Critical Thinking in United States History*. In four volumes, for grade five to adult, this critical approach to history from the early settlers to the assassination of JFK encourages students to look at historical sources with a discerning eye in order to teach them to be more aware of varying viewpoints in historical events. All of these materials are extremely well done and will be appreciated by parents/teachers who want to develop thinking students with a lifelong love of learning.

Eagle's Wings
P.O. Box 502
Duncan, OK 73534
405-252-1555

This is your source for some unique phonics, math, and science programs. *Alphabet Island* is a series of fifteen-minute lessons including stories, songs, poems, games, and workbook activities. *Kinder Math* is a sequential program using worksheets, flash cards, and word problems to teach all basic math concepts. One of their new products is called *Remembering God's Awesome Acts*. It is a social study/Bible study covering creation through the exodus. Finally, *Considering God's Creation* offers an in-depth study of natural science from a biblical perspective for second to seventh graders. It can be used in an age-integrated setting for a broad span of grade levels.

Hewitt Educational Resources
P.O. Box 9
Washougal, WA 98671
800-348-1750

Hewitt offers to put together a curriculum that is flexible and varied for grades K–12. They also offer a readiness program in addition to formal education for the upper grades. They offer curriculum counseling, achievement testing, written evaluation of a child's work, and guidance and assistance for students with special needs. Their approach is not overly workbook oriented but rather draws from a variety of sources.

Home Study International
P.O. Box 44137
Silver Spring, MD 20914-4437
301-680-6570

This organization offers a complete curriculum for preschool through grade twelve. They also administer the Columbia Union College External Degree Program. The "Partnership Plan" offers teacher assistance, grading, recordkeeping, and report card/transcript services. Parents may also choose to purchase supplies only.

Konos Character Curriculum
P.O. Box 1534
Richardson, TX 75083
214-669-8337

In a typical Konos unit study, your student will "do, discover, dramatize, dialogue, and drill." Because these units involve the whole child in education, children are excited about learning and have better retention. Konos units are organized around character traits. In the *Attentiveness* unit, for example, children study the physical eye, learn that the eye is a window to the heart, do a study of blindness, and more. Bible, science, social studies, art, music, literature, health, and safety are all integrated around a character trait theme. All required subjects (except math and phonics) are covered. Three volumes are currently available. The activities have recommended age levels, so older and younger children can work together, with the younger students dropping off where appropriate and the older ones digging deeper. Konos is also well known for their time lines. Many other supportive products are also available.

The Moore Foundation
Box 1
Camas, WA 98607
360-835-2736

A variety of services and materials are available through the Moore Foundation, the organization of Raymond and Dorothy Moore. You may enroll in the "Startup Program," which provides you with curriculum planning and phone consultation. Independent study allows you to enhance your own curriculum with Moore-based counseling. Their "Satellite Program" is full-service, from curriculum planning to consultation, to state registration and academic evaluation.

Pathway Publishers
2580 N. 250 W.
LaGrange, IN 46761

This publisher began printing books for use in Amish schools. The materials are now available for sale to home schoolers. The reading program is a traditional phonics program using readers and workbooks. The Pathway Reading Series features wholesome stories of farm families. Each has a reading lesson as well as a life lesson. My children enjoyed these readers very much. Workbooks and teachers' editions are available at each level. Pathway offers other interesting storybooks, devotionals, and child-training information.

Dr. Arthur Robinson
Robinson Self-Teaching Curriculum
c/o Oregon Institute of Science and Medicine
Box 1279
Cave Junction, OR 97523

Dr. Robinson developed a self-teaching curriculum for grades 1–12, consisting of twenty-two CD-ROMs. The curriculum provides a program of self-study, using high quality books and materials that may be printed out for use. The only area of supplementation required is in the area of math, and Dr. Robinson integrates Saxon Math into his curriculum.

Rod and Staff Publishers
Route 172
Crockett, KY 41413
606-522-4348

Rod and Staff is a Mennonite publisher offering a traditional curriculum that relies heavily on biblical material. They offer complete curriculum for grades K–12 at a very reasonable cost. These books are graceful, simple, respectful, and full of the Word of God. Their big catalog contains a complete curriculum guide of materials to be used at each grade level.

School of Tomorrow
P.O. Box 299000
Lewisville, TX 75029-9000
800-925-7777

The School of Tomorrow is an individualized curriculum that allows each student to work at his own level of achievement. The curriculum includes five major academic disciplines—math, English, social studies, science, and word building, which are taught via individual worktexts called PACES. The student works through an average of twelve PACES per course, per year. The material requires little (if any) parental preparation. This company also offers a variety of videos, CD-ROMs, and other software material. They are on the cutting edge of this educational technology.

Sonlight Curriculum
8185 S. Grant Way
Littleton, CO 80122
303-730-6292

Sonlight Curriculum provides user-friendly teacher's manuals and a nicely done literature-based curriculum for grades K–8. They put tried-and-true programs, such as Saxon Math, together with a rich literature and history base.

The Sycamore Tree
2179 Meyer Place
Costa Mesa, CA 92627
800-779-6750
http://www.sycamoretree.com

Bill and Sandy Gogel are in their fifteenth year with The Sycamore Tree. Credentialed teachers help you with curriculum choices, monitor your program, and send you sixty to eighty pages of enrichment material each month. Their catalog, from which you build your curriculum, is wonderful. It is a book-lover's paradise with variety, choice, and fun. They feature the best standard material, like Saxon Math and Pathway Readers, but they also have a ton of materials that are not the usual run-of-the-mill stuff. Their fees are reasonable. Each child is charged an enrollment fee, but the monthly tuition fee is per family, not per child. The services they provide are extensive and professional. If you are looking for a family program offering a lot of choice combined with a lot of experienced guidance, then you must check out The Sycamore Tree.

*Curriculum Do-It-Yourself Style*

Design-a-Study
408 Victoria Avenue
Wilmington, DE 19804-2124
302-998-3889

Would you like the freedom to provide a quality education on a limited budget—the freedom to really match a curriculum to your child without worrying
about gaps, and the freedom to allow your child to learn at his own pace? These
thorough, intelligent, interesting resources may be just what you're looking for.
Author and speaker Kathryn Stout has a bachelor's degree in elementary education and a master's degree in special education. In addition to a long teaching
career in the schools, she has taught her own children at home for twelve years.

These materials are a gold mine for those of us who want to break away from a
structured curriculum and take a more tailored approach. Kathryn Stout not only
tells us what can be covered at each grade level, but gives ideas for how to cover the
material as well as appropriate projects and hands-on activities for individual learners. Her spiral-bound books are: *Maximum Math, Science Scope, Guides to History,
Natural Speller, Comprehensive Composition,* and *Critical Conditioning.* She also
offers *Teaching Tips and Techniques* and a unit study on the Maya. A complete set
of convention workshop audiocassettes is available that covers much of the material above. These materials can guide you to wonderful, thorough unit studies.
They can also help you cover the math and spelling areas that trouble many home
educators. These materials are definitely worth checking out carefully.

## Preschool/Readiness Materials

Alphagator Al Preschool Curricula
c/o Praise Hymn
P.O. Box 1325
Taylors, SC 29687
800-729-2821

This is a fun, easy way to teach beginning sound recognition, letter formation,
and alphabetical order using activity sheets, stories, games, and songs. There is a
teacher's book, a letter book with games and activities for the child, and a writing
tablet for when the child is ready to begin practicing letter formation. This is a
neat, inexpensive system for those who are just beginning to teach or want to just
cover a letter a day with their child. The materials are bright and fun, and my
younger children really enjoyed them!

At Home Publications
2826 Roselawn Avenue
Baltimore, MD 21214
410-444-5465

Jean Soyke has written a complete curriculum for parents of preschoolers and kindergartners in one easy-to-use, inexpensive volume. *Early Education at Home* covers all the subject areas for your youngest students with lots of fun activities, reading lists, field trip activities, and snack ideas. It is activity based because children learn best by doing, especially at this age. It is complete in its content yet can be used with as much flexibility as your situation requires. To top it all off, the price is extremely reasonable and it can be used over and over again with each succeeding child.

Bio-Alpha, Inc.
P.O. Box 7190
Fairfax Station, VA 22039
Fax: 703-323-0743
Phone: 703-323-6142

This is a wonderful book for parents who are interested in home schooling their very young children. It is a book of weekly developmental activities for each year of a child's life up to age five. There is one simple activity per week that can be done with materials found around the house. For example, at age two, week forty-nine, your child should be ready to kick or move a soft ball with his foot. For this week, your child works on his eye-foot coordination, awareness of boundaries, and listening to instruction. We love this book and have used it with two of our children. These are brief, stimulating activities that you and your child will really enjoy. The author is a career kindergarten teacher and also offers an accompanying video and checklist to help monitor your child's development. The book itself is a bargain (around twenty dollars) and will give you many ideas for educational activities.

*Learning at Home: Preschool and Kindergarten*
*Learning at Home: First Grade and Second Grade*
by Ann Ward
Smiling Heart Press
P.O. Box 229
Corbett, OR 97019

These books present a full year's curriculum to use with your child. I used the preschool one with my oldest child and enjoyed it a great deal. It was a systematic way to ensure that she was exposed to certain topics and experiences that I felt were important. The only expense in using this is the purchase of the manual because the course uses the public library as a resource. In the preschool/kindergarten volume, the author even gives the library call letters for nonfiction books to use to complement the lesson. This is very structured, but it can be modified to meet your family's needs. We enjoyed preschool with this very much!

The manual is available through Great Christian Books, a discount book distributor, or Christian Life Workshops.

*Playful Parenting: An Alternative Approach to Preschool,* 1986
by Anne Engelhardt and Cheryl Sullivan
La Leche League International
1400 N. Meacham Road
P.O. Box 4079
Schaumburg, IL 60168-4079
800-LALECHE

This book is an oldie but a goodie. They talk about setting up a neighborhood cooperative preschool, but the projects and ideas can easily be utilized by an individual home schooling family. The book is available at most public libraries.

TLC—Terry Learning Company
P.O. Box 268
Elmore City, OK 73035
405-788-4765

This is a complete preschool curriculum in one fat, spiral-bound volume. Through fun activities, these materials teach a progression of skills, with a suggested yearly schedule. There are many fun accessories in this program—a cassette tape of eleven songs, reward stickers, a "Can Do" calendar full of poems, games, activities, recipes, crafts and experiments, ready-to-use game boards, lace-up shapes, flash cards, concentration cards, and much more. The materials are printed on heavy card stock and are very well done. Four units can be covered in a suggested day: calendar, movement, fine motor skills, and nursery rhymes. This is a complete program for your young child that you will both find delightful.

## Specific Subjects

### Art

At Home Publications
2826 Roselawn Avenue
Baltimore, MD 21214
410-444-5465

*Art Adventures at Home* is a complete art curriculum for grades K–5. In a two-volume package, you can inexpensively provide a rich art experience for your home school family. The lessons present the basics of art and provide experience in drawing, printmaking, painting, sculpture, and crafts. It is well organized and can be used by parents who have little art experience. Written by a home schooling mom, it is a very well-done, satisfying art experience for the home schooling family. The lessons are fun, yet they have an objective so your child will have a foundation in a variety of art experiences. The volumes can be used for a variety of ages and for any number of children. This is an impressive art curriculum at an impressive price.

Gordon School of Art
P.O. Box 28208
Green Bay, WI 54324-8208
800-210-1220

Are you looking for a complete sequential art curriculum for you and your child? This course covers a full studio arts curriculum arranged in a logical sequence for students from about age six and up. The creator of this fabulous program isolated some two hundred technical skills associated with the mastery of art concepts. The course teaches these concepts by breaking down the process of drawing and painting into tasks that anyone can manage, even those who may not consider themselves artistic. The instructor believes that if basic tasks can be learned and managed, students can eventually master it all. The lessons are taught on videotape. The course comes with a student art book, a teacher manual, videotapes, a supply packet, and two free mail-monitoring sessions in which your work will be evaluated by trained teachers. This is a very impressive home study art course that the whole family can enjoy.

How Great Thou Art
Dept. 17, 10802 Bishopville Road
P.O. Box 211
Bishopville, MD 21813
410-352-3319

Barry Stebbing is an artist and teacher with many years of experience. He has created a series of art lessons that have been designed to be both simple and precise. He offers his art books, along with instructional videos and art supplies. These books can be used with children as young as three years of age!

National Gallery of Art
Gallery Shops
Mail Order Department
2000 B South Club Drive
Landover, MD 20785
301-322-5900

Although their reproductions catalog is no longer available, they have just about any reproduction you would want in stock. The size is eleven by fourteen inches and the cost is $1.25 each. These are very useful for studying the work of individual artists or periods in art history. They also sell posters of famous paintings.

Parent Child Press
P.O. Box 675
Hollidaysburg, PA 16648-0675
814-696-7512

These are the creators of the program formerly known as *Mommy! It's a Renoir!* The art appreciation program has been renamed *How to Use Child-Size Masterpieces for Art Appreciation.* This book and accompanying art prints provide a rich, hands-on introduction to art for your children. At the program's simplest level, your child will match identical paintings. As it advances, the children learn to identify works from the same artist and finally learn to classify the schools of art history. This is really great stuff that you and your child will both love. This company also sells postcard-size reproductions, posters, time line cards, and a few other books on the theme of Montessori education.

University Prints
21 East Street
Winchester, MA 01890
617-729-8006

Are you looking for a source for art prints to use in your home school? University Prints has a huge collection. Their detailed brochures contain listings for special art study sets, topic study sets, and visual surveys for library reference. The prints are five and a half by eight inches and are very nicely done. Brochures are free, or a complete 246-page catalog is available for three dollars.

### Bible and Character Studies

Abba Ministries
1621 Baldwin Avenue
Orange, CA 92665
714-282-0496

This is the ministry of Peter and Beverly Caruso, who have spoken and ministered around the world. They have some wonderful books available. I was especially impressed with *Developing Godly Character in Children: A Handbook and Resource Guide.* This is a unit-study approach to the study of ninety-three character qualities. It is designed to be covered over three years and can be used with all ages. It is carefully and creatively written with memory verses, songs, activities, and more for each character trait. There is a bibliography for each trait as well, referring you to novels and children's books on the subject, many of which are available in your church library. This is a resource my family has needed! Other books available include *Faith Builders from Around the World,* which includes stories of faith in action from workers in over ninety countries. The stories exhibit the work of God firsthand in the lives of people around the world. Also available is *Loving Confrontation: Biblical Relationships Principles.* Drawing on their years of experience in the ministry, the Carusos talk about biblical and practical principles that transformed their individual lives, their marriage, and their church. The Carusos are also available to do seminars and workshops.

Bradshaw Publishers
P.O. Box 277

Bryn Mawr, CA 92318
909-796-6766

This company publishes a very nice collection called *Bible Stories for Early Readers*. Two reading levels are available. Each small, inexpensive booklet features stories that are easy to read with colorful pictures and quality writing. These will encourage even young children to read the Bible.

Doorposts
5840 SW Old Hwy 47
Gaston, OR 97119
503-357-4749

This is a gold mine! The Forster family, authors and distributors of the Doorposts products, can really help your family apply Scripture in your home with their Bible-based, parent-designed, family-tested products. *For Instruction in Righteousness* is a topical reference guide for biblical child training. Each topic includes ideas for discipline, stories about people in the Bible who indulged in the same sin, and memory verses. This is a great resource for teaching your children that right and wrong are based on God's Word—not yours! We have used this in our family as a resource in our character studies, where we pick a character trait and study it for a period of time. Another book available is *Plants Grown Up: Projects for Sons on the Road to Manhood.* This five-hundred-page manual offers ideas for Bible study projects, reading material, and everyday activities to help train sons for manhood. As of this writing, the Forsters are working on a book for girls, tentatively titled *Polished Cornerstones,* so be sure to look for that as well. Doorposts offers other fabulous products as well:

- The "If-Then" chart lists infractions such as whining, hitting, or teasing, and lets the parent write in the consequences of the behavior. It gives children a consistent measure of discipline.
- The "Blessing" chart is designed to help you acknowledge and reward godly attitudes and behavior. One column lists qualities you want to see developed along with supporting Scripture verses. The final column is left blank for you to plan creative rewards for blessing behavior.
- The "Brother-Offended" checklist is a cartoon-illustrated chart and book set that outlines steps for an offended person to follow, steps to encourage the offender to confess and forsake his sin, and Scripture-based guidelines for parents to follow when they must assume the role of judge.
- "Checklist for Parents" is an eye-opener to help parents examine themselves in light of God's Word.
- "A Young Lady of Valor" is a little booklet study of Proverbs 31 for girls. Illustrated by cartoons, it encourages young girls to think about their biblical roles and responsibilities.
- The "Go-to-the-Ant" chart arms parents with Bible references for working with the easily distracted child. It covers areas like laziness

and allows you to take your child to the chart, identify his action, and read what God says about it. This has been very helpful in dealing with my bright but less-than-attentive oldest child.

These materials are wonderful and will give you lots of help in dealing with character issues with your children.

Lynn's Bookshelf
P.O. Box 2224
Boise, ID 83701
208-331-1987

This is the publisher of the highly acclaimed *Proverbs for Parenting*. It is a topical guide from the Book of Proverbs for child raising. Organized in helpful categories, the book can be used for reference in any family situation. For example, if your children are complaining, you can turn to the section on that topic and have quick access to verses such as Proverbs 17:22: "A cheerful heart is good medicine, but a crushed spirit dries up the bones." The publisher also offers two coloring books, *A Coloring Book of Proverbs* and *A Coloring Book of Bible Verses from the Epistles* in both King James and New International versions.

Memlok
420 E. Montwood Avenue
LaHabra, CA 90631
800-373-1947

I have a terrible memory. I blame it on having small children, but I still need to hide God's Word in my heart. Memlok is a Bible memory system that really works for me. I am a woman who cannot recall what she did two hours ago, but I am memorizing Scripture thanks to this great system. I think that one of my highest duties as a home schooling parent is to teach my children Bible memory skills. Memlok can help. It has a word picture for the first key words of Scripture verses to get you started. Working about five minutes a day, you can memorize one verse a week, or more if you are highly motivated. The system comes with memorization cards organized by topic and checklists for you to chart your progress. One of their other products is *Say the Books!* This little book uses a series of cartoons to illustrate each book of the Bible with a caption and a running story line. Quizzes are included and the illustrations may be colored. These are great resources for the whole family.

Pearables
P.O. Box 9887
Colorado Springs, CO 80932

If you believe that Bible and character training are the most important subjects you can cover in your home school, you must check out Pearables. *The Narrow*

*Way* is a curriculum devoted solely to building godly character, beginning around age four. You can work in a family setting with multiple ages of children. The lessons take only a few minutes a day and will help instill a solid foundation of faith that is based totally on God's Word. *Pearables Character Building Kingdom Stories,* vols. 1–3 are illustrated books that use a simple parable or allegory to illustrate biblical views on issues such as television, obedience, or blaming others for our own mistakes. These stories make great family reading and are followed by scriptural references and discussion questions. These gentle yet very solid materials are beautifully done and will bless your home school experience.

Praise Hymn
P.O. Box 1325
Taylors, SC 29687
800-729-2821

These materials teach the Bible using a story approach. Formatted for grades 1–6 with one twenty-minute lesson per day for four days a week, students will receive a survey of all major stories and New Testament books once in grades 1–3 and again in grades 4–6. Students add to their knowledge each year, rather than stalling at one section or topic. The materials are inexpensive and come with a song tape for grades 1–3. The student books are bright and fun, and my kids really enjoyed them. They wanted to snatch them all from me and immediately begin coloring and cutting and pasting the fun activities. The teacher's manuals are very thorough and carefully cover each lesson and topic.

### *Foreign Languages*

Audio-Forum
The Language Source
96 Broad Street
Guilford, CT 06437-2612
203-453-9794

Many home schoolers want to study a foreign language as a family. Audio-Forum provides a broad selection of languages, from Arabic to Native American. They offer complete courses for adults as well as some materials for children.

This company offers a variety of other products. They have grammar tapes, folk song anthologies, and films. Send for their catalogs to browse this collection.

International Linguistics Corporation
3505 East Red Bridge
Kansas City, MO 64137
800-237-1830

This is your source for *The Learnables,* foreign language courses that have been used by home schoolers since 1976. Using pictures and audiocassettes, children and parents can learn a new language together. Current languages offered are Spanish, French, German, Russian, Chinese, Czech, Hebrew, and Japanese.

Power-Glide Language Courses
988 Cedar Avenue
Provo, UT 84604
801-373-3973
http://www.power-glide.com

In this exciting new approach to language acquisition, students take on the identity of a secret agent who must go to a foreign country to solve a mystery. This immersion study includes six ninety-minute audiotapes. The program is available in Spanish, French, Russian, Japanese, and German and covers all the material typically studied in two years of high school. It is most appropriate for junior high level or above. The home teacher does not need to know the language, so student and parent can learn together. The exciting accompanying workbook uses drawing, storytelling, grammar games, and familiar stories to establish fluency, as well as providing traditional exercises. This is an extremely creative and interesting approach that should be thoroughly explored by home schooling families seeking to study a foreign language.

*Handwriting*

Concerned Communications
P.O. Box 1000
Siloam Springs, AR 72761
501-736-2244

Would you like to see your child practice handwriting and Bible verses at the same time? This series of handwriting books called *A Reason for Writing* combines basic handwriting practice with Bible memorization. Even the earliest books use "Jesus" for the letter "J" rather than something like "jack-in-the-box." As ability progresses, the verses become more challenging. Practice pages are attractively decorated with borders that may be colored and displayed. Some parents use these to have their children send messages to friends and family members. There is one word to describe these books—inspired! They combine handwriting, Scripture, art, and sharing in one lesson. They truly give your students "a reason for writing." You will love them and so will your children.

*History*

Greenleaf Press
1570 Old LaGuardo Road
Lebanon, TN 37087
800-311-1508

If you are raising history students who want a serious approach to history, you have to see these materials. Most noted for their study packages of ancient Egypt, ancient Greece, and ancient Rome, Rob and Cyndy Shearer have a rich collection of history resources to offer your family. They even have a suggested schedule as to when to teach what topics to your children. They can also suggest wonderful resources to enrich the experience. For example, if you want to do an in-depth study of Egypt, start with the *Greenleaf Guide to Ancient Egypt*. In this in-depth study, you and your child will learn history and geography, study Egyptian hieroglyphics, and do a hands-on project to illustrate irrigation in ancient Egypt. The book will guide you to other resources, such as *The Pharaohs of Ancient Egypt* (Elizabeth Payne), *Pharaohs and Pyramids* (Usborne Books), and *Pyramid* (David Macaulay).

With the Greenleaf guides and other recommended materials, history comes alive for you and your family. Their other materials can take you through *Famous Men of Rome, Famous Men of Greece, Famous Men of the Middle Ages,* as well as their highly acclaimed *Greenleaf Guide to Old Testament History.* Many other materials are available, including some important books on special education.

Peter Marshall Ministries
81 Finlay Road
Orleans, MA 02653
800-879-3298

Do you want your history studies to focus on God's plan as well as man's story? There is no better place to start than the writings of Peter Marshall. He has many resources available, but the most popular are two books: *The Light and the Glory* and *From Sea to Shining Sea.* They are available in two formats: One is for older children and the other is for children ages five to eight. There is also a children's activity book available for ages five to eight for *The Light and the Glory.* Our children are never too young to learn that our country was founded by godly men who listened to God's calling for their lives.

*Mathematics*

Cuisenaire Company of America
P.O. Box 5026
White Plains, NY 10602-5026
800-237-0338

Cuisenaire rods are math manipulatives used to teach place value, fractions, and other concepts. This catalog offers these as well as other imaginative materials.

Delta Education
Hands-On Math
P.O. Box 3000
Nashua, NH 03061-3000
800-282-9560

Manipulatives galore! Although specifically geared to the classroom setting, this colorful catalog is a wonderful source for finding excellent math materials.

Everyday Learning Corporation
P.O. Box 1479
Evanston, IL 60204-1479
800-382-7670

This is the distributor for the highly touted University of Chicago School Math Project called *Everyday Mathematics*. Available for grades K–6, the program emphasizes verbal interactions and the use of manipulatives. Math is also linked to other subjects. The materials are very well done, are fun for the children, and encourage students to be excited about math. I have heard from several families who use this program and think it is wonderful.

Hands-On Equations
Borenson & Associates
P.O. Box 3328
Allentown, PA 18106
215-820-5575

What an interesting approach to basic algebra concepts! For third or fourth graders, this approach presents a physical and intuitive model of algebra through the use of game pieces on a laminated picture of a balance. The students are given an equation. They first set up the equation with pawns and cubes on the balance. Through a series of "legal moves" they work through simple instructions and solve the problem. What a confidence builder for your young math student! While it is not a substitute for an algebra class, this is an easy way to introduce some higher math concepts. The student who is given this foundation will have a great head start in upper-level math courses.

Mathematics Program Associates
P.O. Box 2118
Halesite, NY 11743
516-643-9300

This is a complete workbook series covering the basic elements of arithmetic into the beginnings of algebra. In each lesson, students go from the lowest level of knowledge to the highest level of mastery. They are ideal for self-paced learning and are the product of decades of research and testing around the world. The goal is not to merely teach the memorization of facts and the steps of computations; rather, these materials seek to lead children through the progression of *how* the facts are derived and *how* the computations are developed. In this program, the main goal is cultivating independent thinking. Each workbook comes with a parent's guide and a diagnostic test. These materials are very well done and thoughtfully presented.

*Miscellaneous*

American Map Corporation
Lande Communications
909 Chesterfield Drive
Ambler, PA 19002
215-654-7950

Maps, maps, and more maps! This company has everything from jumbo wall maps
to pocket maps. Maps cover cities, towns, states, the country, and the world. The
types of maps include political reference maps, road and street maps, physical
maps, and business maps. They offer atlases as well as some unusual items, such
as map puzzles. This is a beautiful catalog, and the maps I have seen are of excellent quality. If you enjoy using maps at your house, contact the American Map
Corporation.

Aristoplay, Ltd.
P.O. Box 7529
Ann Arbor, MI 48107
800-634-7738

Games, glorious games! They have wonderful educational games, such as *Made
for Trade*—an early American shopping game. Or *Knights and Castles*—an adventure in chivalry game. Our favorite is *Music Maestro*. My four-year-old learned all
the sounds of orchestra instruments with this one. There is lots of variety here for
the game player in all of us.

Audio Memory Publishing
501 Cliff Drive
Newport Beach, CA 92663
800-365-SING

They say you never forget what you sing! If your children are singers, get these
tapes. They can listen to catchy tunes and learn any number of things. Tapes available include *Grammar Songs Kit, Geography Songs Kit, States and Capitals Kit, Multiplication Songs* (*Division Drills Book* and *Fraction Drills Book* sold separately),
*Addition Songs,* and *Subtraction Songs.* Whether you listen to tapes in the car or
have a child who likes to wear headphones, these tapes will make drilling and
memorization fun! The songs are sung first with the answers, then without the
answers for self-testing. My kids are singing all the time anyway. These tapes give
them something useful to sing that really sticks in their brains. They love them!

The math tapes each come with a big chart. The geography tape has thirty-two
songs and an informative book. The states and capitals tape comes with a huge
poster map to label and color. The grammar kit has a seventy-two-page book and
sixteen songs on the cassette. Although most appropriate for upper elementary

grades, some of the earlier material can be learned by much younger children. Check these out!

Back Home Industries
P.O. Box 22495
Milwaukie, OR 97269-2495
503-654-2300

This is your source for Wanda Sanseri's *Teaching Reading at Home*. This supplements Romalda Spaulding's *The Writing Road to Reading*, which is an intensive phonics program instructing the teacher in phonics methods. Mrs. Sanseri also offers seminars in this complete method of teaching phonics, reading, spelling, handwriting, and grammar. Other interesting materials available from Back Home Industries include *The New England Primer of 1777*, a reprint of the famous primer from an earlier time. Every page is based on Scripture! Wanda Sanseri has written a beautiful Bible study called *God's Priceless Woman*. In it, she encourages us to return to Scripture to regain our true identity as women. It is more than the usual fill-in-the-blank type of Bible study and will make you think! Gary Sanseri has written some material on personal finance and money management in light of biblical truth. His book, *A Banker's Confession: A Christian Guide to Getting out of Debt*, challenges us to look at the real meaning of financial freedom and gives practical advice on how to save money. Many other fine materials on Bible, history, and economics are also available.

Back to Basics
P.O. Box 30513
Cleveland, OH 44130

Dan Taddeo is a very wise man. He is a husband, father, teacher, counselor, and grandparent. He also loves the Word of God and offers two outstanding publications: *Words of Wisdom: Character Building Family Values for Your Refrigerator Door* is a little book packed with thoughts from the greatest thinkers of the world. The booklet is designed to have the pages detached and displayed on the refrigerator door. This would make a great gift or a touchstone for your own family's devotional studies. Taddeo's other book, *Back to Basics: Parenting Principles: A Biblical Perspective* offers sixty-one readings on everything from accountability to worry. This is a precious volume that can help us train our children's character—and our own.

Bealls' Learning Games
5220 Lone Jack Lane
Garden City, CA 95633
Phone or Fax: 916-333-4589

Do you want to have fun with your kids while reinforcing math facts, spelling rules, phonograms, or geography? The Bealls have some great ideas. Using their game boards, the whole family can play games that use cards from a variety of subjects to reinforce needed areas for each child. Or games can be played with the *Phonogram Fun Packet, Math Fact Fun Packet, U.S. Geography Fun Packet,* or *U.S. States and Capitals.* The object is not to get to the end of the game board, but to get as many cards as possible. Each retained card represents a fact that has been successfully drilled. There is also a complete *Early Learner's Special* available that uses hands-on activities and games to teach basic concepts. The game boards are bright and colorful, and my kids have had a great time trying out some of the games. The game cards are on good quality paper stock. You can also create a game of your own using these materials, depending on the needs of your children. This is a unique little company with some great ideas. If you like games, hands-on learning, and smiles on your children's faces, send for the Bealls' brochure.

> Bendt Family Ministries
> 333 Rio Vista Court
> Tampa, FL 33604
> 813-238-3721

Valerie Bendt is well known for her unit-study books, *How to Create Your Own Unit Study* and *The Unit Study Idea Book.* We have used these to create many interesting unit-study experiences for our children. Ms. Bendt has many other resources as well. *For the Love of Reading* is a beautiful book that shows us how to make reading the focal point of our learning. She discusses using dictation and narration, turning children's stories into their own readers, keeping a reader's journal, and motivating your children to take an active part in family reading. She has also created a literature study guide for the books of Russell Hoban about that loveable character Frances. The *Frances Study Guide* is full of fun, hands-on activities and oral discussion questions and projects, with reading and writing integrated into the study. My kids liked this guide, and it gave us a chance to really explore an author and a character. The Bendt Family Ministries brochure is full of other neat stuff as well. Send for it today!

> Bluestocking Press
> P.O. Box 2030
> Shingle Springs, CA 95682-2030
> 800-959-8586

Bluestocking Press is a publisher as well as a distributor of "materials to challenge the student's thinking as well as the teacher's." Bluestocking titles include these by Jane Williams: *How to Stock a Home Library Inexpensively, The Home School Market Guide,* as well as the *Laura Ingalls Wilder and Rose Wilder Lane Historical Timetable.* They have also published the works of Richard J. Maybury, *Uncle Eric's Model of How the World Works.* They carry an incredible collection of history and literature books and much, much more. This is a must-have catalog for the serious reader or the serious home schooler.

> Budgetext
> 1936 N. Shiloh Drive

Fayetteville, AR 72704
800-643-3432 or 888-888-2272

Budgetext carries over five hundred thousand used textbooks from a variety of
publishers at budget prices, including textbooks, workbooks, biographies, and
classical literature. Publishers include A Beka, Bob Jones, Modern Curriculum
Press, and many others. Check out these prices!

The Carpenter's Son Woodcraft
3209 Willowbrook Circle
Waco, TX 76711
817-756-5261

This neat catalog seeks to introduce children to the joy of hands-on learning
through practical woodworking projects. They carry woodworking kits and some
other really interesting craft kits.

Christian Life Workshops
P.O. Box 2250
Gresham, OR 97030
800-225-5259

This is the organization of Gregg Harris and his family. He is one of the most
respected, sought-after speakers and writers in the home school movement. His
tapes and conferences are enormously helpful and inspiring. You may obtain Harris's book, tapes, and planners from C.L.W. as well as many other materials. Their
big catalog is an education in home schooling.

The Cornerstone Curriculum Project
2006 Flat Creek Place
Richardson, TX 75080
214-235-5149

These are the people who bring you *Making Math Meaningful* (a complete multisensory math program for home instruction), *Principles from Patterns, Algebra I,
Science: The Search, Learning Language Arts through Literature, Adventures in Art,
Music and Moments with the Masters,* and *World Views of the Western World* for
high school students.

The Courtship Connection
3731 Cecelia
Toledo, OH 43608
419-729-4594

Alan and Kathie Morrissey have a twenty-page catalog dedicated to materials that
deal with their strong belief in the importance of courtship over dating and other

character training issues. Kathie is also a delightful convention speaker on many
topics, and tapes of her materials are also available.

Cranbrook Software and Publications
1607 Cranbrook Drive
Saginaw, MI 48603
517-793-2316

Cranbrook has developed several programs for the home schooling family. *Create-a-Story*, for K–8, includes calendars with a starting phrase for a daily writing assignment. The *Home School Report Card* program allows you to print your own report cards. The *Home School Organizer* is designed to allow you to print your own assignment sheets. *Home School Transcript* can be used to organize the information needed for college applications.

Cygnet Press
The Swanns
HC 12, Box 7A
116 Hwy 28
Anthony, NM 88021
505-874-3306

Have you heard of the Swann family and their phenomenal success with accelerated home education? The oldest child, Alexandra, graduated from college at fifteen and earned her master's degree at age sixteen. Her nine brothers and sisters have a similar track record. What is really impressive is that they have accomplished these academic feats in a way that honors God, promotes family unity, and recognizes the unique strengths of each child.

Alexandra's story is chronicled in her book, *No Regrets: How Home Schooling Earned Me a Master's Degree at Sixteen*. In her own words, she tells the story of her individual striving and of her family's commitment to excellence. The family also sells an eight-tape audio-album called *the Swann Family's Family Life Series* in which various family members discuss time management, socialization, and college at home. I particularly appreciated mother Joyce Swann's tape in the series on discipline. Finally, two of the Swann sisters, Alexandra and Francesca, have written *Writing for Success: A Comprehensive Guide to Improved Creative Writing Skills,* for students in seventh grade and above. It covers basic grammar, punctuation, and word exercises and has imaginative assignments in a usable format. The teaching is thorough and the exercises call for both knowledge and creativity. This course looks like a winner for older writing students. All their resources are self-published and available from their home business, listed above.

D.P. & K. Productions
2201 High Road
Tallahassee, FL 32303
904-385-1958

Do you want your children to be proficient in research skills? One of the most important things we can give our children is the ability to find the information they need, when they need it. This is your source for the *Information, Please!* books. They are a fun and exciting way to teach children research and critical-thinking skills. Available in beginning (K–5), intermediate (grades 6–8), and advanced levels (grades 9–12), these books are filled with questionnaires to be completed once a week for a year. Children are required to look in traditional sources, such as almanacs, atlases, and dictionaries, as well as less traditional sources, such as etiquette books, concordances, and phone books.

Another resource entitled *Information, Please! Getting Started* is available to introduce your child to the many forms of reference material available. Other products available from this company include a wonderful unit study on the Civil War and a book called *Big Ideas, Small Budget.* A newsletter is also available with the same title. This interesting family also presents workshops. (By the way, D.P. & K. stands for Don, Pat, and the kids. They have eight kids and have been home schooling for twelve years.)

Dover Publications
31 East 2nd Street
Mineola, NY 11501
516-294-7000

What a neat catalog! With incredibly affordable prices, Dover offers stickers, tapes, punch-out books, art and craft instruction, illustration reference books, clip art, and much, much more. You will find something educational, fun, and affordable to complement any curriculum or study.

English from the Roots Up
Literacy Unlimited Publications
P.O. Box 278
Medina, WA 98039-0278

Subtitled *Help for Reading, Writing, Spelling, and SAT Scores,* this program is really unique. Many people in my generation had the opportunity to study Latin. I believe this gave them a literacy advantage. By seeing and recognizing Latin root words, they were able to figure out the meanings of many more words. This program exposes your child to Greek and Latin root words that will greatly expand their vocabulary and word skills. The book exposes your child to one hundred Latin and Greek root words and provides information about words that are related to the derivatives. This requires little preparation and takes about fifteen minutes per card. It's simple and fun and can really give your child a depth of language understanding.

Family Christian Academy
487 Myatt Drive
Madison, TN 37115
615-860-3000

email: FCAPub@aol.com
web site: http://www.fcahomeschool.com

Robin Scarlata, along with Lynda Coats, is the creator of *Far above Rubies: A Unit Study Based on Proverbs 31:10–31 for High School Girls* and *The Far above Rubies Companion.* The study is designed to train girls to become godly women by providing a well-rounded curriculum useful for college preparatory purposes as well as offering a number of business and vocational skills. The program needs supplementation in the math area. There are twenty units based on one or more verses from the passage under study. Each unit includes the following areas: Bible and Christian character, cultural studies, reading and literature, composition, math and personal finance, science, health and physical fitness, practical arts, and creative and performing arts. Together with *The Far above Rubies Companion,* this work can be used during the high school years when supplemented with the many resources recommended. This is a valuable resource for families who wish to instill in their daughters a solidly biblical worldview.

Family Christian Academy is your source for two other in-depth works. *A Family Guide to the Biblical Holidays* is a thick volume that creatively explores biblical holidays and provides activities for all ages of family members. The author explores the historical purpose and meaning of each holiday. The book is devoted to helping families see how the festival celebrations were a foreshadowing of the life of Jesus. This meaty unit study will help your family delight in the celebrations of the Bible holidays and give everyone a deeper understanding of their significance.

Family Christian Academy also offers a new, expanded edition of *What Your Child Needs to Know When* by Robin Scarlata. This reassuring and informative book is a great starter book for home educators. Mrs. Scarlata includes a major discussion of a philosophy of education, an explanation of state achievement tests, a section on teaching wisdom, which describes how to use the Bible as the core of the curriculum, and a major section of evaluation checklists. She lists all basic skills in all subject areas for grades K–8. Perhaps most importantly, she provides a Bible reading checklist and a character quality checklist. The materials presented, along with selected resources, will enable you to train your child to have a heart of wisdom (H.O.W.), which is Mrs. Scarlata's name for her teaching approach. This is an encouraging and informative book whether you are creating your own curriculum or using prepared materials.

Fireside Games
P.O. Box 82995
Portland, OR 97282-0995
503-231-8990

This is the source for a really neat card game called *Rhymes and 'Nyms™ Card Game.* This is a game that uses one-word rhymes, homonyms, synonyms, or antonyms. The dealer chooses a starter word and players must respond with a designated category of response from one of the above. The winner is the first person to get rid of all their cards. This game is a challenge as players try to come up with unique words. As an added benefit, players explore the nuances of language and reinforce spelling and pronunciation. The game is most appropriate for ages eight to adult and can be played with some variations, such as a speed version or a solitaire version.

Follett Home Education
5563 S. Archer Avenue
Chicago, IL 60638
800-554-5754

This thick catalog is full of books that we all use at incredible bargain prices. It features workbooks and texts from A Beka, Bob Jones, Macmillan, Modern Curriculum Press, Saxon, and many others.

Gallaudet University Press
800 Washington Avenue N.E.
Washington, DC 20002
800-451-1073

Do you have a hearing-impaired child? Are you doing a study of deafness? This is an incredible resource for either. The Gallaudet Press is the publishing arm of the only liberal arts university for deaf and hard-of-hearing students. Their catalog includes scholarly works, general interest works, children's books, and sign language books.

Thomas Geale Publications, Inc.
P.O. Box 370540
583 Sixth Street
Montara, CA 94037
800-544-5457

This company offers aids to creativity and problem solving. *Young Think* (for preschool or kindergarten); *Just Think, Books 1–7; Stretch Think, Books 1, 2, and 3;* and *Think Quest, Books 1–4* are activity books that explore different approaches to problem solving. For example, a child might be asked to design and describe a machine for washing dogs, or to design a machine to peel, slice, and put apples into jars. These books require no extra teaching aids, so preparation time is minimal. The literature clearly spells out the various levels of ability required for each activity.

Great Christian Books
229 South Bridge Street
P.O. Box 8000
Elkton, MD 21922-8000
800-775-5422

Almost anything you are looking for can be found here at a discount. This organization carries curriculum and general books from a variety of publishers and suppliers, and the savings are wonderful. If you're thinking of buying anything, check here first!

Hear an' Tell Adventures
320 Bunker Hill
Houston, TX 77024
Fax: 713-784-7689

Hear an' Tell Adventures offers a unique way to learn foreign languages, math facts, or Scripture memory. The creator, Patricia Al-Attas is a speech therapist working with learning disabled children. She is also a musician, composer, artist, writer, and conference speaker. These products bring together all of her talents to make learning fun. Her foreign language tapes introduce children to a new language by reading familiar stories with a careful pace and phrase-by-phrase translations. Materials are also available for math. *Musical Math* sets each series of counting into an easy-to-remember musical story. Patricia Al-Attas works with mnemonic numbers and has a tape called *Adding Is Easy.* Other materials are Scripture memory and Bible study aids.

Helping Hands
7532 Lakota Springs Drive
West Chester, OH 45069
513-755-8230

Home schooling mom Terry Lustig has written *The Blueprint for Excellence in Home Education.* She is a veteran home educator who helps us learn to go to school with God, solve problems, increase creativity, remain accountable, discipline our children, free ourselves from curriculum bondage, and live the lifestyle of home education. The book sells for about fifteen dollars plus shipping. Helpful appendices have some nice forms, book lists, and resource lists.

International Learning Systems of North America, Inc.
1000 112th Circle N., Suite 100
St. Petersburg, FL 33716
800-321-8322

Sue Dickson is the author and creator of the award-winning program *Sing, Spell, Read, and Write.* This is a multisensory approach to teaching reading that appeals to all learning styles. In thirty-six steps, this program will take your child to independent reading ability through catchy songs on cassettes, storybook readers, games, prizes, and a built-in lap desk/storage box. The materials are bright, colorful, and fun. Children learn through singing, cutting and pasting, playing games, and more. Also available is a manual and a training video to take you through the thirty-six steps of learning. This corporation also offers tapes entitled *Grammar Plus Kit, Remedial Reading and Spelling, Musical Math Facts, Songs of the U.S. Presidents, Songs of America's Freedoms, Grammar Songs Kit, States and Capitals Songs Kit,* and *Geography Songs Kit.* All these materials are very nicely done and work well with different types of learners. We have used and enjoyed several of these products in our home and highly recommend them.

J & K Schooling
5350 Sunset Lane
Loretto, MN 55357
612-479-2286

Finally, an affordable time line! Their basic set includes figures from a variety of disciplines. (We mounted ours on a big cardboard sewing board.) They also have the *Celebration Life Line* and an American history/presidential card game.

Keepers of the Faith
P.O. Box 100
Ironwood, MI 49938-0100
906-663-6681

Many feel that scouting and other activities are too value-neutral for their children. Keepers of the Faith is a program "that Jesus could join." It is a club for boys or girls that can be done at church or support group or with just your own family. Boys and girls each have a handbook and can earn achievement badges. For boys, some of the badges are for chess, electricity, and the use of a pocket-knife. For girls, some of the badges are for knitting, visitation, and housekeeping. Each can earn badges on Bible memory, pets, and many other subjects. For older teens or adults, *The Joy of Womanhood* by Susan Zakula is available. Keepers of the Faith also has an encouraging newsletter and a complete catalog of crafts, supplies, resources, how-to books, and Christian reading selections. If you are tired of sending your family off in different directions for club activities, you must check this out.

KidsCo
Family Legacy
Suite 152, 8510 N. Knoxville
Peoria, IL 61615
800-207-7229

Do you have an eight- to twelve-year-old looking for ways to make money? KidsCo can help your child begin his own business with a focus on biblical principles. The child learns Bible verses, forms a biblical worldview of marketplace concepts, and builds business skills. The program teaches your child planning, goal-setting, recordkeeping, and time management. These materials look very interesting. My six-year-old wants to start a pet-sitting business. We will use these materials to launch her venture.

Kits 'n' Kaboodles
35819 Ramada Lane
Yucaipa, CA 92399
909-790-4050

Kits, kits, kits, and kaboodles of stuff for arts and crafts, geography and civiliza-
tion, history, industrial arts and science, nature, science, and virtue and values.
This is no ordinary kit catalog. Yes, you will find bead kits and skeleton bones,
but you will also find house framing construction kits, telephone kits, and a prairie
bonnet pattern. This is a neat catalog with lots of stuff for the hands-on family
learner.

The Learning Heart Workshop
HC 33, Box 3265
Boise, ID 83706-9708
208-385-9069

*The Learning Heart Memory System* was developed by Lynn Barry to address a
common problem in any area of study—memory work. This notebook is uniquely
designed, containing pockets for daily, weekly, and monthly review of small memory cards. The cards, called either Vis-Ed or Compact Fact Cards, are available in
a blank form or for SAT preparation, foreign language drills, algebra, sciences,
social studies, history, statistics, and more. You may use the preprinted cards or
create your own for any level of vocabulary, phonics, spelling, math, music, or
Bible memorization. You can customize the system for any subject.

The other aspect of this family business is *The Language Connection,* a language
arts and Latin correspondence course. A monthly newsletter contains four weeks
of Latin instruction and assignments, a feature article that teaches background
and historical information, four weeks of reading assignments and dictation passages from literary classics, and four weeks of writing assignments.

Library and Educational Services
8784 Valley View Drive
P.O. Box 146
Berrien Springs, MI 49103
616-471-1400

The lowest prices on book series you may want to collect, such as *The Sugar Creek
Gang, The Mandie Series, Men and Women of Faith Series,* or *Great Illustrated Classics.* Check their catalog before you invest in any of these resources.

Little Folks Visuals
39620 Entrepreneur Lane
Palm Desert, CA 92211
619-345-5571
800-537-7227

Do you have children who need to touch and feel things before they learn? Little Folks Visuals has something for you. From Bible sets, to nursery rhymes, to fairy tales, to math concepts, to social studies, to science, to dolls and games and puppets, Little Folks has something for your hands-on learner. We especially enjoyed working with "Early Math Concepts" with our five-year-old. She loved the colorful fish, dolls, balls, and numbers used to illustrate basic math concepts. If you want to make Bible stories come alive, there is nothing like felt figures that your children can touch and feel to help them to remember the stories. Mine also enjoy using the figures to act out Bible stories and tell them in their own words. Little Folks Visuals can help you to make a lasting impact on your child.

M & M Software
P.O. Box 15769
Long Beach, CA 90815-0795
800-642-6163

This company has educational public domain and shareware software as low as three dollars per disk. There is something for everyone in this little catalog.

McQueen Publishing
RR 1, Box 264
Tiskilwa, IL 61368
815-646-4591

The McQueen program offers an integrated phonics and language arts program for preschool, kindergarten, and elementary grades. Along with a teacher's guide, the books are simple and charming. They also offer a program for remedial reading for grades 1–12.

Memory Joggers
24 Nuevo
Irvine, CA 92612
888-854-9400

Memory Joggers is a series of interactive picture cards that tell visual stories to help children learn their multiplication and division facts. The system employs multiple learning modalities—seeing bright illustrations, hearing lively stories, speaking, drawing, and moving through suggested games. This is a delightful way to learn multiplication and division facts.

National Writing Institute
810 Damon Court
Houston, TX 77006
800-688-5375

David Marks is the creator of the popular *Writing Strands* program. The program teaches rules of writing as children need to know them, not in some artificial context. The detailed instructions in the assignments teach how to write in four major modes—argumentative, explanatory, research and report, and creative. Each book covers ninety days of training and yields a report, an essay, or a piece of fiction. As a writer, I believe these materials look very interesting. They foster a positive attitude toward the writing process and provide a lot of encouragement for the student.

> Pencil Playground
> Estella Graphics
> RR 3, Box 369
> Montrose, PA 18801
> 717-278-4504

This is an interesting creative writing curriculum in a fill-in-the-blank format for the elementary level. The graphics are clear and appealing and are designed to nurture enthusiasm and appreciation in your child for his or her own creative writing. Through the course, the child writes a story about his name, an autumn story, a thankfulness story, a story about a snapshot, an autobiography, and more. My oldest can't wait to get her pencils and markers out to do this program! It really looks like fun.

> Pleasant Company
> 8400 Fairway Place
> Middleton, WI 53562-0998
> 608-836-4848

The creator of these materials is a genius. The American Girl dolls, although a bit pricey, are a big hit. The company has taken that popularity and created educational materials for each segment of history represented by each doll. One curriculum unit, called *America at School,* examines education during five periods in American history. In addition, a teacher's guide is available for each of the American Girls that includes maps, background information, and project suggestions. Another book called *Five Plays: Teacher's Guide and Scripts* can be used in a group setting to stage an American Girl production. Of course, the company also offers the dolls and their accessories, the sets of books, a monthly magazine, and many other books, kits, and materials. I wish I had thought of this!

> Progeny Press
> 200 Spring Street, Suite A
> Eau Claire, WI 54703-3225
> 715-833-5259

Progeny Press offers Bible-based study guides for literature. Each study includes vocabulary exercises, comprehension, analysis, and application questions, introduction of literary terms, background information, discussion of related biblical themes, suggested activities related to the reading, an answer key, and more. Guides start at the lower elementary grades with titles such as *Frog and Toad Together.* Upper elementary, middle school, and high school titles are available as well. Some of the high school titles include *Hamlet, To Kill a Mockingbird,* and *The Adventures of Huckleberry Finn.* I used *The Josephina Story Quilt* and *The Best Christmas Pageant Ever* with my kids and enjoyed them a great deal.

Rainbow Re-Source Center
P.O. Box 491
Kewanee, IL 61443
309-937-3385

A meaty catalog of learning tools for homes and schools that has everything a parent or student might need. A wonderful assortment of books and supplies.

The Re-Print Corporation
P.O. Box 830677
Birmingham, AL 35283-0677
800-248-9171

This thick catalog bills itself as a source for deep-discount school supplies, teaching aids, and preschool supplies. If you're looking for lots of art supplies, bulletin board stuff, or other teaching helps, these prices are pretty good. The colorful catalog is worth taking a look at before going to your local retailer for these items.

Royal Fireworks Publishing Co.
First Avenue, Box 399
Unionville, NY 10988
814-726-4444

This company offers an interesting catalog called *Materials for Educating Gifted Children* as well as a monthly magazine called *Our Gifted Children.* The catalog contains materials for educators, parents, and children, including math and science materials, novels, and creative thinking materials.

Ruark's Home and School Accessories
8232 N. County Road 150 East
Pittsboro, IN 46167-9466
317-892-4791

A nice selection of reading books and fun stuff, such as craft kits, doll bonnets, coonskin caps, and kites.

Shareware Source
P.O. Box 925

Greenville, SC 29602-0925
864-232-7102

Over five hundred shareware programs for IBM-compatible computers for as low as two dollars per disk.

Small Ventures
11023 Watterson Drive
Dallas, TX 75228
214-681-1728

A nice catalog featuring a little bit of everything, especially Bonnie Dettmer's *Phonics for Reading and Spelling* and Ann Ward's *Learning at Home* series and lots more. Do-it-yourself curriculum constructors will appreciate this catalog.

Timberdoodle Company
E. 1510 Spencer Lake Road
Shelton, WA 98584
800-478-0672

Variety, variety, variety—that is what Timberdoodle is all about. Their motto is "Meeting the Needs of Home Educators." You will find the everyday fare and a lot of unusual items in their catalog.

Whole Heart Ministries
P.O. Box 228
Route 1, Box 617A
Walnut Springs, TX 76690
817-797-2142

Whole Heart Ministries is the creator of *Educating the Whole-Hearted Child.* This is one of the best books I have ever read about how to approach the spiritual, emotional, and academic training of our children. They also have a catalog business of family-affirming books. Titles are available on Bible study, general home schooling, language arts, children's books, fine arts, and more. The catalog itself is delightful, with little snippets of wisdom and encouragement.

*Music*

Davidsons Music
6727 Metcalf
Shawnee Mission, KS 66204
913-262-4982

Madonna Woods has created a piano course for Christians. This is a boon for home schoolers because the explanations are clear and easy to understand. Ms.

Woods has a master's degree and many years of teaching experience. The course starts at the beginning of piano training and explains all the basics of music. The full course is in six levels from preparatory through level five, and all the lessons are based on religious music. A workbook is accompanied by the encouraging reassurance of Ms. Woods on a cassette tape. It is like having a loving, caring piano teacher right there—on tape. Davidsons Music has a full catalog of many interesting items, such as play-by-ear courses, video piano lessons, songbooks, guitar music books, and more.

Praise Hymn
P.O. Box 1325
Taylors, SC 29687
800-729-2821

This is a K–7 music series, with one thirty-minute lesson per week recommended (a total of thirty-four lessons). The lessons cover elementary music theory and notation, singing, instrument studies, classical listening appreciation, composer studies, composition, harmonization and flutophone (grade three), and recorder (grade four) instruction. You don't need to be a musician to use these materials! If you want to have a systematic way of exposing your home educated children to music, these bright, attractive, inexpensive books might be useful for your family.

The Progressive Pianist
North Island Productions
14950 Sun Forest Drive
Penn Valley, CA 95946
916-432-5355

This music course was designed specifically for home schoolers. The work incorporates music pieces, theory worksheets, exercise programs for finger development, studies on the science of music, great composers, and information on other types of instruments. The books, accompanied by tape sessions, are available in levels one through five. Supplemental material is available through Christmas music, hymns, and performance pieces. The words to the practice songs emphasize important family concepts such as thrift, politeness, father's involvement, mothers at home, reading, or working hard at school. This is a method that the whole family can use at a great price. The cost of the starter kit (which can cover a year or so of work) is less than what one month of private lessons would cost. These materials are very well done and the tapes are professional. The program is thorough and unique.

### Reading

Play 'n' Talk
7105 Manzanita Street
Carlsbad, CA 92008
619-438-4338
800-472-7525

This complete phonics program has been around for thirty-five years and is now available on records, cassette tapes, or CDs. The recordings feature a professional teacher. They save the home teacher preparation and training time and they include motivational games. Presentation is multisensory and has been successful with children, adults, and those with learning problems. The set comes with student books, alphabet cards, a teacher-training video, an instructor's manual, and more.

### Science

Backyard Scientist, Inc.
P.O. Box 16966
Irvine, CA 92623
714-551-2392

These award-winning books are delightful! They can be the basis of a science fair project or the backbone of your science curriculum. Jane Hoffman, author and science educator, believes that early, positive, hands-on experiences in science are essential for a lifetime interest in learning. Her work has been acknowledged by the National Science Foundation as a unique teaching resource.

There are five volumes of *The Backyard Scientist* each full of experiments, thought-provoking questions, and fun. The original book, series one, and series three are for ages 4–12. Series four is for all ages and series two is for children ages 9–12. She has also recently released *Exploring Earthworms with Me* and plans to release *A Science Wonderland for the Very Young*. Recently added to her repertoire are a series of science kits that my children absolutely loved. *Magic Slime, Magic of Rocks,* and *Magic Crystals* can form the basis for a fun unit of discovery for you and your children. Each kit includes a twenty-four-page experiment book with experiments and projects.

Finally, Ms. Hoffman has available a booklet called *Backyard Scientist Parent Guide to Teaching Science*. She wrote this book for home schooling parents who want to use her materials but want to ensure that their students are learning the material typically taught in a school setting. For each grade level, she discusses the scientific concepts to be covered, giving you the peace of mind of thoughtfully building a hands-on science curriculum for your child. With her books, supplemented by some general reading from library books, you could plan a thorough, exciting, fun, hands-on science curriculum. If that is your goal, check out these materials.

Bible Science Association, Inc.
P.O. Box 260
Zimmerman, MN 55398-0260
800-422-4253

The purpose of this group is to teach the literal truth of the Genesis account of divine creation and a universal flood. They also have a radio ministry and offer seminars and a magazine. Their book catalog has over two hundred titles relating to creation and the flood and creation/evolution issues.

Braden Road Farm and Garden
Rt. 1, Box 55
Walla Walla, WA 99362
509-522-4253

If you are interested in gardening, you must see this catalog. They sell a complete line of seeds as well as offering a gardening unit-study packet. It is a multilevel study for families to use to learn about gardening. Really fun and informative!

Castle Heights Press
1610 W. Highland, Box 228
Chicago, IL 60660
800-763-7148

Castle Heights Press offers *Science Notebooks* and other materials with simple, easy-to-understand procedures, common equipment, directions on how to make scientific write-ups, questions to help the student in critical thinking, and applications to the real world. The science notebooks are nicely written and can be used to create a real science lab experience in the home.

Creation Resource Foundation
P.O. Box 570
El Dorado, CA 95623
800-497-1454

These beautiful materials seek to integrate the study of science, Bible, and history. They will help you and your family to develop a confidently biblical worldview. Materials available include textbooks, videos, and workbooks.

Delta Education
Hands-On Science
P.O. Box 3000
Nashua, NH 03061-3000
800-442-5444

This bright, colorful catalog features science kits, books, and other items. Many of the materials are geared toward the classroom setting, but we regularly order our butterfly kits and a few other items from here.

Home Training Tools
2827 Buffalo Horn Drive
Laurel, MT 59044
800-860-6272

This catalog offers over eight hundred products for the serious science student. They have everything from field guides to microscopes—all at reasonable prices.

Dissection kits, preserved materials, and rocks and minerals are a few of the other items available.

Helen Nelson
P.O. Box 251
Wheaton, IL 60187
708-653-8750

Mrs. Nelson has produced a series of unit studies for the whole family to enjoy. There are currently three titles available: *The Deep Blue Sea: A Study of Oceans; Buzz, Chirp, and Hum: A Study of Insects;* and *The Sun and Beyond: A Study of the Solar System.* Each book sells for fifteen dollars and is full of ideas and information for multiple ages of children. The studies are structured to last twelve weeks. Each incorporates science, Bible, art, and language arts. There are weekly outlines, vocabulary lists, bibliographies, and project instructions. If you are looking for thorough, fun science unit studies, I highly recommend these. Your whole family will learn to love these!

Media Angels
16520 S. Tamiami Trail, #18-193
Ft. Myers, FL 33908
email: whitlock@sprynet.com
web site: http://www.noahzark.com

This is a publishing company offering a series of science and creation unit studies created by home schooling moms Felice Gerwitz and Jill Whitlock. Their cornerstone book is called *Teaching Science and Having Fun,* which features a scope and sequence for all levels and provides a wealth of information about what and how to teach. A small booklet called *The Science Fair Handbook* is a complete, inexpensive guide to organizing a fair as well as helping your child choose and prepare a topic. Their other publications are called *Creation Science, Creation Geology, Creation Astronomy,* and *Creation Anatomy.* Each volume provides an exciting unit study including reading lists, experiments, vocabulary, spelling and grammar, other language arts ideas, math reinforcement, geography and history ideas, and art and music ideas. These books are a great aid in teaching science and having fun!

Science-by-Mail™
Museum of Science
Science Park
Boston, MA 02114-1099
800-729-3300

This is an innovative program whereby your child (grades 4–9) is paired with a scientist pen pal to work on science activity packets. In each packet, they will perform eight to nine hands-on experiments and may correspond with their scientist pen pal on their projects. Send for their brochure to see if this will work for your family.

Solomon Resource Guide
Solomon Publishing
5830 Sovereign Drive
Cincinnati, OH 45241
513-489-3033

Are you interested in teaching science without textbooks? These resource guides look fascinating. Offered in two volumes, *Solomon Resource Guides* provide over forty different thematic units that cover an entire elementary science scope and sequence. Each chapter contains teaching resources, reading selections, and activities in creative writing or the arts. Volume one covers weather, the solar system, plants, animals, energy, and machines. Volume two covers the earth, habitats, the human body, matter, and ecology. I reviewed some sample pages on the subject of ecology and they really look great!

Tobin's Lab
P.O. Box 6503
Glendale, AZ 85312-6503
800-522-4776 (orders)
602-843-3520 (help line)

This catalog is the brainchild of a home schooling family that loves science. The products are arranged in the order of creation. For example, products on the subject of color, light, and solar power are listed under the first day of creation. The fifth day offers materials about birds and marine biology. They do not feature an entire curriculum, but if you need a camera kit or a frog to dissect, you can find it in this delightful catalog. If you are into hands-on science in your home, you've got to look at this catalog.

TOPS Learning Systems
10970 S. Mulino Road
Canby, OR 97013

This group publishes an idea magazine/catalog that is distributed free to educators twice a year. Each issue features a couple of experiments and some ideas. The purpose of the catalog is to sell their learning modules or activity kits. A fun catalog!

## Magazines for Parents

*An Encouraging Word*
P.O. Box 599
Idabel, OK 74745

What a wonderful magazine! I wish it had been available years ago. The magazine is dedicated to providing encouragement, featuring articles on topics such as marriage, child training, herbal remedies and nutrition, arts for the home, home schooling, recipes, resources, and more. It is like an encouraging friend coming to your mailbox to share ideas and support your lifestyle. They carry a few products in their small catalog, such as Playmobil toys, Victorian doll houses and furniture, a choice selection of books, and a really neat product called Lauren's Locket. This is an ingenious idea; it's a pretty locket that comes with Scripture inserts to wear in the space where the picture would usually go. They can also be used as a reminder to work on certain character traits or as a witnessing tool. What a neat idea! What a wonderful magazine!

*Coming Home*
P.O. Box 367
Savannah, TN 38372-0367
615-722-5026

This is a really nice magazine, although not specifically about home schooling. It offers articles on home education, home births, home business, home crafts, and so on. Very encouraging and spiritually grounded.

F.U.N.—Family Unschoolers Network
1688 Belhaven Woods Court
Pasadena, MD 21122-3727
410-360-6265
http://members.aol.com/FUNNews

Also ask for their catalog of F.U.N. Books.

*Growing without Schooling*
2269 Massachusetts Avenue
Cambridge, MA 02140
617-864-3100

Also has a catalog of books from John Holt's bookstore.

*Home Education Magazine*
P.O. Box 1083
Tonasket, WA 98855
509-486-1351

*Home School Digest*
Wisdom Publications
P.O. Box 249
West, TX 76691

*The Home School Exchange*
26 Colony Street
St. Augustine, FL 32095-1208
904-824-8247

A free newspaper that publishes free classified ads for private parties. Use to sell books, curriculum, and so on.

*Home Schooling Today*
P.O. Box 1425
Melrose, FL 32666

*Moore Report International*
Moore Foundation
P.O. Box 1
Camus, WA 98607
206-835-5500

*The Parents Review*
Charlotte Mason Research and Supply
P.O. Box 172
Stanton, NJ 08885

This magazine features articles from the original Charlotte Mason magazine as well as contemporary articles about Mason's teaching philosophy.

*Patriarch*
P.O. Box 725
Rolla, MO 65402

This is a magazine dedicated to giving men a regular diet of biblical teaching and application in order to equip them to be godly leaders in family, church, and society.

*Practical Home Schooling*
P.O. Box 1250
Fenton, MO 63026-1850
800-346-6322

*The Teaching Home*
Box 20219
Portland, OR 97294
503-253-9633

*Quit You Like Men*
152 Maple Lane
Harriman, TN 38663

This is a men's magazine devoted to the pursuit of true Christian manliness. The name refers to 1 Corinthians 16:13–14: "Watch ye, stand fast in the faith, quit you like men, be strong. Let all your things be done with charity" (KJV).

## Magazines for Students

*Calliope—World History for Young People*
7 School Street
Peterborough, NH 03458

Features articles about world history, arts, crafts, adventure, and biographies for ages eight to fifteen. Offers an exciting look at world history for the young historian.

*Cobblestone—The History Magazine for Young People*
7 School Street
Peterborough, NH 03458

Each issue has a theme focusing on biographical and historical information, travel, plays, recipes, crafts, and activities for ages eight to fifteen. Very nicely done. Also has a nice catalog of history resources.

*Cricket*
P.O. Box 300
Peru, IL 61354

Fiction, poetry, nonfiction for ages nine to fourteen.

*Faces*
7 School Street
Peterborough, NH 03458

Fiction, legends, tales, and crafts based on an anthropological theme for ages eight to fifteen. Recent issues have been dedicated to rice, insects and spiders, and Ireland.

God's World Publications
P.O. Box 2330
Asheville, NC 28802

A children's newspaper available twenty-six times a year for grades pre-K to adult. News stories show how God is alive in the events around us every day. Plus, they have teaching resources each week and full color posters almost every month. Discounts are available for quantity orders. Also ask for their educational catalog— a nice collection of resources for the home school.

*Highlights for Children*
803 Church Street
Honesdale, PA 18431

An old favorite that has stories, nonfiction, and lots of regular features like hidden pictures. Most appropriate for ages eight to twelve.

*Hopscotch for Girls*
*Boys Quest*
P.O. Box 164
Bluffton, OH 45817
800-358-4732

Really nice magazines with strong family values and *no ads*. Interesting fiction, nonfiction, puzzles, crafts, science, and more.

*Kindred Spirits*
6628 E. Beryl Avenue
Scottsdale, AZ 85253

This is a lovely magazine for Christian young women from ages ten to twenty to encourage them to walk in Jesus' steps. Features articles, book reviews, recipes, and more.

*National Geographic World*
1145 Street NW
Washington, DC 20036

*National Geographic* for ages eight to twelve.

*Nature Friend*
22777 State Road 119
Goshen, IN 46526

Animals, science, and nature projects for ages eight to fourteen published by Pilgrim Publishers, a nondenominational Christian publisher. This magazine is extremely popular with home school families.

*New Attitude*
6920 SE Hogan
Gresham, OR 97080

Magazine for home schooled teens.

*Odyssey*
Cobblestone Publishing, Inc.
7 School Street
Peterborough, NH 03458

Do you have a young science enthusiast? This is a very well done science publication for middle childhood. Each issue features a major topic as well as puzzles, activities, and science news.

*Ranger Rick Nature Magazine*
8925 Leesburg Pike
Vienna, VA 22184

Wildlife and out-of-doors material for ages six to nine.

# *Appendix B*

# Home School Organizations

## Statewide Home School Organizations

These organizations can keep you informed concerning legal matters, events, state newsletters, and local support groups in your state. Please include a self-addressed, stamped envelope when writing.

*Alabama.* Christian Home Education Fellowship of Alabama, Box 563, Alabaster, AL 35007, 205-664-2232.

*Alaska.* Alaska Private and Home Educators Association, Box 141764, Anchorage, AK 99514, 907-696-0641.

*Arizona.* Arizona Families for Home Education, Box 4661, Scottsdale, AZ 85261, 602-443-0612.

*Arkansas.* Arkansas Christian Home Educators Association, Box 4025, N. Little Rock, AR 72190, 501-758-9099.

*California.* Christian Home Educators Association of California, Box 2009, Norwalk, CA 90651, 800-564-2432.

*Colorado.* Christian Home Educators of Colorado, 3739 E. 4th Ave., Denver, CO 80206, 303-388-1888.

*Connecticut.* The Education Association of Christian Homeschoolers, 25 Field Stone Run, Farmington, CT 06032, 800-205-7844; out-of-state 860-677-4538.

*Delaware.* Delaware Home Education Association, Suite 172, 1712 Marsh Rd., Wilmington, DE 19810, 302-475-0574.

*Florida.* Florida at Home, 4644 Adanson, Orlando, FL 32804, 407-740-8877.

*Georgia.* Georgia Home Education Association, 245 Buckeye Lane, Fayetteville, GA 30214, 770-461-3657.

*Hawaii.* Christian Homeschoolers of Hawaii, 91-824 Oama St., Ewa Beach, HI 96706, 808-689-6398.

*Idaho.* Pocatello Regional Christian Home Educators, 13191 N. Smith Rd., Chubbuck, ID 83202, 208-237-8163.

*Illinois.* Illinois Christian Home Educators, Box 261, Zion, IL 60099, 847-670-7150.

*Indiana.* Indiana Association of Home Educators, 850 N. Madison Ave., Greenwood, IN 46142, 317-859-1202.

*Iowa.* Network of Iowa Christian Home Educators, Box 158, Dexter, IA 50070, 800-723-0438; out-of-state 515-830-1614.

*Kansas.* Christian Home Educators Confederation of Kansas, Box 3564, Shawnee Mission, KS 66203, 316-945-0810.

*Kentucky.* Christian Home Educators of Kentucky, 691 Howardstown Rd., Hodgenville, KY 42748, 502-358-9270.

*Louisiana.* Christian Home Educators Fellowship of Louisiana, Box 74292, Baton Rouge, LA 70874, 504-775-9709.

*Maine.* Homeschoolers of Maine, HC 62, Box 24, Hope, ME 04847, 207-763-4251.

*Maryland.* Maryland Association of Christian Home Educators, Box 247, Point of Rocks, MD 21777, 301-607-4284.

*Massachusetts.* Massachusetts Homeschool Organization of Parent Educators, 5 Atwood Rd., Cheffy Valley, MA 01611, 508-544-7948.

*Michigan.* Information Network for Christian Homes, 4934 Cannonsburg Rd., Belmont, MI 49306, 616-874-5656.

*Minnesota.* Minnesota Association of Christian Home Educators, Box 32308, Fridley, MN 55432, 612-717-9070.

*Mississippi.* Mississippi Home Educators Association, Box 945, Brookhaven, MS 39601, 601-833-9110.

*Missouri.* Missouri Association of Teaching Christian Homes, 307 E. Ash St. #146, Columbia, MO 65201, 573-443-8217.

*Montana.* Montana Coalition of Home Educators, Box 43, Gallatin Gateway, MT 59730, 406-587-6163.

*Nebraska.* Nebraska Christian Home Educators Association, Box 57041, Lincoln, NE 68505, 402-423-4297.

*Nevada.* Northern Nevada Home Schools, Box 21323, Reno, NV 89515, 702-852-6647.

*New Hampshire.* Christian Home Educators of New Hampshire, Box 961, Manchester, NH 03105, 603-569-2343.

*New Jersey.* Education Network of Christian Home Schoolers of New Jersey, 120 Mayfair Ln., Mt. Laurel, NJ 08054, 609-222-4283.

*New Mexico.* Christian Association of Parent Educators of New Mexico, Box 25046, Albuquerque, NM 87125, 505-898-8548.

*New York.* New York State Loving Education at Home, Box 88, Cato, NY 13033, 716-346-0939.

*North Carolina.* North Carolinians for Home Education, 419 N. Boylan Ave., Raleigh, NC 27603, 919-834-6243.

*North Dakota.* North Dakota Home School Association, Box 7400, Bismarck, ND 58507-7400, 701-223-4080.

*Ohio.* Christian Home Educators of Ohio, 430 N. Court St., Circleville, OH 43113, 614-474-3177.

*Oklahoma.* Christian Home Educators Fellowship of Oklahoma, Box 471363, Tulsa, OK 74147, 918-583-7323.

*Oregon.* Oregon Christian Home Education Association Network, 2515 NE 37th, Portland, OR 97212, 503-288-1285.

*Pennsylvania.* Christian Home School Association of Pennsylvania, Box 3603, York, PA 17402, 717-661-2428.

*Rhode Island.* Rhode Island Guild of Home Teachers, Box 11, Hope, RI 02831, 401-821-7700.

*South Carolina.* South Carolina Association of Independent Home Schools, Box 2104, Irmo, SC 29063, 803-551-1003.

*South Dakota.* South Dakota Christian Home Schools, Box 528, Black Hawk, SD 57718, 605-923-1893.

*Tennessee.* Tennessee Home Education Association, 3677 Richbriar Ct., Nashville, TN 37211, 615-834-3529.

*Texas.* Home-Oriented Private Education for Texas, Box 59876, Dallas, TX 75229, 214-358-2221.

*Utah.* Utah Christian Home Schoolers, Box 3942, Salt Lake City, UT 84110, 801-296-7198.

*Vermont.* Christian Home Educators of Vermont, 214 N. Prospect #105, Burlington, VT 05401, 802-658-4561.

*Virginia.* Home Educators Association of Virginia, Box 6745, Richmond, VA 23230, 804-288-1608.

*Washington.* Washington Association of Teaching Christian Homes, N. 2904 Dora Rd., Spokane, WA 99212, 509-922-4811.

*West Virginia.* Christian Home Educators of West Virginia, Box 8770, S. Charleston, WV 25303, 304-776-4664.

*Wisconsin.* Wisconsin Christian Home Educators Association, 2307 Carmel Ave., Racine, WI 53405, 414-637-5127.

*Wyoming.* Homeschoolers of Wyoming, Box 907, Evansville, WY 82636, 307-237-4383.

This information is provided courtesy of *The Teaching Home* magazine.

## Other Organizations

Home School Legal Defense Association
P.O. Box 159
Paeonian Springs, VA 22129
540-338-5600

Provides legal services to home school families (for a membership fee) who are experiencing legal conflicts with local authorities regarding home schooling.

National Homeschool Association
P.O. Box 290
Hartland, MI 48353-0290

Provides a quarterly magazine, an annual conference, networking, and referrals.

# Appendix C

# The Law in the Fifty States

The home schooling laws of the United States take one of three forms:

1. Home education is allowed as a specific exemption to the state's compulsory attendance laws.
2. Home schools are regulated as private schools subject to only minimal regulation.
3. A specific statutory scheme deals with the establishment and regulation of home schools.

Each state's law is briefly examined below.

## Summary of State Laws

The laws for home education are changing rapidly. Before you begin home schooling, check with your state to verify the status of the laws. Legislators and regulators are constantly responding to the growth of the home schooling movement. You must be in compliance with the latest law.

The information below is not to be construed as legal advice. For competent legal advice, consult your private attorney or the Home School Legal Defense Association (see address in appendix B).

### Alabama

Coordinator-Student Instructional Services
Gordon Persons Building
P.O. Box 302101
Montgomery, AL 36130-2101
334-242-9700

*See Code of Alabama, section 16-1-11 et. seq.* Requires that children be instructed by a competent private tutor, being a person who holds a certificate issued by the state superintendent of education. Must teach the same branches of study as the public school, for at least three hours a day between 8:00 A.M. and 4:00 P.M. and must use the English language in giving instruction. Parents must contact the local school superintendent stating intent to home school. Must maintain a register of work, showing daily the hours used for instruction. Provision is made for a waiver of teacher certification where the child is enrolled in a church school, such as a church satellite school.

## Alaska

Alaska Department of Education
Office of Teacher Education and Certification
801 West 10th Street, Suite 200
Juneau, AK 99801-1894
907-465-2026

See Alaska Statute 14.45.100-200. Parents may teach their own children in a private or religious school (which has numerous requirements) or as a home school in which only that family participates. To operate as a private or religious school, they must file a notice of intent, maintain attendance records, have a 180-day schedule and take a standardized test at grades four, six, and eight. If your school is a home school in which your children are the only students taught, you are not required to have fire, safety, or asbestos inspections and do not need a corporal punishment policy, whereas the private or religious school must provide them.

## Arizona

Arizona Department of Education
1535 West Jefferson
Phoenix, AZ 85007
602-255-4361

See Arizona Revised Statutes 15-310 et. seq. Parents must file an affidavit of intent with the superintendent of schools. Testing is not required while the child is receiving home instruction, but testing is required if the child subsequently enters public school. Home schooled children may enroll part-time for certain classes and are allowed to participate in interscholastic athletic competition subject to district requirements.

## Arkansas

Arkansas Department of Education
4 State Capitol Mall
Little Rock, AR 72201-1071
501-682-4475

*See Arkansas Statutes Annotated, section 6-15-501 et. seq.* Parents who wish to home school may do so after giving written notice to their local superintendent and providing curriculum information. Requires that each child age seven or older must take a standardized achievement test. If results are unsatisfactory, a student who is eight or older shall be enrolled in a regular school unless the test is retaken with satisfactory results.

### California

Office of Nonpublic Schools Unit
721 Capitol Mall, P.O. Box 944272
Sacramento, CA 94244-2720
916-445-4338

*See California Education Code, section 48200, et. seq.* Provides three vehicles for home instruction: (1) private tutoring by a tutor who holds a valid California teaching credential, (2) enrolling in a private full-time day school, or (3) pursuing independent study through the local public school system.

### Colorado

Colorado State Board of Education
Department of Education
201 East Colfax Avenue
Denver, CO 80203
303-866-6817

*See Colorado Revised Statutes 22-33-104.5.* Recognizes home-based education as a legitimate alternative to classroom attendance. Program shall include no less than 172 days per year, averaging four hours per day. There are also curriculum requirements. Parents must notify the local school district of intent to home educate. Child must be evaluated at grades three, five, seven, nine, and eleven either by standardized achievement test or by other qualified evaluator. Standardized test score must be at or above the 13th percentile to continue to be eligible for home education.

### Connecticut

Department of Education
P.O. Box 2219
Hartford, CT 06145
203-566-5458

*See Connecticut General Statutes Annotated 10-184.* Parents must file notice of intent with superintendent of schools. Education received must be equivalent to the studies taught in the public schools. An annual portfolio review will be held with the parent and school officials to determine if instruction in the required courses has been given.

## Delaware

State of Delaware Department of Public Instruction
Townsend Building
P.O. Box 1402
Dover, DE 19903-1402
800-624-5434

*See Delaware Code 14-2702 et. seq.* Children are exempt from compulsory attendance if it can be shown to the satisfaction of the superintendent of schools that a child is elsewhere receiving regular and thorough instruction in the subjects prescribed for the public schools of the state. Home schooling parents must report the enrollment, age, and attendance of each student to the state board of education on or before July 31.

## Florida

State of Florida Department of Education
844 Florida Educational Center
Tallahassee, FL 32301
904-488-8974

*See Florida Statutes Annotated 232.01.* Parents may home educate if they either (1) hold a valid Florida teaching certificate, or (2) notify superintendent of intent to home school, maintain a portfolio of records and materials, and provide an annual educational evaluation.

## Georgia

Georgia Department of Education
Twin Towers East
Atlanta, GA 30334-5001
404-656-2446

*See Code of Georgia Annotated 20-2-690.* Parents may teach their children at home but must submit a declaration of intent to home school to the superintendent of schools. Parents who teach their own must have at least a high school diploma or a G.E.D. If a parent teaches children outside their own family, they must have at least a baccalaureate degree. The course of study must include reading, language arts, math, social studies, and science and must provide 180 school days of instruction of at least four and one-half hours per day for each twelve-month period. Standardized tests are required every three years after third grade. The home teacher must submit an annual progress assessment for each of the areas of study above.

*Hawaii*

Department of Education
Office of Instructional Services
P.O. Box 2360
Honolulu, HI 96813

*See Hawaii Revised Statutes, section 298-9(a) and Hawaii Administration Rules, title 8, subtitle 2, chapter 12.* Home schoolers must notify the local public school of their intention to home educate on a specific form provided by the department or via a letter. Home teachers do not need certification, but must keep a record of curriculum and arrange for standardized testing at grades three, six, eight, and ten. Testing may be arranged through the local public school. Parents must submit an annual report of the child's progress to the principal of the local school.

*Idaho*

Idaho Department of Education
P.O. Box 83720
Boise, ID 83720
800-432-4601

*See Idaho Code 33-202.* Parents shall cause the child to attend a public, private, or parochial school unless the child is otherwise comparably instructed. Children are allowed to enroll in selected public school classes or activities.

*Illinois*

Illinois State Board of Education
100 North First Street
Springfield, IL 62777
217-782-3950

*See Illinois Compiled Statutes 5/26-1.* Compulsory school attendance is required for children between the ages of seven and sixteen, except where the child is attending a private or parochial school and the children are being taught the same branches of education as in the public school and the instruction is in English. A specific case, *People v. Levinson* (90 N.E. 2nd 213), determined that home schools were to be considered private schools. Illinois families are not required to register, submit statements of assurance, or seek state approval for their home schools.

*Indiana*

Indiana Department of Education
Room 229, State House
Indianapolis, IN 46204-2798
317-232-9100

*See Indiana Statutes Annotated 20-8.1-3-17 and 20-8.1-3-34.* Children must attend a public school unless they are being provided with instruction equivalent to that given in the public schools. Home schools must keep attendance records and register with the state when requested.

### Iowa

Department of Education
Grimes State Office Building
Des Moines, IA 50319-0146
515-281-5001

*See Iowa Code Annotated 299.1.* Parent may home school if child is provided with competent private instruction and parent files a report to the school district on forms provided by the school and parent ensures that child is evaluated annually.

### Kansas

Kansas State Education Building
120 East 10th Street
Topeka, KS 66612
913-296-3201

*See Kansas Statutes Annotated 72-1111.* Parents may home school only if they meet all the statutory requirements of a private school. Home school must meet statutory course of instruction requirements, children must be taught by a competent instructor, and instruction must be in English for the prescribed time.

### Kentucky

Kentucky Department of Education
500 Mero Street
Frankfort, KY 40601
502-564-4770

*See Kentucky Revised Statutes 159.010 et. seq.* Parents must notify board of education of intent to home school, instruction must take place 175 days per year in the English language and in the branches of study that are taught in the public schools.

### Louisiana

Department of Education
Home Study Program
P.O. Box 94064
Baton Rouge, LA 70804-9064
504-342-3473

*See Louisiana Revised Statutes 17:236 and 17:236.1.* Parent must submit application for home study and must submit satisfactory evidence that the program of instruction is of a quality at least equal to that offered in the public schools.

### Maine

Maine State Department of Education
23 State House Station
Augusta, ME 04333-0023
207-287-5922

*See Maine Revised Statutes Annotated 20A-5001A, 4706, 4711.* Parents must provide equivalent instruction to that of the public schools and must submit an application to the local board for approval. Teaching must be by a certified tutor or a tutor who will be assisted by a satisfactory support system, such as: (1) a certified teacher who will work with the parent four times a year, (2) a tutor who receives regular assistance from a public school or approved private school, (3) a tutor who receives regular assistance from another approved home instruction program, or (4) other support systems, such as local area home school support groups. Parents must submit curriculum outline and annual assessment.

### Maryland

Maryland State Department of Education
200 W. Baltimore Street
Baltimore, MD 21201
410-767-0100

*See Annotated Code of Maryland 7-301(a).* Parent must submit a form indicating their intent to home school to the local superintendent of schools and must maintain a portfolio of student materials that shall be reviewed by the superintendent at regular intervals.

### Massachusetts

Legal Office
1385 Hancock Street
Quincy, MA 02169
617-770-7300

*See Massachusetts General Laws 76-1.* Students shall attend a public school unless they are otherwise instructed in a manner approved by the superintendent of schools. Superintendent may review curriculum and operation and may require periodic testing.

### Michigan

Office of Legislation and School Law
Michigan Department of Education

Lansing, MI 48909
517-335-4074

*See Michigan Compiled Laws 380-1561.* As of July 1996, Michigan law recognizes the validity of home schools. Provides an exemption to compulsory attendance if "the child is being educated at the child's home by his or her parent or legal guardian in an organized educational program in the subject areas of reading, spelling, mathematics, science, history, civics, literature, writing, and English grammar."

### Minnesota

Minnesota Department of Children, Families, and Learning
550 Cedar Street
St. Paul, MN 55101-2273
612-296-6595

*See Minnesota Statutes Annotated 120.10.* A person providing instruction must meet at least one of the following requirements: (1) hold a teaching license, (2) be directly supervised by someone with a teaching license, (3) successfully complete a teacher competency exam, (4) provide instruction in an accredited school, (5) hold a baccalaureate degree, or (6) be the parent of a child who is assessed yearly on a nationally norm-referenced standardized achievement test.

### Mississippi

Mississippi Department of Education
P.O. Box 771
Jackson, MS 39205-0771
601-359-3602

*See Mississippi Code Annotated 37-13-91.* The Mississippi Code states that the child must be educated in a legitimate home instruction program. Parents must submit a certificate of enrollment stating the names of the children and a simple description of the type of education the children are receiving. A legitimate home instruction program is one that is not operated for the "purpose of avoiding or circumventing the compulsory attendance law." Teacher certification or standardized tests are not required.

### Missouri

Department of Education
P.O. Box 480
Jefferson City, MO 65102
314-751-3527

*See Annotated Missouri Statutes 167.031 through 167.042.* Any parent may educate at home. Must provide one thousand hours of instruction with at least six hundred hours in the basics, such as reading, language arts, math, social studies, and science. At least four hundred of the six hundred hours must be taught in the home location. Parent must maintain a plan book or daily log, a portfolio of student's work, and a record of evaluation.

### Montana

Office of Public Instruction
State Capitol Room 106
Helena, MT 59602
406-449-3554

*See Montana Code Annotated 20-5-109.* Parents are not required to notify the county, but must maintain records providing evidence of regular instruction, keep a portfolio of work, and abide by curriculum and school hour requirements.

### Nebraska

Nebraska Department of Education
301 Centennial Mall South
Lincoln, NE 68509-4987
402-471-2784

*See Title 92, Nebraska Administrative Code, chapter 13.* In order to be exempt from Nebraska compulsory attendance laws, home schooling parents must file the "Statement of Objection and Assurances." This statement asserts that the rules and regulations adopted by the state board of education violate sincerely held religious beliefs. When/if the exemption is granted, the parents must sign an affirmation that states they understand their duties and will make arrangements for a school visit or testing as requested by the commissioner or county superintendent. Parents agree to hold school for 175 days, submit a chart or written summary to show the scope and sequence of instruction, and submit to testing at the discretion of the department of education. Forms are supplied by the above office.

### Nevada

Department of Education
Capitol Complex
400 W. King Street
Carson City, NV 89719
702-885-3100

*See Nevada Revised Statutes 392.070.* Child may be excused from school attendance if satisfactory evidence is presented that the child is receiving equivalent instruction of the kind and amount approved by the state board of education. Parents must file an exemption with the board of education, along with a calendar, sample weekly schedules, and a list of materials. Parent either (1) must be a certified teacher, (2) consult with a certified teacher, or (3) enroll in an approved correspondence school. Students must be tested in grades two, three, four, five, six, and seven.

### New Hampshire

New Hampshire Department of Education
State Office Park South
101 Pleasant Street
Concord, NH 03301
603-271-3144

*See New Hampshire Revised Statutes Annotated, section 193:1 and New Hampshire Code of Administrative Rules, Part Ed. 315.* Compulsory school attendance is required for children between ages six and sixteen unless that child is receiving home instruction. There is an established home education program administered by the department of education. Home schooling families must notify the commissioner of education, resident district superintendent, or principal of the commencement of home education within thirty days of commencement. The notification must include children's names and birth dates and a curriculum description. Parents must maintain a portfolio of records and materials and must provide an annual educational evaluation.

### New Jersey

Commissioner of Education
225 West State Street
Trenton, NJ 08625
609-984-7814

*See New Jersey Statutes Annotated 18A.38-25.* Children must attend school or receive equivalent instruction elsewhere. Instruction must be academically equivalent to that provided in the local public school.

### New Mexico

New Mexico State Department of Education
515 Don Gaspar
Santa Fe, NM 87501-2786
505-827-3876

*See New Mexico Statutes Annotated 22-1-2.* A home study program is one "which provides a basic education" operated by a parent. Parent must notify superintendent of schools, maintain records of attendance; teacher must have at least a high school diploma or equivalent; and students must be tested annually.

*New York*

Office for Nonpublic School Services
New York State Education Department
Room 475, Education Building Annex
Albany, NY 12234
518-474-7948

*See section 100.10 of the Regulations of the Commissioner of Education.* Parents must supply annual notice to the local superintendent of schools. Parents are instructed to submit an individualized home instruction plan (IHEP) for each child. Specific courses are required for each grade level. If the plan is not approved, the superintendent may require the child to enroll in school. Parents must submit an annual assessment report, including standardized test results. Provides for an alternative form of evaluation as well. The packet of information from the state department of education is very helpful in preparation of all of these materials.

*North Carolina*

Division of Nonpublic Education
530 N. Wilmington Street
Raleigh, NC 27604
919-733-4276

*North Carolina General Statutes 115C-547 through 115C-565.* A home school is defined as a nonpublic school in which a child receives his academic instruction from his parent, legal guardian, or a member of the household. Must file notice of intent, provide documentation that teacher has at least a high school diploma or equivalent, and abide by requirements for recordkeeping and standardized testing.

*North Dakota*

Department of Public Instruction
Bismarck, ND 58505
710-224-2260

*See North Dakota Centennial Code 15-34.1-06.* Home-based instruction is "an educational program for students based in the child's home and supervised by the child's parent or parents." Parent must file statement of intent and maintain an annual record of courses taken and the child's academic progress assessments, including achievement tests at grades three, four, six, eight, and eleven. Parent is qualified to teach if (1) certified as a teacher, (2) has a baccalaureate degree, (3) has passed a teacher's exam, or (4) has high school diploma or equivalent and is monitored by a certified teacher for the first two years of instruction.

*Ohio*

Nonpublic Schools
65 S. Front Street

Columbus, OH 43266-0308
614-466-2937

*See Ohio Revised Code 3321.03.* Recognizes home education as that primarily directed and provided by the parent or guardian. Parents must supply information to superintendent, including assurance that curriculum requirements are being met, a list of textbooks used, and so on. Teacher must have a high school diploma or equivalent or work under the direction of a person holding a baccalaureate degree. Must submit an academic assessment to superintendent of schools, including achievement tests and work portfolios.

### Oklahoma

Oklahoma State Department of Education
2500 North Lincoln Boulevard
Oklahoma City, OK 73105-4599
405-521-3301

*See Oklahoma Statutes Annotated, section 229, Article X.* Home education which is provided in good faith is equivalent to that afforded by the state. The law "suggests" that parents notify the local school district by letter that they are home schooling. Teacher certification is not required, the state furnishes no materials, and does not issue diplomas. A core curriculum is available from the department of education document section.

### Oregon

Oregon Department of Education
Office of Student Services
255 Capitol Street NE
Salem, OR 93710-0203
503-378-5585

*See Oregon Revised Statutes 339.030.* Children are exempt from compulsory attendance if they are being taught for a period equivalent to that required of children attending public schools by a parent or private teacher and are being taught the course of study usually taught in grades 1–12 in the public school. Parents must notify superintendent of home instruction and must have the child examined annually in the work covered.

### Pennsylvania

Pennsylvania Department of Education
Office of School Services
333 Market Street, 5th Floor
Harrisburg, PA 17126-0333
717-787-4860

*See 24 Pennsylvania Statutes 13-1327 et. seq.* Home schooling is specifically provided for in the statute. Parents, guardians, and legal custodians may home educate upon filing an affidavit with the superintendent of the school district. Must include an outline of objectives and subjects that are specified in the statute. The home teacher must maintain a portfolio of records for each child with titles of reading materials and samples of writing and other projects. The work in the portfolio is examined at least annually. Students must take a standardized achievement test in grades three, five, and eight that may not be administered by the home educating parents.

### Rhode Island

Department of Education
2225 Westminster Street
Providence, RI 02903
401-277-2031

*See Rhode Island General Laws 16-19-1.* Parents may home school as long as (1) the period of attendance is substantially equal to that of the public school, (2) an attendance register is kept, and (3) the teaching in the required subjects is thorough and efficient. Home schooling must be approved by the school committee of the town where the child resides. Standardized tests are not required by state law, but local school districts have authority to require some kind of evaluation.

### South Carolina

Office of Leadership and School Improvement
Rutledge Building
1429 Senate Street
Columbia, SC 29201
803-734-8492

*See South Carolina 59-65-40.* Parents may teach their children at home if the instruction is approved by the district or if instruction is conducted under the auspices of the South Carolina Association of Independent Schools. Parents must have a high school diploma or equivalent, teach 180 days per year for at least four and one-half hours per day, have a curriculum of regular instruction, maintain a plan book and student portfolio, and submit to annual statewide testing.

### South Dakota

Division of Education
Department of Education and Cultural Affairs
700 Governors Drive
Pierre, SD 57501-2291
605-773-6934

*See South Dakota Compiled Law 13-27-2 and 3.* The parent of a child who places the child in an alternative instruction program shall file the "Application for Public School Exemption" certificate. Must provide instruction for 175 days per year, maintain records of attendance and academic progress, deliver instruction in English, and provide courses in specified areas of study.

## Tennessee

Department of Education
Fifth Floor, Andrew Johnson Tower
710 James Robertson Parkway
Nashville, TN 37243
615-532-4711

*See Tennessee Code Annotated 49-6-4050(b)(1).* Home schooling families may choose one of two options: Independent home school or (state recognized) church-related home school. Either group must notify the local superintendent of intent to home school. Independent home schools must be taught by a teacher at grades K–8 who holds a high school diploma or a G.E.D. Home teachers at the 9–12 grade level must have a baccalaureate degree. All independent home school students must take achievement tests at grades two, five, seven, and nine. Parent/teachers who enroll in a state recognized church-related home school must have a high school diploma or G.E.D., and an annual standardized test is required for grades 9–12.

## Texas

Texas Education Agency
Legal Division
1701 N. Congress
Austin, TX 78701
512-463-9720

*See Texas Code Annotated 21.032 through 21.040.* Child is exempt from public school attendance who attends a private or parochial school that includes in its course of study the subject of good citizenship. Statute specifically provides that this exemption includes home schools.

## Utah

Utah State Office of Education
250 East 500 South
Salt Lake City, UT 84111
801-533-5431

*See Utah Code Annotated, section 53-24-1 et. seq.* Parents who wish to home school must contact the district in which their children would attend school. Most dis-

tricts have a form that parents must complete. The school year for home schooling must be the same as the public school year (180 days), and must be two and
one-half hours per day for kindergarten, four and one-half hours per day for first
grade, and five and one-half hours per day for second through twelfth grade, exclu-
sive of the lunch period. Students must receive instruction in the state core curriculum, which may be obtained from the above office.

## Vermont

State of Vermont
Department of Education
120 State Street
Montpelier, VT 05602
802-828-5406

*See Vermont Statutes Annotated Title 16, 1121; 16(11); 1666.* Parent shall send
enrollment notice to commissioner including data on children and a detailed outline of course of study. Parents must annually assess students choosing from a variety of available assessment procedures.

## Virginia

Superintendent of Education
Box 6-Q
Richmond, VA 23216-2060
804-225-2023

*See Virginia Code 22.1-254.1.* Parents who wish to home educate must (1) hold
a baccalaureate degree, (2) be a certified teacher, (3) enroll the child in an approved
correspondence school, or (4) provide a program of study that provides evidence
the parent is able to provide an adequate education for the child. Must notify the
superintendent of intent to home educate and must submit evidence of child's
academic achievement via achievement testing or independent assessment. Student may also be excused from school attendance by reason of bona fide religious
training or belief.

## Washington

Department of Education
Old Capitol Building FG-11
Olympia, WA 98504
360-664-3574

*See Washington Revised Code 28A.225.010.* Provides for home based instruction if
it consists of planned and supervised instructional and related educational activities. Parent/teacher must (1) be supervised by a certified teacher, (2) have forty-five
college level credit hours, or (3) be deemed sufficiently qualified to provide instruc-

tion by the superintendent. A declaration of intent must be filed with the superintendent and child must either take an annual standardized achievement test or parent must arrange for an annual assessment.

## West Virginia

West Virginia Department of Education
1900 Kanawha Boulevard
Charleston, WV 25305
304-558-3667

*See West Virginia Statutes 18-8-1.* Parent must file request to home educate with the county board of education. The person providing instruction must have a high school diploma or equivalent and formal education at least four years higher than the most academically advanced child for whom instruction is provided. Parent/teacher must provide an outline of instruction plans and each child must take an annual achievement test.

## Wisconsin

Department of Home-Based Instruction
125 S. Webster Street, Box 7841
Madison, WI 53707-7841
608-266-3390

*See Wisconsin Statutes Annotated 118.165 and 118.15.* Parents may provide a program of educational instruction if parent registers with the department of public instruction and provides a "sequentially progressive curriculum of fundamental instruction in reading, language arts, mathematics, social studies, science, and health" for at least 875 hours each school year.

## Wyoming

Department of Education
Hathaway Building
Cheyenne, WY 82002
302-777-7673

*See Wyoming Statutes 21-4-101.* Parents may provide a basic educational program if they submit an acceptable curriculum to the board of trustees and written documentary proof of immunization.

# Notes

## Chapter 1: How We Fell into Home Schooling

1. Nola Kortner Aiex, "Home Schooling and Socialization of Children," *ERIC Digest* (1994): 1, ED372460.

2. Dr. Brian Ray, "Home Education Research Fact Sheet III," National Home Education Research Institute, P.O. Box 13939, Salem, OR 97309, 1995.

3. Dana Hawkins, "Homeschool Battles," *U.S. News and World Report* (February 12, 1996): 58.

4. Mark Weston, "Reformers Should Take a Look at Home Schools," *Education Week* (April 3, 1996): 34.

5. Clay and Sally Clarkson, *Educating the Whole-Hearted Child* (Walnut Springs, Tex.: Whole Heart Ministries, 1996), 57.

6. Tom Wells, "Home Is Where the School Is for Families Fed Up with System," *The Daily Herald* (December 15, 1995): 3.

7. Christopher J. Klicka, *The Right Choice* (Gresham, Oreg.: Noble Publishing Association, 1993), 239.

8. Ibid., 242.

9. Dr. Brian Ray, "A Nationwide Study of Home Education: Family Characteristics, Legal Matters, and Student Achievement," National Home Education Research Institute, P.O. Box 13939, Salem, OR 97309, 1990.

10. Candy Berkebile, "Home: The Heart of Education," *Family Voice* (September 1994): 14.

11. Linda Dobson, *The Art of Education* (Tonasket, Wash.: Home Education Press, 1995), 164.

12. J. Richard Fugate, *Successful Home Schooling* (Tempe, Ariz.: Aletheia Press, 1990), 68.

13. James Michaels, "Do-It-Yourself Schooling," *Forbes* (October 11, 1993): 10.

14. Mary Hood, *Onto the Yellow School Bus and through the Gates of Hell* (Cartersville, Ga.: Ambleside Educational Press, 1995), 100–101.

15. "Classless Society," *The Economist* (June 11, 1994): 27.

16. John W. Kennedy, "Home Schooling Grown Up," *Christianity Today* (July 17, 1995): 51.

17. Susan Schaeffer Macaulay, *For the Children's Sake* (Wheaton: Crossway Books, 1984), 15.

18. Ferenc Mate, "Are We Losing Our Children?" *Country Journal* (January/February 1994): 49.

## Chapter 2: Why Home School Now?

1. Joel Riemer, "Perspectives from a Home-Schooling Educator," *Educational Leadership* (September 1994): 53.

2. Llewellyn Davis, *Going Home to School* (Knoxville: The Elijah Co., 1991), 97.

3. Christopher J. Klicka, *The Right Choice* (Gresham, Oreg.: Noble Publishing Association, 1993), 62–63.

4. Davis, *Going Home,* 54.

5. Klicka, *Right Choice,* 77.

6. John J. Dunphy, "A Religion for a New Age," *The Humanist* (January/February 1983): 26.

7. J. Richard Fugate, *Successful Home Schooling* (Tempe, Ariz.: Aletheia Press, 1990), 10.

8. Mary Hood, *Onto the Yellow School Bus and through the Gates of Hell* (Cartersville, Ga.: Ambleside Educational Press, 1995), 13.

9. Maralee Mayberry, J. Gary Knowles, Brian Ray, Stacey Marlow, *Home Schooling: Parents as Teachers* (Thousand Oaks, Calif.: Corwin Press, 1995), 102.

10. Krista Ramsey, "Home Is Where the School Is," *The School Administrator* (January 1992): 22.

11. Hood, *Onto the Yellow School Bus,* 54, 58.

12. Fugate, *Successful Home Schooling,* 33.

13. Klicka, *Right Choice,* 124.

14. Cheryl Gorder, *Home Schools: An Alternative* (Tempe, Ariz.: Blue Bird Publishing, 1990), 32.

15. Dr. Raymond and Dorothy Moore, *The Successful Homeschool Family Handbook* (Nashville: Thomas Nelson Publishers, 1994), 45.

16. Ray E. Ballman, *The How and Why of Home Schooling* (Wheaton: Crossway Books, 1995), 37.

17. Davis, *Going Home,* 137.

18. Klicka, *Right Choice,* 101.

19. Davis, *Going Home,* 57.

20. Gregg Harris, *The Christian Home School* (Brentwood, Tenn.: Wolgemuth & Hyatt Publishers 1988), 50–51.

21. Gorder, *Home Schools,* 29.

22. Sue Welch and Cindy Short, "Questions and Answers Concerning Home Schooling," *The Teaching Home* (March/April 1995): 13.

23. Ballman, *How and Why of Home Schooling,* 83.

24. Dana Hawkins, "Homeschool Battles," *U.S. News and World Report* (February 12, 1996): 58.

25. Klicka, *Right Choice,* 18.

26. Rick Medlin, "There's No Effective Learning Environment Like Home," *Homeschooling Today* (July/August 1996): 16.

27. Christopher Klicka, Presentation to Illinois Christian Home Educators, 1996 Convention, Naperville, Ill.

28. Welch and Short, "Questions and Answers," 13.

29. David Elkind, *The Hurried Child* (Reading, Mass.: Addison-Wesley Publishing, 1981), 3.

30. Terry Dorian and Zan Peters Tyler, *Anyone Can Home School* (Lafayette, La.: Huntington House Publishers, 1996), 33.

31. Susan Schaeffer Macaulay, *For the Children's Sake* (Wheaton: Crossway Books, 1984), 22.

32. Ibid.

33. Welch and Short, "Questions and Answers," 13.

34. David Guterson, *Family Matters: Why Homeschooling Makes Sense* (New York: Harcourt Brace Jovanovich, 1992), 71.

35. Chris Jeub, "Why Parents Choose Home Schooling," *Educational Leadership* (September 1994): 51.

36. Ballman, *How and Why of Home Schooling,* 91.

37. Gorder, *Home Schools,* 27.

38. David Rosenthal and Lenore Jacobson, *Pygmalion in the Classroom* (New York: Holt, Rinehart, and Winston, 1968).

39. Nancy Gibbs, "Home Sweet School," *Time* (October 31, 1994): 63.

40. Shari Henry, "Heartbeat," *Heart of Homeschooling* (May 1995): 1.

41. Dorian and Tyler, *Anyone Can Home School,* 32.

42. Bill Roorbach, "Mommy, What's a Classroom?" *New York Times Magazine* (February 2, 1997): 37.

43. Guterson, *Family Matters,* 220–21.

44. Ibid., 226.

45. Harris, *Christian Home School,* 65.

46. Ted Wade, *The Home School Manual* (Bridgeman, Mich.: Gazelle Publications, 1995), 34.

47. Ibid., 35.

48. Linda Dobson, *The Art of Education* (Tonasket, Wash.: Home Education Press, 1995), 167.

49. Dorian and Tyler, *Anyone Can Home School,* 25.

## Chapter 3: Why Not the Public School?

1. Mary Hood, *Onto the Yellow School Bus and through the Gates of Hell* (Cartersville, Ga.: Ambleside Educational Press, 1995), 53.

2. David and Micki Colfax, *Homeschooling for Excellence* (New York: Warner Books, 1988), 33.

3. Llewellyn Davis, *Going Home to School* (Knoxville: The Elijah Co., 1991), 25–26.

4. Peter Brimelow and Leslie Spencer, "The National Extortion Association?" *Forbes* (June 7, 1993): 79.

5. Linda Dobson, *The Art of Education* (Tonasket, Wash.: Home Education Press, 1995), 158.

6. National Commission on Excellence in Education, "A Nation at Risk: The Imperative for Educational Reform," 1982, 20.

7. Ray Ballman, *The How and Why of Home Schooling* (Wheaton: Crossway Books, 1995), 20.

8. Christopher J. Klicka, *The Right Choice* (Gresham, Oreg.: Noble Publishing Association, 1993), 28.

9. Ibid., 31.

10. Ibid., 33.

11. Ballman, *How and Why of Home Schooling,* 48.

12. Klicka, *Right Choice,* 34.

13. Ballman, *How and Why of Home Schooling,* 56.

14. Dobson, *Art of Education,* 52–53.

15. Ballman, *How and Why of Home Schooling,* 58.

16. Hood, *Onto the Yellow School Bus,* 63.

17. Christian Home Educators Coalition, P.O. Box 47322, Chicago, IL 60647, "Homeschoolers and Goals 2000," 1995, 2.

18. Mark and Helen Hegener, *Alternatives in Education* (Tonasket, Wash.: Home Education Press, 1992), 60.

19. Cathy Duffy, *Government Nannies* (Gresham, Oreg.: Noble Publishing, 1995), 17.

20. Ibid., 27.

21. CHEC, "Homeschoolers and Goals 2000," 12.

22. Hegener and Hegener, *Alternatives in Education,* 60–61.

23. Larry and Susan Kaseman, "School-to-Work: Problems and Alternatives," *Home Education Magazine* (January/February 1997): 17.

24. Duffy, *Government Nannies,* 175.

25. Hegener and Hegener, *Alternatives in Education,* 61.

26. Duffy, *Government Nannies,* 79.

27. Ibid., 61.

28. Ibid., 61–62.

29. Ibid., 62.

30. Terry Dorian and Zan Peters Tyler, *Anyone Can Home School* (Lafayette, La.: Huntington House Publishers, 1996), 51.

31. Jennifer Ferranti, "Federal Infiltration," *Focus on the Family CITIZEN* (August 21, 1995): 10.

32. CHEC, *Homeschoolers and Goals 2000,* 5–6.

33. Linda Page, "OBE: What You Don't Know Could Hurt Your Children," Focus on the Family, Education Policy Department, 1995.

34. Jeff Hooten, "Outcome-Based Deception?" *Focus on the Family CITIZEN* (August 21, 1996): 1.

35. Ibid., 3.

36. Ibid., 4.

## Chapter 4: Home Schooling Success

1. Charles S. Clark, *Congressional Quarterly Researcher* (September 9, 1994): 778.

2. Dr. Brian Ray, "Test Scores of 16,320 Students Continue to Confirm Home-School Research," *The Teaching Home* (March/April 1995): 27.

3. Dr. Brian Ray, "Home Schoolers' Academic Achievement and Critical Thinking Skills Studied and Reported," *The Teaching Home* (November/December 1995): 23.

4. Christian Home Educators Coalition, P.O. Box 47322, Chicago, IL 60647, Report, 1995, 4.

5. Ray, "Home Schoolers' Academic Achievement," 25.

6. Home School Legal Defense Association, "Marching to the Beat of Their Own Drum: A Profile of Home Education Research," 1992, 7.

7. Clark, *Congressional Quarterly Researcher,* 775.

8. Ibid., 777.

9. Dr. Brian Ray, "Positive Home-School Research Accumulates," *The Teaching Home* (March/April 1996): 28.

10. Home School Legal Defense Association, "Marching to the Beat of Their Own Drum," 12.

11. Ray, "Positive Home-School Research," 28.

12. Home School Legal Defense Association, "Marching to the Beat of Their Own Drum," 12.

13. Christopher J. Klicka, "Socialization: Home Schoolers Are in the Real World," *Home School Court Report* (September/October 1993): 3.

14. Home School Legal Defense Association, "Marching to the Beat of Their Own Drum," 11.

15. Ray, "Positive Home-School Research," 28.

16. Raymond and Dorothy Moore, *Home Style Teaching* (Waco: Word Books, 1984), 36.

17. Home School Legal Defense Association, "Marching to the Beat of Their Own Drum," 11.

18. Dale Fenton, Assistant Director, Career Development Center, Wheaton College, article in progress.

19. Christopher Shea, "From Home to College," *The Chronicle of Higher Education* (February 2, 1996): 12

20. Dale Fenton, article in progress.

21. Ibid.

22. Home School Legal Defense Association, "Marching to the Beat of Their Own Drum," 12–13.

23. Klicka, "Socialization," 4.

### Chapter 6: How Does Janey Learn?

1. Mary Pride, *The Big Book of Home Learning,* vol. 1, *Getting Started* (Wheaton: Crossway Books, 1991), 40.

2. Ibid.

3. Ibid., 41.

4. Cathy Duffy, *Christian Home Educators' Curriculum Manual: Elementary Grades* (Westminster, Calif.: Home Run Enterprises, 1995).

5. Ibid., 11.

6. Christopher J. Klicka, *The Right Choice* (Gresham, Oreg.: Noble Publishing Association, 1993), 206.

7. Mary Hood, *The Relaxed Home School* (Westminster, Md.: Ambleside Educational Press, 1994), 7–8.

8. Gregg Harris, "Home Schooling and the New World Order," The Advanced Home Schooling Workshop Cassette Series, tape 1, Christian Life Workshops, 1992.

9. Clay and Sally Clarkson, *Educating the Whole-Hearted Child* (Walnut Springs, Tex.: Whole Heart Ministries, 1996), 82.

10. Ferenc Mate, "Are We Losing Our Children?" *Country Journal* (January/February 1994): 50.

## Chapter 7: Getting Started

1. Dr. Raymond and Dorothy Moore, *The Successful Homeschool Family Handbook* (Nashville: Thomas Nelson Publishers, 1994), 165.

2. Ibid., 115.

3. Lewis Carroll, *Alice in Wonderland* (New York: Grosset and Dunlap), 62.

4. Mary Hood, *The Relaxed Home School* (Westminster, Md.: Ambleside Educational Press, 1994), 12.

5. Bill and Cindy Short, "Preparing Your Children for Adulthood," *The Teaching Home* (April/May 1989): 26–27.

6. Ted Wade, *The Home School Manual,* 6th ed. (Bridgeman, Mich.: Gazelle Publications, 1995), 33.

7. J. Richard Fugate, *Successful Home Schooling* (Tempe, Ariz.: Aletheia Press, 1990), 3.

8. Moore and Moore, *Successful Homeschool Family Handbook,* 150.

9. Fugate, *Successful Home Schooling,* 46.

10. Annette Vittetoe, "Simplify to Reach Spiritual Goals," *The Teaching Home* (July/August 1995): 43.

11. Terry Dorian and Zan Peters Tyler, *Anyone Can Home School* (Lafayette, La.: Huntington House Publishers, 1996), 169.

12. Moore and Moore, *Successful Homeschool Family Handbook,* 96.

13. Luanne Shackelford and Susan White, *A Survivor's Guide to Home Schooling* (Westchester, Ill.: Crossway Books, 1988), 17.

14. Rick Boyer, *The Socialization Trap* (Rustburg, Va.: Rickey G. Boyer, 1993), 121.

15. Ray Ballman, *The How and Why of Home Schooling* (Wheaton: Crossway Books, 1996), 137.

16. Jane M. Healy, *Endangered Minds: Why Our Children Don't Think* (New York: Simon and Schuster, 1990).

17. Dorian and Tyler, *Anyone Can Home School,* 129.

18. Elijah Company Catalog, "What's New, Great Holiday Ideas, The Best of the Old and New," 1996, 3.

19. Ibid., 20.

20. Ibid., 11.

21. David Guterson, "When Schools Fail Children," *Harper's Magazine* (November 1990): 58.

## Chapter 8: Positive Relationships with the Public Schools and Community

1. Diane Brockett, "Home-School Kids in Public-School Activities," *Education Digest* (November 1995): 68

2. Debra E. Blum, "Home-Schooled Athletes," *The Chronicle of Higher Education* (June 7, 1996): A33.

3. Ibid., A34.

4. Brockett, "Home-School Kids," 67.

5. The Rutherford Institute, P.O. Box 7482, Charlottesville, VA 22906, "Access of Home Schooled Children to Public School Activities," 1995.

6. Mike Shepherd, "Home Schoolers as Public School Tutors," *Educational Leadership* (September 1994): 56.

7. Mary Terpstra, "A Home School/School District Partnership," *Educational Leadership* (September 1994): 57.

8. Krista Ramsey, "Home Is Where the School Is," *The School Administrator* (January 1992): 22.

9. Ibid., 25.

10. Mark Weston, "Reformers Should Take a Look at Home Schools," *Education Week* (April 3, 1996): 34.

11. Jo Anna Natale, "Understanding Home Schooling," *The Education Digest* (March 1993): 60–61.

12. Maralee Mayberry, J. Gary Knowles, Brian Ray, Stacey Marlow, *Home Schooling: Parents as Teachers* (Thousand Oaks, Calif.: Corwin Press, 1995): 89.

13. Ibid., 97.

14. Betty Jo Simmons, "Classroom at Home," *The American School Board Journal* (February 1994): 49.

15. M. Larry and Susan D. Kaseman, *Taking Charge through Home Schooling* (Stoughton, Wis.: Koshkononk Press, 1990), 106.

16. Christian Home Educators Coalition, P.O. Box 47322, Chicago, IL 60647, "Homeschoolers and Goals 2000," 1995, 9.

17. Christian Home Educators Coalition, P.O. Box 47322, Chicago, IL 60647, "Vouchers: How Will Homeschoolers Respond?" 1995.

18. The Rutherford Institute, P.O. Box 7482, Charlottesville, VA 22906, "School Choice and Tax Credits for Home Education," 1995.

19. Christopher J. Klicka, *The Right Choice* (Gresham, Oreg.: Noble Publishing Association, 1993), 220.

20. Ibid., 223.

21. Ibid., 219.

22. Terry Dorian and Zan Peters Tyler, *Anyone Can Home School* (Lafayette, La.: Huntington House Publishers, 1996), 22.

23. The Rutherford Institute, P.O. Box 7482, Charlottesville, VA 22906, "Use of Standardized Tests to Measure Home Schooling Success," 1996.

24. The Rutherford Institute, P.O. Box 7482, Charlottesville, VA 22906, "Administrative Searches and Home School Visits," 1995.

25. Klicka, *Right Choice,* 283.

26. The Rutherford Institute, P.O. Box 7482, Charlottesville, VA 22906, "Home School Bill of Rights."

### Chapter 9: The Question of Socialization

1. Linda Dobson, *The Art of Education* (Tonasket, Wash.: Home Education Press, 1995), 78.

2. Dr. Raymond and Dorothy Moore, *The Successful Homeschool Family Handbook* (Nashville: Thomas Nelson Publishers, 1994), 49.

3. Ibid., 51.

4. Rick Boyer, *The Socialization Trap* (Rustburg, Va.: Rickey G. Boyer, 1993), 7.

5. Dobson, *Art of Education,* 43.

6. Bill Roorbach, "Mommy, What's a Classroom?" *New York Times Magazine* (February 2, 1997): 33.

7. Christopher J. Klicka, *The Right Choice* (Gresham, Oreg.: Noble Publishing Association, 1993), 183.

8. David Guterson, *Family Matters: Why Homeschooling Makes Sense* (New York: Harcourt Brace Jovanovich, 1992), 69.

9. Boyer, *Socialization Trap,* 18.

10. Ibid., 36–48.

11. Llewellyn Davis, *Going Home to School* (Knoxville: The Elijah Co., 1991), 115.

12. Dobson, *Art of Education,* 78

13. Jonathan Lindvall, "The Bold Parenting Seminar Tape Series," P.O. Box 820, Springville, CA 93265, 1992.

14. Cheryl Gorder, *Home Schools: An Alternative* (Tempe, Ariz.: Blue Bird Publishing, 1990), 42

15. Nola Kortner Aiex, "Home Schooling and Socialization of Children," *ERIC Digest,* ED372460, 1994, 2.

16. Isabel Lyman, "Better Off at Home?" *National Review* (September 20, 1993): 61.

17. Brian D. Ray, "New Studies Address Socialization and Academic Achievement," *The Teaching Home* (January/February 1996): 23.

18. Aiex, "Home Schooling and Socialization," 3.

19. Carol Silverman Saunders, *Safe at School* (Minneapolis: Free Spirit Publishing, 1994), 22.

20. Ibid.

21. Ibid., 24

22. Donna Carroll, "Is Socialization Overrated?" *Home Education Magazine* (March/April 1996): 33.

23. Dr. Raymond and Dorothy Moore, "When Education Becomes Abuse," *Journal of School Health* 56, no. 2 (February 1986): 74.

24. Mary Hood, *Onto the Yellow School Bus and through the Gates of Hell* (Cartersville, Ga.: Ambleside Educational Press, 1995), 99.

25. J. Richard Fugate, *Successful Home Schooling* (Tempe, Ariz.: Aletheia Press, 1990), 8.

26. Ibid., 12.

27. Susannah Sheffer, *A Sense of Self* (Portsmouth, N.H.: Boynton/Cook Publishers, 1995), 38.

28. Ibid., 108.

29. Fugate, *Successful Home Schooling,* 11.

30. Dr. Raymond and Dorothy Moore, *Home Grown Kids* (Waco, Tex.: Word, 1981), 34–35.

31. Ibid., 37

32. Myra and David Sadker, *Failing at Fairness: How America's Schools Cheat Girls* (New York: Charles Scribner's Sons, 1994), 11.

33. Ibid., 78.

34. Ibid., 13–14.

35. Susan Spaeth Cherry, "Helping Young Girls Be Strong, Focused, Resilient," *Chicago Parent* (February 1997): 23.

36. Sheffer, *A Sense of Self,* 23.

37. Christopher J. Klicka, *The Right to Home School* (Durham, N.C.: Carolina Academic Press, 195), 16.

38. Ibid., 17.

39. Ibid.

40. Klicka, *Right Choice,* 135.

41. Gregg Harris, *The Christian Home School* (Brentwood, Tenn.: Wolgemuth & Hyatt Publishers, 1988), 96.

42. Ibid.

### Chapter 10: Positively Promoting Home Schooling

1. Lynn Schnaiberg, "Staying Home from School," *Education Week* (June 12, 1996): 25.

2. Charles S. Clark, *Congressional Quarterly Researcher* 4, no. 33 (September 9, 1994): 772.

3. Luanne Shackelford and Susan White, *Survivor's Guide to Home Schooling* (Westchester, Ill.: Crossway Books, 1988), 9.

4. Clark, *Congressional Quarterly Researcher,* 774.

5. Christopher J. Klicka, *The Right Choice* (Gresham, Oreg.: Noble Publishing Association, 1993), 375.

### Chapter 11: The Home School Support Group

1. Lynn Schnaiberg, "Home Rule," *The American Spectator* (June 1994): 52.

2. Harley Soltes, "Live and Learn," *Bazaar* (September 1991): 268.

3. Cheryl Gorder, *Home Schools: An Alternative* (Tempe, Ariz.: Blue Bird Publishing, 1990), 41.

4. Terry Dorian and Zan Peters Tyler, *Anyone Can Home School* (Lafayette, La.: Huntington House Publishers, 1996), 4.

## Chapter 12: Home Schooling Parents

1. Luanne Shackelford and Susan White, *A Survivor's Guide to Home Schooling* (Westchester, Ill.: Crossway Books, 1989), 2.

2. J. Richard Fugate, *Successful Home Schooling* (Tempe, Ariz.: Aletheia Press, 1990), 46.

3. Michael Farris, "Who Thanks the Real Heroes?" *The Teaching Home* (November/December 1995): 61.

4. Mary Hood, *Onto the Yellow School Bus and through the Gates of Hell* (Cartersville, Ga.: Ambleside Educational Press, 1995), 25.

5. Dr. Joseph Stowell, Proclaim Radio Broadcast, Moody Bible Institute, 1997.

6. Charlotte Mason, "A Father's Place in Home Training," *Parents Review* 5 (winter 1995): 24.

7. Clay and Sally Clarkson, *Educating the Whole-Hearted Child* (Walnut Springs, Tex.: Whole Heart Ministries, 1996), 169.

8. Gary Wyatt, "Homeschooling Fathers," *Home Education Magazine* (January/February 1997): 24.

## Appendix A: Home School Resources

1. Gayle White, "Home Schooling Appeals to All Faiths," *Publishers Weekly* (July 15, 1996): 27.

**Christine Moriarty Field** practiced law for many years before becoming a full-time mom. She is the author of *Coming Home to Raise Your Children* and *Should You Adopt?* She and her husband live and home school in Wheaton, Illinois, where they are the proud parents of four children, three girls and a boy. She is active in her home school support group, maintains an energetic public speaking schedule, and serves as a referral attorney for the Home School Legal Defense Association.

If you would like to share your home schooling experiences, tips, or ideas, you may contact Christine at:

Christine Field
P.O. Box 261
Wheaton, IL 60189-0261
email: MField7842@aol.com

The Field family also has a web page. To find out about their latest activities, to receive encouragement for mothering, adoption, or home schooling, or to view Christine's speaking schedule, visit their home page on the World Wide Web at:

http://members.aol.com/MField7842/index.html